Twayne's United States Authors Series

EDITOR OF THIS VOLUME

Kenneth Eble

University of Utah

W. H. Auden

Revised Edition

TUSAS 144

W. H. Auden on the lawns of Christ Church, Oxford

W. H. AUDEN

REVISED EDITION

By GEORGE T. WRIGHT

TWAYNE PUBLISHERS

A DIVISION OF G. K. HALL & CO., BOSTON

Published in 1981 by Twayne Publishers,
A Division of G. K. Hall & Co.
All Rights Reserved

Printed on permanent/durable acid-free paper and bound
in the United States of America

First Printing

Photograph of W. H. Auden by Bill Potter,
used with permission of Camera Press, London

Library of Congress Cataloging in Publication Data

Wright, George Thaddeus.
W. H. Auden.

(Twayne's United States authors series ; TUSAS 144)
Bibliography: pp. 213–25
Includes index.
1. Auden, W. H. (Wystan Hugh), 1907–1973—Criticism
and interpretation.   I. Title.   II. Series.
PS3501.U55Z94   1981   811'.52   81–4153
   ISBN 0–8057–7346–0   AACR2

*To my mother
and the memory of my father*

Contents

About the Author

George T. Wright is Professor of English at the University of Minnesota, where he teaches courses in poetry and in modern British literature. He received his B.A. and M.A. degrees from Columbia and his Ph.D. from the University of California at Berkeley, and he has taught English at the University of Kentucky, at San Francisco State College, at the University of Tennessee, and, as a Fulbright lecturer in American literature, at the University of Aix-Marseille in France (1964-66) and at the University of Thessaloniki in Greece (1977-78). His publications include *The Poet in the Poem: The Personae of Eliot, Yeats, and Pound* (1960) and numerous essays, poems, and reviews. Among his scholarly articles are "The Lyric Present: Simple Present Verbs in English Poems," which appeared in *PMLA* and won the Modern Language Association's William Riley Parker Prize in 1974; "Hendiadys and *Hamlet*," *PMLA* (1981); the introductory essay in *Seven American Literary Stylists from Poe to Mailer* (1973); and essays on Donne, Gray, Eliot, and Auden. His poems have appeared in *The New Yorker, Esquire, American Review, Sewanee Review, Nation, Centennial Review, Poetry Northwest,* and many other journals. Mr. Wright is currently writing a book on English iambic pentameter in the Renaissance.

Preface to the Revised Edition

Since 1966, when the text of this book's first edition was mainly written, the state of Auden studies has changed in four ways: (1) a great many more books and articles have appeared, several of them written independently of each other at about the same time as this one; (2) Auden wrote a few more volumes, and he died in 1973; (3) on his death, friends of his began to write much more frankly about his life; and (4) the texts of his poems began to be republished in new and presumably definitive form under the editorship of Auden's literary executor, Edward Mendelson.

The present edition takes these changes into account. The bibliography has been brought up to date, and the most recent books, some notable articles, and Auden's posthumous texts have been annotated, some at length; the chapter on Auden's later poetry has been extended to treat his last three volumes of verse; a biographical sketch of Auden's later years has been added, as Chapter 13; a new and wider-ranging appraisal of Auden and his verse, and of Auden's place in twentieth-century literature, appears now as Chapter 19. In addition, a few passages have been slightly or much rewritten, notably the section on *The Orators* in Chapter 4. Otherwise, I have let my earlier descriptions and judgments stand, conscious that they might be improved upon but unwilling to disown *en masse* my earlier insights or confusions. The new material adds some considered readings of the man and his work to what I still hope are helpful analyses of Auden's stylistic and philosophical stages.

In reading through Auden again and trying to see clearly what is distinctive and essential in his work, I have kept trying to imagine some audience of the future to whom it would not appear, as it does to many readers today, that Auden's later poems leave out something essentially human, something for which the symbolic resonance he avoids is the only poetic correlative.

Not living in advance of my own age, I have found this difficult to do. I suspect that this sense of something missing will keep Auden's admirers from ever claiming for him the overpoweringly human appeal of Homer, Dante, Shakespeare, or even of Wordsworth, Yeats, and Eliot. In clarity and intelligence, however, in sharpness of phrase, precision of thought and form, and aptness of image, Auden seems to me to have no equal in this century. What he wished his poetry to do was not to overpower but to help, and all the instruments suggest that his wish will be granted.

GEORGE T. WRIGHT

University of Minnesota

Acknowledgments

The quotations from the works of W. H. Auden are copyrighted and reprinted by permission of Random House, Inc.

Passages from Christopher Isherwood's *Lions and Shadows* are reprinted by permission of the publisher, New Directions Publishing Corporation. Copyright 1947 by New Directions.

Passages from Stephen Spender's *World Within World* (New York: Harcourt, Brace & World, 1951) are reprinted by permission of the present copyright holder, Harold Matson Company, Inc.

I thank Edward Callan for permitting me to quote at length from his articles on Auden's long poems; and the editors of *Tennessee Studies in Literature* (and the University of Tennessee Press) for permission to reprint, much changed, an article that first appeared in Volume X (1965).

I am grateful also to Leslie Palmer, Mary Stanley Weinkauf, Larry Yates, and other graduate students at the University of Tennessee, who, in seminars on Auden, helped me understand his work better; to the Fulbright Program, especially the Franco-American Commission for University Exchange, which made it possible for me to stay two years in France as Fulbright Lecturer at the University of Aix-Marseille, a position that gave me time to write this book; to the University of Tennessee (and especially my department chairman, Kenneth L. Knickerbocker) for granting me a two-year leave of absence; and, for helping with various problems of research, writing, and morale, to Professor Bain Tate Stewart (of the University of Tennessee), my mother, and my wife.

Permission to quote from Hannah Arendt's essay "Remembering Wystan H. Auden," as it appeared in *W. H. Auden: A Tribute*, edited by Stephen Spender, has been granted by Harcourt Brace Jovanovich, Inc.

Permission to quote from other writing in *W. H. Auden: A*

W. H. AUDEN

Tribute, edited by Stephen Spender (Copyright © 1974, 1975 by George Weidenfeld & Nicolson Ltd.) has been granted by Weidenfeld and Nicolson and by Macmillan Publishing Co., Inc.

In preparing the revised edition, I have received help from other persons and powers, for which I am very grateful. I wish particularly to thank Edward Mendelson for responding helpfully to several questions about Auden; Nancy Lestina for superb typing of an often very difficult revised manuscript; and the University of Minnesota's College of Liberal Arts for providing this typing service for its harried faculty.

The frontispiece photograph of W. H. Auden, by Bill Potter, is used with permission of Camera Press, London.

A Note on Auden's Texts

Auden believed that a poet's poems in some sense belonged to the poet until death, that readers and critics should accept the poet's final text as definitive, and that earlier versions should, if published, be ignored and, if unpublished, remain so. The drafts of *The Waste Land,* he felt, should never have been published. Not even the most sympathetic of Auden's critics has been able to share these views. For one thing, the chance of watching a poet arriving at his best text through several stumbling stages is too fascinating to give up—every critic is willing to be a *voyeur* to this degree—and the light it throws on the poetic process seems of genuine theoretical interest. In addition, a poet may turn out not to be the most satisfactory reviser of his own earlier poems; if he has changed his views or his stylistic habits, if he has lost sympathy with the younger self he was, his changes may actually damage the poems, particularly if they were, to begin with, very good poems of their kind.

This is, in fact, Auden's case, as it is not, for example, Yeats's. Auden's tireless revising of many an early poem—from its journal appearance to its collection in a volume, to its inclusion in a collected edition, and even from one collection to another—has puzzled or angered or dismayed his critics. Joseph Warren Beach's book *The Making of the Auden Canon* is only the most public expression of this critical pique. Nothing, after all, is more irritating to a critic than to express his admiration for a poem, only to have its author call it "trash," especially when the reasons the poet gives seem trivial or silly. But even if critics acknowledge that poets till they die have some rights over their poems, the *historical* interest in a poet's early work, especially when the poet has been part of a literary movement of considerable historical importance, would appear to demand that his early poems be available in something close to the form in which they first became widely known.

When Auden died in 1973, a large number of his early poems had been revised, shortened, discarded, suppressed, printed out of context, incorporated into new contexts, reviled by Auden himself, given new titles, deprived of titles, or collected in differing versions. Almost any given early poem by Auden has appeared, over its career, in such different form or company that anyone interested in reading it accurately may feel obliged to study its different versions and embeddings. However much one wants simply to read the words on the page, as Auden suggested we do, when the poems are elusive it may help to know what else is on the page, or was there once.

It is not hard to imagine what a chaos might have been made of Auden's published work if it had been left to chance or to a careless publisher or executor to put his literary remains in order. Luckily for this poet, and for all his readers, Auden chose Edward Mendelson for his literary executor, and the early results show how wise a choice it was. Mendelson had already collaborated on the revised edition of the standard Auden bibliography first compiled by B. C. Bloomfield, and his command of Auden's writings has the authority and completeness an executor of such a vast and miscellaneous literary estate must have. Furthermore, to judge by the bibliography, by *Forewords and Afterwords* (1973), the collection of prose writings he selected with Auden's approval, by the tactfully presented posthumous volume of poems *Thank You, Fog* (1974), and by the first two volumes of collected poems published after Auden's death, Mendelson is an admirably sensitive and scrupulous editor who can be depended on to make intelligent decisions about the hundreds of tough problems involved in the editing of such mercurial texts.

Auden's principal previous collections had various limitations. In *Collected Poetry* (1945) he arranged his lyric poems alphabetically by first line instead of chronologically; this collection, too, was available only in an American, not in an English, edition. The equivalent British edition, *Collected Shorter Poems, 1930–1944* (1950), also arranged the poems alphabetically but revised many of them further and omitted the long poems included in the American collection. A later version, *Collected Shorter Poems, 1927–1957*, was issued in 1966 in England and in the United States in 1967; this volume (already a decade out of date) presented the poems in chronological order but omitted some famous ones which Auden no longer cared for—notably "Petition" ("Sir, no man's enemy . . .), "Spain 1937," and "September 1, 1939." A companion volume, *Collected Longer Poems* (1968), gathered together Auden's more extended poems, some of which had appeared in none of the earlier collections. Many of Auden's essays, in the meantime, had been collected in *The Dyer's Hand* (1962).

By the time of Auden's death, then, the poems in his four most recent volumes remained uncollected, and no collection since 1945 included both his long and short poems. In addition, his plays, libretti, and criticism had gone almost entirely unassembled. It was difficult for a short-of-funds Auden admirer to know which of his books to buy, and the most convenient "collected" texts were seriously incomplete.

The problem is not entirely solved now, but Mendelson's editorial work has gone a long way toward solving it. His selection of essays in *Forewords and Afterwords*, made with Auden's approval, rescued many of the poet's most intriguing critical pieces from their widely scattered oblivion in the library stacks. His edition of *Collected Poems* (New York, 1976) presented Auden's poems, long and short, as the poet apparently wanted them to appear. The volume omits poems that Auden wished to forget, and it includes his later versions of many earlier poems. The pieces are generally arranged in chronological order—the order is stricter for the early poems than for the later—and the dates of composition are given for each poem. As a result, except for the difficulty that many earlier poems are not permitted to stand as they were in their early appearances (or even to stand at all), the reader for the first time can feel that he has in this volume almost all of Auden's poetical works.

But for any reader who wants to see the early work in its own terms, *The English Auden* (New York, 1977) is indispensable. Here Mendelson has collected not only the short and long poems of the period 1927–39, but he has included as well some important prose writing of these years. The poems, too, are all here, even the ones rejected by Auden, and the text of each poem is given "in the form it reached at the end of 1939" (xxi)—i.e., before Auden's later revisionary hand did its work. Separable poems from the plays are also included, but Mendelson expects to issue "a complete edition of Auden's plays and librettos, including the radio plays and narratives for documentary films." He also plans a "complete edition of Auden's prose, probably in four volumes."[1] When these are issued, virtually all of Auden's writing will be available in a few large volumes.

In short, Auden's work is fast becoming accessible to interested readers in skillfully edited texts. When one considers that, more than forty years after his death, W. B. Yeats's poems are still not available in a satisfactory edition—the order of *Last Poems* is a jumble that the Macmillan Company apparently proposes never to set right—and that T. S. Eliot's poems and plays, even fifteen years after his death, have never been collected in a complete edition, every reader of Auden ought to be grateful for the devoted editorial work of Edward Mendelson.

Because I have wanted to trace Auden's development as a poet through his successive phases, I have in this edition almost always quoted his early work from *The English Auden* (*EA*) and not from *Collected Poems*. The later poems, however— those of the American Auden—are normally quoted from *Collected Poems* (*CP*). Where the text I quote differs slightly from the source I cite, I have kept the reading of an earlier version but have wanted the reader to be able to find the poem in the more available text. In a few cases, I have quoted from one or another of those slimmer volumes of verse which Auden published every few years during his long career, and which, even now that we are on the verge of having satisfactory editions of the complete poems and plays, still mark important stages of his intellectual and formal development.

Chronology

1907   Wystan Hugh Auden born at York, February 21, third son of George Augustus Auden and Constance Rosalie (Bicknell) Auden.

1908   Family move to Birmingham.

1914–   Father away at war.
1918

1915–   St. Edmund's preparatory school, Grayshott.
1920

1920–   Gresham's School, Holt (Norfolk).
1925

1925–   Christ Church College, Oxford.
1928

1928   *Poems* (about thirty copies printed at Oxford by Stephen Spender).

1928–   Lives in Berlin.
1929

1930   *Paid on Both Sides* in *The Criterion*. *Poems*, his first important book, brought out by Faber and Faber.

1930–   Teaches at Larchfield, Helensburgh, Scotland; and at the
1935   Downs School, Colwall (near Malvern).

1932   *The Orators*. Begins 'In the year of my youth . . .'

1933   *The Dance of Death* (not produced till 1935). *Poems*, second edition, with seven new poems.

1935   *The Dog Beneath the Skin* (with Christopher Isherwood). Film work for six months. Marries Erika Mann.

1936   Visits Iceland with Louis MacNeice, July to September. *The Ascent of F6* (with Isherwood). *Look, Stranger* (American edition: *On This Island*, 1937).

1937   Visits Spain, January to March. *Spain*. *Letters from Iceland* (with MacNeice). Wins King's Gold Medal.

1938   Visits China with Isherwood, January to July, returns by way of Japan and United States; later in Brussels. *On the Frontier* (with Isherwood).

1939   Moves permanently to the United States in January. *Journey to a War* (with Isherwood). Meets Chester Kallman.
1939–   Teaches at St. Mark's School, Southborough, Mass.
1940
1940   *Another Time.* "The Dark Valley" (radio play). Becomes a Christian.
1940–   Teaches at the New School for Social Research, New
1941   York.
1941   *The Double Man* (British edition: *New Year Letter*).
1941–   Teaches at the University of Michigan.
1942
1942   Wins Guggenheim fellowship.
1942–   Teaches at Swarthmore College.
1945
1943–   Teaches at Bryn Mawr College.
1945
1944   *For the Time Being* (including *The Sea and the Mirror*).
1945   *Collected Poetry* (American edition only). "Sent overseas in April by the United States Air Force to investigate the effect of strategic bombing on German morale" (Spears, *The Poetry of W. H. Auden*, 169). Wins Guggenheim fellowship. Awarded $1000 prize by the American Academy of Arts and Letters.
1946   Becomes a United States citizen. Teaches at Bennington College.
1946–   Teaches at New School for Social Research.
1947
1947   *The Age of Anxiety.* Teaches at Barnard College.
1948   Auden and Kallman begin to spend every spring and summer on the island of Ischia. Wins Pulitzer Prize.
1949   Gives Page-Barbour Lectures at the University of Virginia.
1950   *Collected Shorter Poems* (British edition only). *The Enchafèd Flood.*
1951   *Nones.* Libretto (with Chester Kallman) for *The Rake's Progress*, by Igor Stravinsky.
1953   "Delia or a Masque of Night," a one-act libretto (with Kallman). Teaches at Smith College, as W. A. Neilson Research Professor.

1954 Wins Bollingen Prize. Is elected to the American Academy of Arts and Letters.

1955 *The Shield of Achilles.*

1956 Wins National Book Award.

1956– Serves as Professor of Poetry at Oxford University.
1961

1957 Buys house in Kirchstetten, Austria, and, with Kallman, begins to spend springs and summers there. Wins Feltrinelli Prize (Rome).

1958 *Selected Poetry* (American edition: 1959).

1959 Wins Guinness Poetry Award. Awarded Alexander Droutzkoy Gold Medal by the Poetry Society of America.

1960 *Homage to Clio.*

1961 Libretto (with Kallman) for *Elegy for Young Lovers*, by Hans Werner Henze.

1962 *The Dyer's Hand.* Elected Honorary Student (Fellow) of Christ Church College, Oxford University.

1964 Awarded Honorary Litt.D. by Swarthmore College.

1965 *About the House.*

1966 Libretto (with Kallman) for *The Bassarids*, by Henze. *Collected Shorter Poems, 1927–1957.* Awarded Austrian State Prize for Literature.

1967 Awarded the National Medal for Literature.

1968 *Collected Longer Poems. Secondary Worlds.* Awarded the National Institute of Arts Gold Medal for Poetry.

1969 *City Without Walls.*

1971 *Academic Graffitti. A Certain World: A Commonplace Book.*

1972 *Epistle to a Godson.* Gives up living in New York and moves to Oxford, where he plans to spend half of every year as a Fellow of Christ Church College.

1973 Libretto (with Kallman) for *Love's Labour's Lost*, by Nicholas Nabokov. *Forewords and Afterwords*, selected by Edward Mendelson. Death in Austria on September 29, of a heart seizure. Burial in Kirchstetten.

1974 *Thank You, Fog.*

1976 *Collected Poems*, edited by Edward Mendelson.

1977 *The English Auden*, edited by Edward Mendelson.

1979 *Selected Poems*, edited by Edward Mendelson.

CHAPTER 1

The Character of the Poet

WHAT KIND of poet is W. H. Auden? Critics have often condemned him for not being one kind or another, but they have seldom succeeded, even when they have wanted to, in describing the kind he *is*. During a career that spans two continents and several faiths, his poetry has seemed, from phase to phase, to alter not merely its loyalties but its character. Is it really British or American? really Freudian, Marxist, or Christian? Is Auden mainly a satirist, a Romantic, a journalist, a song writer, or what? Every new poem or new style of his seems to challenge what we thought we knew about him. Randall Jarrell, with delicate malice, once placed at the head of an article hostile to Auden a quotation he attributed to Heraclitus: *We never step twice into the same Auden.*[1]

Two or three characteristics, however, seem fairly permanent. For one thing, although Auden, sometimes very obviously, borrows techniques or mannerisms from dozens of other writers, he has to an extraordinary degree the poet's ability to make what he borrows his own, to mold it into something we think of as recognizably Auden. All readers will probably see as essential qualities of his style a quickness and lightness of touch; a cleanness of phrase and sentence; a caustic wit; an ironic hardness that, even as it recommends love as the answer to modern anxiety and injustice, is seldom in danger of sentimentality. At times Auden's wit is so exuberant and zestful as to produce, in the service of the most serious ideas, fanciful and even outrageous extravaganzas. At other times the wit is restrained and the verse austere; his writing achieves an Augustan, a Latin, a rococo, elegance.

But, in spite of the feeling we have of an undeniable precision,

21

most readers of Auden have had the experience, after reading one of his poems, of being thoroughly mystified—the thing doesn't make sense; the point vanishes between two stanzas; and the reader is left with a blurred image, an obscure situation, a half understood, possibly misunderstood point. It may be that Auden intends this uncertainty as a way of saying that, among all our precise instruments for measuring, computing, refining, we still have no sure knowledge of where we are. But among the causes of Auden's obscurity are some which account in large part for both the blur and the zest of his writing: his concern at once with inner experience and with society, his frequent shifts in perspective, his readiness to interpret anything as a parable of human experience, and his tireless experimentation.

I *Perspectives*

Although Auden's poems always probed the illnesses of modern society he usually approached this subject through the examination of inner motives and conflicts. A consistent student of the inner life—of anxiety, guilt, fear, self-doubt, anguish, love —he brought himself for a time in the 1930s to maintain that our inner lives could be put right only if certain social changes occurred; but he always found more congenial the opposing view that, whatever its causes, the center of our *malaise*, as well as the focal point of any cure, is the lonely human being. His work tends to make the outer world symbolic of an inner reality that is the scene of all finally significant action or at least the testing ground on which all action must be tried out and evaluated. Intellectual as Auden's poetry often seems—removed, detached, impersonal—the center of it is nevertheless the inner man who is thinking, feeling, comparing, refining, mocking, doubting, believing. As Auden puts it in a poem of the 1930s: "For private reasons I must have the truth" (*EA*, 142).

Still, from another point of view the *public* reasons are important. Skeptical of utopias, critical of society's administrators and managers, Auden is always alert to the contradictions between the personal and the public; and his poetry constantly shifts its angles of vision in order to show graphically the distance between the feeling inner self and what that self looks like from the point of view of the state, or of an objective observer. Even such an observer is at successive moments a social scientist, an interplanetary visitor, a psychoanalyst. The perspectives are often different, often changing; but all of them are needed to correct one another, to fill out Auden's view of the whole man: anguished self, citizen, organism, outsider.

Outer perspectives, however, may be fairly clear (although some of their intricate combinations can be puzzling); it is the *inner* perspective that often makes poems hard for us to focus. In the early work Auden uses syntactical ellipsis to give us that hard, gruff, urgent sense of meaning deeper than words: "Can speak of trouble, pressure on men/Born all the time, brought forward into light/For warm dark moan." (*EA*, 2) Frequently, too, both here and later, the syntax, though always crisp, is very involved; in fact, no other modern poet uses such various or such elaborate sentences.

Auden's poems are also full of unexplained pronouns, concepts, jokes, and contexts. Especially in the early poems (1928–32) we have a decisive sense of something happening, but not in a clearly defined place or time or situation. Many of these early poems revolve around the fighting of some unspecified war or an unexplained exile, but we do not know exactly who the enemy is, or what war we are engaged in, what its purpose is, or what we hope to gain. Although we may sometimes identify the cause with Marxist revolution (and early readers often did), we are not told enough to justify this identification; and the war is usually more intelligible as a conflict between inner forces of a Freudian kind, perhaps between a child and his elders.

The deliberate blurring is necessary to Auden's aims in these poems. The effect is that of dream-symbolism; for Auden, in exploring the inner life, is trying to present objects and events which are strong in felt, not reasoned, significance. What is important in the early poems is not the intellectual exposition of a social or psychological doctrine but the feeling that accompanies ambiguous commitment: what it feels like to go into voluntary, purposeful, if regretful, exile or partly to see one's way out of smothering anxieties and guilts. Even later on, when Auden's poetry becomes more discursive, the inner reality is still

central. As with more obvious stream-of-consciousness techniques, Auden's aim is to avoid explaining what the feeling self
already knows and he presents landscapes, statements, and
dream-imagery as correlatives of inner anxiety or polished corruption. Indeed, much of the best of Auden's work is expressionist
in character; and even the rational statements, however analytical
they sometimes become, normally function in poetic structures
which distort outer reality to conform to the self's feelings of
anguish, dread, hope, faith, or worry.

For example, the opening stanza of this poem seemed quite
opaque when I first read it:

> Wrapped in a yielding air, beside
> The flower's soundless hunger,
> Close to the tree's clandestine tide,
> Close to the bird's high fever,
> Loud in his hope and anger,
> Erect about his skeleton,
> Stands the expressive lover,
> Stands the deliberate man.   (*EA*, 217)

Gradually I realized that Auden is speaking of man in general
and of the universe that surrounds him: the air that stirs as he
moves; the plant life whose thirst, when we come to think of it,
is unlike that of other thirsty things in being silent; trees in
which the sap rises like a tide (the image echoes one of Rainer
Maria Rilke's), but also silently and secretly; birds that seem
intense and live in the air above us—hence the pun "high fever."

Later on Auden speaks of this man as

> The brothered and the hated
> Whose family have taught him
> To set against the large and dumb,
> The timeless and the rooted,
> His money and his time.

And, because I have read Auden's essays of this period, I see
at once that he is not condemning the strong man's exploitation
of the less gifted—"the large and dumb" working class, for example. No, the "timeless and the rooted" clearly refers, respec-

tively, to animals and plants. As with "high fever," the juxtaposition of money and time is a passing joke, which temporarily distracts us from seeing, and later adds emphasis to the fact, that "time" means "conception of time." And when we see this, we see that "money" signifies something like "the human capacity to deal with symbols and hence to develop elaborate social structures," which we then use to lay waste the natural world.

Although all of these phrases generalize certain aspects of air, flowers, trees, birds, plants, and animals, and therefore seem abstract, they nevertheless present these objects from the point of view of the man who experiences them all, who feels the air give way, who is aware of the flower's silence and the tree's unseen activity, who looks up at the bird, who observes the plant's immobility and the animal's imperfect comprehension of futurity. The bird is high, the plant rootless, the animal timeless, mainly in respect to man, so that these descriptions, though abstract, are still expressionist distortions because the point of view is included in the description.

II *Parables*

Another permanent feature of Auden's work is his delight in parables, in all literary or mythological structures that symbolize the relations between parts of the self or the self's relation to elements of society or nature: the unidentified war, the Marxist conception of history, the Christian picture of a world fallen but capable of redemption through miracle. Fairy tales, fantasies, dreams, or any stylized model of events may express for him certain fundamental spiritual conditions in the life of men for which he is always seeking analogues and symbols—the relations between members of a family, between master and servant, between doctor and patient, or the relations that hold in quests, in detective stories, in legends and landscapes.

Auden thus subordinates the usual practical, objective categories of value, of time, and of political order in favor of a world of parabolic relationships that are symbolic of real but inner conditions. He subordinates appearance to what he feels is deeper reality. The surfaces of life are still important to him, for it is through the physical and the immediate that a man works out his salvation. But, although in Auden's perspective one actual event may be empirically more important than another, *any* apparently trivial object, action, or system of relationships—a room, a meal, a forest—may have a capacity for illuminating our lives far beyond what we would expect from its modest position in ordinary life.

Holding such a view, Auden is remarkably attentive to the surfaces of ordinary life; for anything may, if we look at it right, suddenly glow with meaning. Looking at it right involves submitting it to sometimes bizarre perspectives, deliberately deranging our usual rational or sensory categories—having Caliban talk like Henry James, or locating a pastoral poem in a city bar. This kind of derangement is constant in Auden; it enters almost always into his imagery and is largely responsible for the blur of meaning that both intrigues and perplexes. It reminds us that his poetry, however rational in tone and structure, is faithful to its source in that unconscious that never gets logical categories straight, that his verse is often wildly playful, and that he is hopelessly in love with variety, improvisation, experiment.

III *Play*

Experiment, like other important things, may look trivial at first, may *be* so at first; but the trivial may lead us to the richest sort of meaning. Auden's experiment often begins in parody and ends in conversion; indeed, Christopher Isherwood recalls in his autobiographical *Lions and Shadows*[2] how Auden (whom he calls "Weston") used to change his personality with his hats:

There was an opera hat—belonging to the period when he decided that poets ought to dress like bank directors, in morning cut-aways and striped trousers or evening swallow-tails. There was a workman's cap, with a shiny black peak, which he bought while he was living in Berlin, and which had, in the end, to be burnt, because he was sick into it one evening in a cinema. There was, and occasionally still is, a panama with a black ribbon—representing, I think, Weston's conception of himself as a lunatic clergyman; always a favourite role. (188–89)

On a bus trip into the country one day in 1926, Auden em-

barrassed Isherwood not only by his hat (which raised snickers)
but also by his pretentious pronouncements

in resonant Oxonian tones: "Of course, intellect's the only thing that
matters at *all*. . . . Apart from Nature, geometry's all there *is*. . . .
Geometry belongs to man. Man's got to assert himself against Nature,
all the *time*. . . . Of course, I've absolutely no use for colour. Only
form. The only really exciting things are volumes and *shapes*. . . .
Poetry's got to be made up of images of form. I hate sunsets and
flowers. And I loathe the *sea*. The sea is formless. . . . (189)

But, Isherwood tells us, such pomposities "never for a moment
made me feel . . . that Weston himself was a sham. He was merely
experimenting aloud; saying over the latest things he had read
in books, to hear how they sounded" (190). And Auden continued to do so throughout his poetic career. He mimics the
tones, the verbal habits, even the imagery of other writers, of
older verse forms, and of political, scientific, or religious points
of view. But this mimicking is not always, or even typically,
hostile. It may even be, at first, a form of reverence, an awe-
stricken trying on of a new hat to see what it feels like on the
head. And who knows? The hat may turn out to fit, to be the
right one for the experimenter. Without the experiment, he might
never have found the hat. Several of Auden's poems in 1939 and
1940 show him "trying on" Christianity before he actually became
a Christian. As he states in *The Age of Anxiety*, "Human beings
are, necessarily, actors who cannot become something before
they have first pretended to be it . . ." (109).

But trying on a hat—or a style or a Church—whatever its serious
side, is also amusing; and, as one of the age's great wits, Auden
is rarely far from a joke. The jokes sometimes undermine serious
purposes, and his poems of the 1930s in particular often suffer
from an uncertainty of feeling: there are too many tones, and
we don't know how to take them. Any sincere stance Auden assumes in a poem—Freudian, Marxist, or even Christian—is always
in danger of being ridiculed by that other, comic side of him.
And perhaps his most remarkable achievement is that, despite
his almost unmanageable multiplicity of attitudes, he has not
wasted his talents in ironic play but has worked through to new

forms, new ironic structures, which do justice to the critical qualifications of the ironic intelligence, and yet affirm.

Auden, then, is a thoroughly serious poet, and a thoroughly amusing one. Never only one thing at once, he keeps shifting his own perspectives on the world and, in the process, reveals different sides of himself. His formal variety is astounding: he performs authentically as satirist, song writer, epigrammatist, didactic poet, meditative poet, elegist, odist; in long lines or short, sonnets or sestinas, octosyllabic couplets or four-stress alliterative verse, loose meter or strict, iambics or syllabics, and all kinds of rhyme. He develops styles and abandons them, a sign not of instability but of versatility—of wide, deep, and various interests. From the oracular early poems to the more direct analyses of social illness; from the quiet music of the early songs to the abstract imagery of the later 1930s that culminates in the earnest poems on Yeats and Freud; and from these to the elegance of "New Year Letter" and *The Sea and the Mirror*, and to the balanced Latin opulence of his more ambitious poems of the last three decades, Auden's poetry is continually changing.

Within these periods, even within single poems, the poetry is rarely single; it plays off mood against mood, reinforces wisdom with wit, enriches its textures with quick changes in feeling. For art, to Auden, is a mixed, a paradoxical, affair. It is play, but play is worth dying for (*DH*, 89); and yet it is, too, "in the profoundest sense, frivolous. For one thing, and one thing only, is serious: loving one's neighbor as oneself."[3] Auden's poetry keeps bringing together the sense of everything as of intense significance, and the sense of everything as trivial and frivolous. But each attitude is coherent only in the light of the other.

In fact, as it explores both the rationalities and suddennesses of the inner life, Auden's poetry asserts as its basic insight the connectedness of everything, even of the most unlikely things. The techniques of wit, the shifting images, the unexpected turns that the prosody often takes, all stress the surprise that life is— "O what authority gives/Existence its surprise?" (*CP*, 311)—its playfulness, its magic, its outlandish order. Inner life and outer spectacle, landscape and self, society and feeling—all are discovered to be connected in mysterious, puzzling, disturbing, yet marvelous ways.

Indeed, the world, touched anywhere, will expose these underground connections—if they are approached with just the right attitude of serious play. Words, ideas, feelings are fun to fool around with, to arrange, to order. They are the landscape of this world, whether it be Freud's or God's; and Auden always loved to name, to map, and to anatomize this landscape. Ultimately, this kind of happy tinkering amounts to reverence: to enjoy the world is perhaps to make the most pious use of it. As Auden's career proceeded, he passed from the nightmare conception of man divided from his own best self by overpowering shadows to the more sanctified fairy tale of man born to evil but capable of enchantment by Grace. Freudian inquisitor and Marxist prophet gave way to the more congenial role of ashamed but hopeful Christian.

In the new perspective, achieved by incongruities, even the wittiest poem is an act of joyful obeisance before this astonishing and beneficent arrangement of the world. "Whatever its actual content and overt interest," said Auden in 1956 (in his Inaugural Lecture as Professor of Poetry at Oxford University), "every poem is rooted in imaginative awe. Poetry can do a hundred and one things, delight, sadden, disturb, amuse, instruct—it may express every possible shade of emotion, and describe every conceivable kind of event, but there is only one thing that all poetry must do; it must praise all it can for being and for happening" (*DH*, 60).

CHAPTER 2

First Things

TO ENTER the world of Auden's poetry, we do well to understand another distinction he makes in his Oxford lecture—the distinction between sacred or profane beings or events. "Sacred" beings and events are those that arouse involuntary awe in us, that seem overwhelmingly significant, though often for reasons too deep for us to analyze; everything that does not have this character is "profane."

> Some sacred beings seem to be sacred to all imaginations at all times. The Moon, for example, Fire, Snakes and those four important beings which can only be defined in terms of nonbeing: Darkness, Silence, Nothing, Death. Some, like kings, are only sacred to all within a certain culture; some only to members of a social group . . . and some are only sacred to a single imagination. . . . One cannot be taught to recognize a sacred being, one has to be converted.   (*DH*, 55–56)

It should be clear that these terms involve no religious commitment at all. Atheists have their sacred beings just like pious Christians. And any poet during his career follows a trail of sacred beings and events—the characteristic images, attitudes, and worlds that seem to him most meaningful. Even certain forms and techniques, certain kinds of verbal gesture, may acquire their own sacredness. As this study proceeds, we shall try, therefore, to follow the ideas, forms, textures, and kinds of encounters that have been successively or continuously sacred to Auden.

I *How to Become a Poet*

Auden began writing poetry at fifteen "because," he tells us, "one Sunday afternoon in March 1922, a friend suggested that I should: the thought had never occurred to me"(*DH*, 34). Until then his interest had been mainly in science, especially in mineralogy; but, in looking back later, as he reports, he realized that he "had read the technological prose of . . . favorite books in a peculiar way. A word like *pyrites*, for example, was for me, not simply an indicative sign; it was the Proper Name of a Sacred Being, so that, when I heard an aunt pronounce it *pirrits*, I was shocked" (*DH*, 34).

Auden's father was a distinguished and scholarly physician who, the year after Auden's birth in York in 1907, "became Medical Officer and Professor of Public Health in Birmingham University";[1] Auden's mother was a trained nurse. The youngest of three brothers, Auden grew up reading fairy tales and Northern sagas, of which his father, conscious of his Icelandic ancestry, was fond. Auden later dedicated *Letters from Iceland* to his father and wrote of him: "Some of the most vivid recollections of my childhood are hearing him read to me Icelandic folk-tales and sagas, and I know more about Northern mythology than Greek" (214).

His scientific passion and the habit of fantasy combined to produce what Auden has called

a kind of daydreaming that was of immense importance to my childhood. Between the ages of six and twelve, I spent a great many of my waking hours in the construction and elaboration of a private sacred world, the basic elements of which were a landscape, northern and limestone, and an industry, lead mining. In constructing it, fantasy had to submit to two rules. In deciding what objects were to be included, I was free to select this and reject that, on condition that both were real objects (two kinds of water turbine, for instance, which could be found in textbooks on mining machinery or a manufacturer's catalogue); I was not allowed to invent one. In deciding how my world was to function, I would choose between two practical possibilities (a mine could be drained either by an adit or by a pump), but physical impossibilities and magic means were forbidden. It is no doubt psychologically significant that my sacred world contained no human beings.[2]

All these early interests left their marks on Auden's poetry, and they help to account for its basic images and situations.

The fairy tale and the saga serve as symbolic frameworks for Auden's intellectual parables; so does the anatomized landscape in which scenes or topographies have their symbolic implications. And the habit of medical diagnosis, the probing of contemporary illness, along with a certain amusement at or contempt for the too easy, too smug, pronouncement of disease or remedy, can be traced throughout Auden's career. In all these modes the stress falls on clear outlines and decisive action.

Perhaps, too, as Monroe Spears suggests,[3] the main problem of Auden as a poet, especially in his early work, was to strike a balance between rational diagnosis (that of the doctor and scientist) and the construction of fantasies (sagalike conflicts and exiles, fairytale quests and punishments, and obscurely significant landscapes). The fantasies always tend, however, to be descriptive of actual situations; for fantasy to Auden is a method of diagnosis, not an escape from, but a revelation of, the actual. Strict realism interests him little; even the novels that most intrigue him are those that can be read parabolically, like fairy tales—Kafka, Dickens, Faulkner, detective stories, late Henry James, and such. For nothing reveals so much about people as fantasy: Touchstone's words to Audrey, "The truest poetry is the most feigning," provide the title for a poem in *The Shield of Achilles* (1955) in which he argues the point.

In his early years Auden also developed a strong sense of musical form. He learned to play the piano with competence, and he sang in school choirs. His musical accomplishments were more extensive than those of any other important poet of our time who writes in English, and this ability is evident in his work. Not only did he produce large numbers of songs to be set to music —and wrote and translated opera libretti as well—but he also modeled many of his poems on various kinds of musical compositions, from the oratorio *For the Time Being* to the highly operatic arias and duets in his volumes of the 1950s and 1960s. Indeed, throughout his career his poems are remarkable for their musical subtlety.

After attending St. Edmund's School, where he first knew Christopher Isherwood slightly, and Gresham's School, where he specialized in biology, Auden went to Oxford, where he soon established himself as a personality and as a poet. His wit and intellectual force made a striking impression on everyone, and he became a central figure for those who cared for poetry. Thomas Hardy, his first poetic model, was followed by such others as Edward Thomas, Wilfred Owen, A. E. Housman, Edwin Arlington Robinson, Robert Frost, Robert Graves, and Laura Riding. But in 1926 at Oxford he was stunned by the impact of T. S. Eliot's verse and probably about this time became aware of the work of Gerard Manley Hopkins. With Charles Plumb he edited *Oxford Poetry 1926;* with C. Day Lewis, *Oxford Poetry 1927.* Auden wrote poetry himself, submitted it to his friends, judged their writing in turn, and explained to them what poets they ought to be reading and what qualities they ought to be aiming at in their own work.

Vivid, decisive, unpredictable, Auden seemed to them not always right, but always impressive. Students, like Stephen Spender, who wished to speak with him made appointments as if he were a don; then, "one was liable to be dismissed suddenly and told the interview was at an end."[4] "I was," Auden later admitted, "insufferably superior with anybody who, when speaking about matters in which I was interested, said something I thought stupid."[5] Spender, at his own first interview, nervously gave wrong answers to Auden's question about the poets he admired, whereupon Auden proceeded to explain his own more developed point of view:

He told me that the subject of a poem was only the peg on which to hang the poetry. A poet was a kind of chemist who mixed his poems out of words, whilst remaining detached from his own feelings. Feelings and emotional experiences were only the occasion which precipitated into his mind the idea of a poem. When this had been suggested he arranged words into patterns with a mind whose aim was not to express a feeling, but to concentrate on the best arrangement that could be derived from the occasion.   (46–47)

As for Auden's own place in the poetry of the future:

He thought that the literary scene in general offered an empty stage. "Evidently they are waiting for Someone," he said with the air of anticipating that he would soon take the center of it. However, he did not think of himself as the only writer of the future. He had the strongest sense of looking for colleagues and disciples, not just in poetry but in all the arts. . . . A group of emergent artists existed in his mind, like a cabinet in the mind of a party leader.   (47)

Isherwood sketches Auden's personality with a freer, more humorous hand:

He smoked enormously, insatiably: "Insufficient weaning," he explained. "I must have something to *suck*." And he drank more cups of tea per day than anybody else I have ever known. It was as if his large, white, apparently bloodless body needed continual reinforcements of warmth. Although this was the height of the summer, he insisted, if the day was cloudy, on having a fire in the sitting-room. At night he slept with two thick blankets, an eiderdown, both our overcoats and all the rugs in his bedroom piled upon his bed. (193–94)

Isherwood had reticences with his other friends, "But Weston left nothing alone and respected nothing: he intruded everywhere; upon my old-maidish tidyness, my intimate little fads, my private ailments, my most secret sexual fears" (194–95). And C. Day Lewis recalls that Auden's exuberance "redeemed . . . the dogmatism, the intellectual bossiness, and the tendency to try and run his friends' lives for them, all of which were by-products of this excess of life."[6]

Curiously enough, Auden was not militantly rebellious. "He rejected, quietly and without fuss," says Spender, "the moral views of both his preceptors and his fellow undergraduates" (48). His originality evidently never required extravagantly anti-social gestures of defiance. But he had a force that grouped people around him, imposed on them many of his own ideas and even much of his own imagery. In consequence, as Spears points out,[7] the Auden who became famous as the central figure of his group in the 1930s did not merely express the general attitudes of that group; to a large extent he created it and gave it its images, its tone, its ways of thinking, feeling, and writing. Although during the 1930s their political positions differed somewhat from his own, they continued to look on him as their most eloquent, if least orthodox, spokesman. And when he later defected from their views, moved to America, and became a Christian, some of his friends—and many liberals who saw Auden as the leader of a radical group—felt his change of allegiance to be a betrayal.

Another important element in Auden's early career was his attachment to German literature and German culture. At the end of his university days his parents offered him the chance to spend a year abroad; and, although most young Englishmen were traveling to France to glimpse "the lost generation," Auden, partly influenced by his enjoyment of Germanic sagas and of Old English poetry, which he had discovered through the Oxford lectures of J. R. R. Tolkien, decided to visit Germany. The effect of his stay there on his poetry and his thinking was considerable. Although his knowledge of French literature was extensive and "he reads and rereads [Dante] in the original,"[8] he owes much more, as later chapters will show, to such German writers as Rilke, Brecht, Kafka, Freud, and Marx, not to speak of German popular songs, the work of Kierkegaard, and the whole German Protestant tradition.

In "Letter to Lord Byron," Auden remembered his childhood this way:

> I must admit that I was most precocious
> (Precocious children rarely grow up good).
> My aunts and uncles thought me quite atrocious
> For using words more adult than I should;
> My first remark at school did all it could
> To shake a matron's monumental poise:
> 'I like to see the various types of boys.'   (*EA*, 192)

The habit of observing, and the habit of classification, remained with Auden to the end of his life. So did his interest in boys. He realized quite young that he was physically attracted to men rather than to women, and although he never addresses this problem openly in his early poetry, it can be sensed as perpetually present in the fables of conspiracy, concealment, exile, and rivalries so prominent in the early verse. Much of this verse, in fact, is concerned to show, with a kind of uneasy assurance, that being different is good, is healthy, that exile from a tainted society is the best response to it. The point is only occasionally put in sexual terms: "voices /Of new men making another love" (*EA*, 55). But if we understand that sexual estrangement and exile precede all other kinds, we can see how easily the myth of exile could later be made to serve first a psychological and then a political view. The early poems justify standing apart, being outside; in terms that Auden came to use later, the characters in these poems choose their Necessity, decide to be authentically what they cannot help being. Indeed, much of Auden's poetry throughout his career is concerned with our need to see what our true condition is and to accept it as given.

Auden wrote love poems all his life, usually in such a way as to disguise the sex of his lover. He wanted the poems, after all, to be valued as expressions of love by people with different patterns of affection. And erotic love is important in all his work. In the 1930s it functions as a figure for the personal life, in competition with the political imperatives that often seem more commanding; later, it serves, for most human creatures, as an imperfect type, and sign, of a more heavenly love. Auden never paraded his homosexuality or his promiscuity, but neither did he conceal them. It is worth pointing out, however, that the increasing clarity in his work probably accompanies his own increasing frankness about his sex life, that the elusiveness of his early verse and the abstraction of his middle period (1937–1945) give way to a much more explicit later poetry, written by the famous New York poet who everyone knew was homosexual.[9]

II *Where Nobody Is Well*

Auden and his friends grew up in the 1920s, an era of widespread disenchantment. They had spent their earliest years in Edwardian England—that well-satisfied, opulent world in which only a few writers and thinkers deeply questioned the validity of the social and moral structures. During World War I, which shook that civilization to its roots, they were children, approaching or passing through their adolescence (Auden was eleven when it ended), not old enough to join brothers, fathers, or neighbors (Auden's father was gone for over four years) in a struggle that made disturbingly clear the disparity between elderly ideals and youthful experience. The poems of Wilfred Owen, which exposed this disparity dramatically, were not lost on young men who later felt both guilty and deprived because they had missed what seemed the most significant experience of their lifetime.

After World War I the West tried to return to normal and to pretend that nothing really crucial had happened. But if there had been a certain falsity in the prewar smugness, the postwar normalcy rang still more obviously hollow. To many young men like Auden, the claims of almost every kind of respectability and orthodoxy had been publicly exposed as sham; and yet the same old phrases, the same old flags, continued to be turned and waved. The disenchantment with heroic Victorian ideals did not begin in 1914, but World War I convinced millions of Englishmen that war was not glorious but vicious, not human and heroic but terrifyingly mechanical, not a series of brilliant strokes but a succession of blunders. To the skeptical young, the traditional façade of public ideals seemed to crumble into fragments of empty oratory—foolish and dangerous platitudes still declaimed by the official guardians of a corrupt civilization: the Press, the Government, the Army, the Church, and even Women.[10]

How does one respond to a world governed by values in which one has ceased to belive? Mockery is a possibility; and there is plenty of it in the literature of the 1920s. Eliot may not laugh at the civilization he shows as exhausted, but writers like James Joyce, Gertrude Stein, and Evelyn Waugh show how playfulness can be turned to serious purposes. All of the Auden group learned at least to be irreverent; Isherwood developed a fine sense of mockery; but Auden became the most playful poet of the century. Deliberately disrespectful, deliberately vulgar, he showed his contemporaries how colloquial language could be used not only to shock conventionality but also to expose and ridicule its sham.

Another natural response is to look for guidance. If the world these young men were entering was not as their elders had described it, who could tell them what it *was*? History seemed to be entering a new phase—the war had perhaps only dramatized the situation—and it was going to be necessary to re-evaluate everything with the help of new lines of thought which were only beginning to make their influence felt. Freudian psychology in particular could throw new light on the nature of man, on the value and function of his social institutions; sociological thought could survey the prospects of individual and national happiness in an industrial civilization productive of both resources and problems that had never existed before.

Again and again, therefore, the young writers of the 1930s speak of their world as new—as a new country requiring new people, new signatures, new verse, new writing. They think of themselves as having the right to step forward to condemn and to remake the age, not only on the grounds that the solutions of orthodoxy have been discredited but also because they felt behind them the undeniable strength of their own prophets—Freud, D. H. Lawrence, later Marx, and a host of lesser but still cogent minds. "I think continually of those who were truly great," says Spender in a memorable poem; and dozens of his contemporaries did so, too.

It is thus worthy of note that, individualistic as most of these writers were, their attack on orthodox authority was not an attack on the principle of authority itself. Ultimately, Auden and his group almost all came to see that the new prophets also had their weaknesses. But this recognition was, for most of them, a gradual one: what they actually did at first was to substitute a new orthodoxy for the old, a new set of heroes, a different moral discipline, a different rigidity and certainty. For Auden, as we shall see, the new crusading faith is at first the psychology of Freud and Homer Lane, which, by curing individuals, may come to cure the world. Later, for himself to some extent but for his contemporaries even more, the faith is Marxism, the trust in a revolutionary social change that will be followed inevitably by universal human happiness (or at least a good chance for it). The religious faith to which Auden came still later, though again an orthodoxy, is, from another point of view, a recognition that his earlier simple faiths were inadequate, that *human* authorities are all flawed.

Even as early as the 1920s, however, the mythology of "the Auden group" includes not only the great intellectual prophets but also "leaders"—those strong personalities to whom weaker ones look for guidance in their struggle to break free of the murderous conventional world. For the other writers Auden became such a leader, and his own writing is filled with similar figures, anonymous in some early poems but more fully developed in such characters as John Nower of *Paid on Both Sides,* Francis in *The Dog Beneath the Skin,* and Ransom in *The Ascent of F6.* What, in this connection, most differentiates Auden's work from that of his contemporaries, however, is that he usually stresses the weakness of the leader himself. Aware no doubt of a discrepancy between his own role of leader and his inner feelings of anxiety and uncertainty, he presents leaders who are even more deeply and fatally divided in themselves, who are not the Truly Strong Men they appear to be (see below, p. 76).

For Auden's interest in politics never superseded his stress on individual moral psychology. And, at least to begin with, the rebelliousness of the Auden group was distinctly nonpolitical. As long as the 1920s lasted, and with them a sufficient British prosperity, the dissatisfaction of these young men was more a defiance of elders in general than a rejection of specific social, political, or economic institutions—of which, in fact, they were often ignorant. Auden even claimed that people at Oxford University were quite unaffected by world events: "Revolution in Russia, inflation in Germany and Austria, Fascism in Italy, whatever fears or hopes they may have aroused in our elders, went unnoticed by us. Before 1930, I never opened a newspaper."[11]

When they did turn to politics—and for some of them left-wing politics was a childish dream of heroic exile—they felt, with some justice, that they were discovering a new life. The very novelty of so many young men from respectable families taking an urgent but nonprofessional interest in politics gave to their activity the feeling of a crusade. And even during the 1930s the crusade was only partly political, only slightly economic. The essential grievance of this generation was always the intellectual and moral dishonesty of the Establishment. Although many of them later accepted, at least temporarily, the Marxist analysis of this situation, almost all of them ultimately—and Auden more consistently than most—retained much of their individualist perspectives, their primary concern with the integrity of private life and love, and their understanding of the contemporary illness as a psychological and even religious problem.

The illness, in any event, is what most impresses them all. The solution, even when it submits to Marxist orthodoxy, is usually conceived in almost religious terms: it is a matter of unaccountable but irresistible conversions and choices of exile. The new convert must break entirely with the past, separate himself from father and mother, and seek purification in an unknown country where he will find other of the faithful. This myth of conversion,[12] largely developed by Auden himself, though it makes an admirable vehicle for conveying the dynamics of Marxian commitment, was actually used by Auden, before he cared about politics, as a means of diagnosing the *psychological* condition of the modern world.

And of England in particular, "this country of ours where nobody is well" (*EA*, 62). We are all ill and must look for help to the great men of thought, the secular saints. If they cannot cure us, we are lost. And what they prescribe—Freud, Lawrence, and others—is a rejection not of political institutions but of conventional pieties and disguises. The proper Englishman makes an effective public appearance. But inside—and in the anatomy of interior conflict Auden is, among this group, uniquely subtle and penetrating—inside, behind the smiling façade, the sick animal, torn by his guilts and fears, is quietly going to pieces.

CHAPTER 3

Symbol, Myth, and Psyche

THE DOUBLE FOCUS—the concern with the relation between public poise and private anxiety—is characteristic of Auden's poetry from the beginning. It can be seen in his first volumes, which are usually spoken of collectively as "early Auden," and which consist of these works: the small *Poems* (1928), privately printed by Stephen Spender; *Paid on Both Sides*, a charade published in T. S. Eliot's journal *The Criterion* in 1930; the more substantial *Poems* (1930), and its second edition (1933) with seven new poems; and *The Orators* (1932). The imagery and ideas of these works, and their treatment of the inner-outer tension, owe much to three sources in particular: the symbolic method of T. S. Eliot, the mythology of Mortmere, and Auden's reading in psychology.

I   *Eliot*

In his poem for T. S. Eliot's sixtieth birthday, Auden, using extravagant detective-story imagery, recalls the 1920s as a time of frightened bewilderment and "drought." At that important moment, he goes on, "it was you/who, not speechless from shock but finding the right/language for thirst and fear, did much to /prevent a panic" (*CP*, 440). Auden's mischievous tone should not obscure the accuracy nor the earnestness of his tribute. What Eliot did for Auden and his friends, and for poets everywhere, was to develop some of the ways in which language could be used to express the contemporary thirst and fear.

For, from its beginning, from the writing of "Prufrock," Eliot's poetry, like his criticism, rested on a moral analysis of society and its institutions. Eliot's was the first significant modern

41

European poetry to see man's social relationships not as a drag
on his more cosmic connections but as the expression of his moral
being. Because Eliot sees man and society as caught up together
in a complex ecology, he never repudiates or withdraws from
society. On the contrary, society is a serious matter in his poetry
as it had hardly been for any poet since the eighteenth century.
It is certainly serious for Auden, too. For him, even more than
for Eliot, society is potentially admirable; it is properly a source
of moral values, a civilizer of men. It goes wrong, of course, but
there is no point in fleeing from it in the hope of escaping its
basic confrontations.

The language Eliot found for his moral studies of man in society is essentially that of symbolism. In *The Waste Land*, instead
of discussing particular governments, cultures, and social problems, Eliot presents a kaleidoscopic landscape of hollow, miserable, lost inhabitants of the modern world. Without personalities,
associated with historical and legendary characters who have
suffered similar situations, moving before us with the frozen
gestures and expressions of people in dreams, these shadowy
archetypal figures seem, nevertheless, to be living in the same
world we know—they cross the same bridges, walk the same
streets, hear the same clocks strike.

The symbolist technique, as Eliot developed it, allowed him to
put together fragments of life in which were fused together the
immediate and the permanent—to merge in a kind of double
exposure the city and the desert, the past and the present, the
particular man and the archetype. The perspective such a technique affords is visionary: each object mentioned ("the brown
land . . . the dull canal . . . the gashouse") becomes the sign of
a spiritual condition; the merest list ("Jerusalem Athens Alex-
andria/Vienna London/Unreal") suggests a history. And the
people who float half-seen through this shadowy landscape of
broken towers, falling bridges, and deserted cities are never
quite distinct from the world they inhabit. All distinction between public and personal is lost in a haze where everyone is
implicated together in the common human loss.

This imagery is the "language for thirst and fear" that Eliot
gave his contemporaries, and in his early poems Auden follows
Eliot in presenting a decayed landscape in bits and pieces which

look two ways at once: inward, to the private predicament; outward, to the public condition. Even when the emphasis is more
strongly on one of these, the other is usually not absent. Scores
of lines in early poems can be read as personal or as cultural
commentary: "And leaning asking from the car/Cannot tell us
where we are . . ." (*EA*, 53). Or:

> Others have tried it and will try again
> To finish that which they did not begin:
> Their fate must always be the same as yours,
> To suffer the loss they were afraid of, yes,
> Holders of one position, wrong for years. (*EA*, 45)

The strength of this early work often derives from the ambiguity. The lines can be read two ways, and it is often the landscape (site of public conflict or diagram of inner conflict) which
mediates between them and seems expressive of both. But if the
method owes much to Eliot, the typical Auden landscape in these
early days is his own. It is developed, in the first place, with a
very different tone—young, surgical, incisive, the directness and
authority contrasting oddly (as Barbara Everett has pointed
out[1]) with the blurred meanings. And, although Auden's decaying world has the same visionary quality as Eliot's, its furniture
is distinctive: a countryside of abandoned mines and power
stations, "derelict works . . . strangled orchards" (*EA*, 47)—
the lead-mine landscape of his boyhood fantasies but in ruin.
   Sometimes this landscape also seems very northern, marked
with glaciers and blizzards: "The ice-sheet moving down" (*EA*,
14); "The snowstorm on the marsh" (*EA*, 24); "the frozen dam"
(*EA*, 441); "Avalanche sliding, white snow from rock-face" (*EA*,
55). The setting seems strange, half known and half envisioned,
a familiar landscape but in an unfamiliar context, the scene of a
mysterious war whose issues are never made explicit, whose
participants even are only vaguely identified: sentries, prisoners,
"the trained spy," conquerors, "the dark squadron," a "leader."
The commonest emotions felt by the personae are fear, anxiety,
guilt, and the sense of isolation or of betrayal.
   Although the tone of most of these war poems is serious, sometimes even sombre, what helps to give them their odd effectiveness is the war imagery reminiscent of boys' adventure stories,

tales of spies, H. G. Wells's narratives of ruined civilizations, or
the war stories of C. E. Montague, from one of whose books
Isherwood derived the title of his autobiography *Lions and
Shadows.* A still more important source is the tradition of Icelandic saga, to which Auden in the late 1920s introduced Isherwood, who promptly noticed a striking similarity between the
heroic Norse warriors "with their feuds, their practical jokes,
their dark threats conveyed in puns and riddles and deliberate
understatements" and "the boys at our preparatory school." When
Isherwood pointed out this resemblance, Auden "was pleased
with the idea: we discussed it a good deal, wondering which of
our schoolfellows best corresponded to the saga characters. In
time, the school-saga world became for us a kind of Mortmere
..." (192–93).

II   *Mortmere*

But what was Mortmere? When Isherwood was at Cambridge,
he and his best friend Edward Upward (whom he calls "Chalmers") constructed an elaborate fictional world which curiously
resembles the early imagery of Auden. They began with a few
isolated figures, particularly with one they called "The Watcher."
"We imagined him," says Isherwood,

as a macabre but semi-comic figure, not unlike Guy Fawkes, or a
human personification of Poe's watching raven. He appeared to us,
we said, at moments when our behaviour was particularly insincere;
one might, for example, be telling a boastful story, or pretending an
interest in heraldry, or flattering the wife of a don—and there, suddenly, he would be standing, visible only to ourselves. He made
no gesture, never spoke. . . . Mutely, he reminded us that the "two
sides" continued to exist, that our enemies remained implacable, beneath all their charming, expensive, scholarly disguises. . . .   (53–54)

The "enemies" of whom Isherwood speaks are largely imagin-
ary, but they are expressive of the sense of isolation, of resistance
to authority, and of nonparticipation in contemporary beliefs
and assumptions that led Isherwood to fail his final examinations
deliberately and that led Upward eventually to communism.
Wherever they walked in Cambridge, they "encountered enemy

agents" (67). Soon they hit on the conception of "The Other Town": the notion that, beneath the Cambridge surface that everyone could see, plots and counterplots of an amazing complexity were being worked out. If one knew the right door, one could enter the world behind the town, a world of quietly plotting enemy agents, but also of some who were on the better side, "medieval bogies" and "the ghosts of our favourite writers" (72).

Later the two young men decided that the "Other Town" wasn't Cambridge at all but (and the description reminds one of Pressan Ambo in *The Dog Beneath the Skin*) "a village somewhere among the enormous downs, on the edge of the Atlantic Ocean" (101). They named it Mortmere, and they peopled it with numerous odd characters—the Reverend Welken, who "had been guilty of moral offenses with a choirboy and had later suffered severe pangs of conscience, persuading himself, at length, that, as a punishment for his crime, his dead wife was appearing to him in the form of a succubus" (102); Ronald Gunball, who "saw wonders and horrors all about him, his everyday life was lived amidst two-headed monsters, ghouls, downpours of human blood and eclipses of the sun—and everything he saw he accepted with the most absolute and placid calm" (102–103); Reynard Moxon, who ran a brothel for necrophiles and kept "a large black serpent which accompanied him on rambles after dark" (106); and a whole villageful of similar grotesques.

In Auden's early poetry, as in Mortmere, the fantastic masks the real; and the fantasy gives to the ordinary details of life a peculiar air of displacement, and to the people a quality of disconnection. The comic characters of Mortmere have been treated with that dimming, mythmaking touch of Eliot's; but otherwise we are in the same world of powerful and obscure enemies, wars without explicit issues, Our Side and whatever We stand for (mainly rebellion) against Them and Their abused authority.

III *Psychology*

Still, the Mortmere landscape has become more than a fantasy setting for vague feelings of rebellion. Where Eliot overlaid his picture of the modern world with the anthropological learning of Sir James Frazer and Jessie Weston—an anthropology that looks both into the self and out to the culture—Auden mounts his adventure myth on two other contemporary conceptual images: the Freudian dream and the vision (eventually Marxist) of a better world. The one faces inward toward the individual and the past; the other, outward toward the society and the future. But each is dependent on the other, each has a view of history to account for the present conflict, and each proposes a cure for today's illness. Marx came later, but Auden's reading in psychology was already extensive by 1928. Hence, while Mortmere in the undergraduate version is a simple game, a framework for continual fanciful improvisation, Auden has deepened the fable by secreting within it a kind of allegorical psychology, by projecting the abstract and inward terms of mental illness and health onto the external landscape of a rather Norse Mortmere.

As Auden diagnoses modern illness in these poems and searches for its cure, he follows his chief mentors of these early years— Freud, Georg Groddeck, Homer Lane, and D. H. Lawrence. The main theme of all these writers, as Auden reads them, is that modern man has lost his capacity for the instinctive life, for the kind of natural and fruitful love that alone can make human relationships satisfying. From Freud, Auden derives the fundamental conceptions of the power of the unconscious over the conscious, of the destructive nature of repression and inhibition, and of the lifelong struggle between the death wish and the life instincts (Eros). From Groddeck, Auden draws (and sometimes mocks) the theory that a peculiar force known as the *It* inhabits each of us, and that all illness is the result of the *It*'s struggle to keep peace between the individual and his environment.[2] From Homer Lane, an American psychologist and educational reformer, Auden takes his emphasis on love and his version of the psychosomatic nature of all illness. Edward Upward allows one of his characters to present this view dramatically in his novel *Journey to the Border* (1938):

"Every disease is a cure if we know the right way to take it. Disease is a result of disobedience to the inner law of our own nature, which works by telling us what we want to do and has no use for 'don't's [*sic*]. From childhood up we are taught that our natural desires are evil, that we must control them, deny them room to grow. But they

will not be denied. Twisted, clogged with moralizings, driven back
from all normal avenues of development, they nevertheless find a way
of asserting themselves, appear in disguise, take on unexpected and
abnormal forms—malaria, murder, neurosis, joining a Storm Troop,
and whatnot." (137–38)

It was from an anthropologist named John Layard, whom
Auden met on his visit to Berlin, that he first heard of Lane and
Groddeck. Under their influence, the young poet evidently be-
came everyone's diagnostician. Once, visiting him at Oxford,
Isherwood contracted the flu; and he subsequently caught cold at
almost every meeting, an affliction to which Auden referred as
"the liar's quinsey" (*Lions and Shadows*, 217). In fact, he gave
Isherwood

a whole catalogue of ailments and physical defects, with their psychic
causes: if you refused to make use of your creative powers, you produced a cancer, instead; excessive obstinacy—a refusal to "bend the
knee"—found expression in rheumatism of the joints; deafness and
short sight were attempts to shut out the exterior world . . . con-
sumption represented a desire to return to early childhood, because
the lungs are the first organs used by the new-born baby; epilepsy
went even farther back—it was an attempt to become an angel, and
fly. (303)

What all these ideas emphasize is the wisdom of letting the
life within us have its way, instead of killing or corrupting it by
rational control. This point D. H. Lawrence particularly makes—
that we think too much and that the stress laid on mind ignores
the lower but purer centers of our being, the solar plexus and
the lumbar ganglion. The aim is to move with the rhythms of
nature—"decent with the seasons," as Auden puts it in an early
poem—to lose one's inhibitions, to be "pure in heart," as Homer
Lane had evidently been: beyond illness, free to love. And free
also to be angry now and then, to loose natural, healthy aggres-
sions. Anger, according to Auden's pantheon, is purgative and
good; pity, destructive and sterile.

The early poems present man confronted with his illness and
required to choose a cure, to choose between death and health.
The present is a time of crisis and possibly of evolutionary
transition: man has the chance to repudiate his death wish by

developing a higher consciousness, one characterized mainly by love. Indeed, by homosexual love, and for an Auden protagonist one early step toward health is to acknowledge what one is, rather than to behave like the "perverted lovers" in *The Orators* "who when the saving thought came shot it for a spy" (*EA*, 63). Often the way to health is presented through the image of a man leaving his community, striking out blindly on a mission he does not understand but one that is his only hope of salvation. We are made to feel, too, that the burden he carries on his shoulders is not only his own salvation but that of his fellow-men: *someone* must reverse the fatal direction of the modern world by recovering at least his own humanity.

Men of good will, therefore, must resist the cultural practices that tend to reduce the life in them—the deadly clichés of feeling (narrow nationalism, petty pride, "self-regard," provincial and immature emotional patterns) and of language. We are told in *The Orators*, only half mischievously, that the good man should beware all the deadly agents of conventionality, people who have the wrong kinds of handshake ("the marsh—the claw—the dead yam") or who ask questions like, "Am I boring you?—Could you tell me the time?—Are you sure you're fit enough?" (*EA*, 81). Healthy people must respond openly to love, without the embarrassments and dodges usual in contemporary life. They must come to see that the illness from which we all suffer is, if understood and properly treated, the first stage of a cure.

The natural, the instinctive, the irrational—these are what Auden, with all his precision, admires and recommends in his early poetry. And the imagery is calculated to support his views, with its mysterious struggle between life and death forces and its investing of topographical strategies with symbolic echoes (faintly reminiscent, perhaps, of *Paradise Lost*). Hence, too, the stern condemnation of evil, the moralistic intolerance of conventional morality. Guilty action and guilty isolation are roundly excoriated, and what Auden in his sometimes pedagogical severity offers to his guilty-schoolboy audience is the path of exile and renunciation—the change of heart that will release man's love.

It ought to be easy, as the schoolmaster's tone suggests. "Man does not choose to love; he *must* love," writes Homer Lane.[3] But, in fact, bad methods of education have so turned us away from the natural and healthy path of love that, even when we come to recognize its superiority, we feel nostalgic for the familiar but deadly life: the past—the conventional, the traditional—is charming in its way, so hard to give up, so richly seductive, even though we know how poisonous it is. "We would rather be ruined than changed" (*CP*, 407)—so Auden wrote many years later—and the typical personage in the early poems exhibits the same ambiguous feeling when confronted by the accusing tone of History, Evolution, or Auden.

It is not enough, Auden tells us, to be born handsome or clever or to see what is best to do. Rather, a man must choose his own path, making choices blindly at times but making them always in favor of what in him is most honest and natural. This basic view of the personal imperative is one that Auden speaks of often; and, in his essays of the 1940s and 1950s, it comes to be expressed, in modified form, as a subordination of the Aesthetic and Ethical attitudes to the Religious (see Chapter 10).

But while Auden indicates throughout his work the honest path that is open to us, he shows us also our inner ambivalence —our wish to be excused from decision, and the difficulty of a firmness that amounts to exile from the normal world of moral slackers. His early poems present this uncertainty in the face of clear (if blind) choices through the imagery of a war played out on an attractively decaying landscape; and the use of this landscape to draw together inner and cultural ambiguities provides him with his own "right/language for thirst and fear."

CHAPTER 4

The Early Poems

I Poems (*1928*)

P OEMS (1928), a severe little volume, consists of twenty untitled poems, most of them obscure. Whether they treat of
love or war, the situations they imply are blurred and vaguely
tragic. The tone is often elegiac: the war—that northern, saga-like
war—is not going well; industry is "already comatose"; and the
most vivid figures are those whose deaths or failures are recalled
in epic manner: "Morgan's who took a clean death in the North,/
Shouting against the gale, or cousin Dodd's,/Passed out, asleep
in her chair, the snow falling" (*EA*, 15). But the tone is also frequently accusing, prescribing, condemning, although, to be sure,
the speaker is often involved in the general guilt and weakness:
"The pointed hand would place/Error in you, in me" (*EA*, 21);
"Returned from that dishonest country, we/Awake, yet tasting
the delicious lie" (*EA*, 24).

From our vantage point of decades and volumes later, we can
see the 1928 Auden experimenting boldly but not wildly. He is
testing tones, combining images and phrases in new ways, imitating the poets he admires, trying to make every line catch fire,
every phrase have its effect. His diction is usually simple, sometimes grand, sometimes theatrical. But he reveals himself already
a master of syntax, which he manipulates with a free hand, tight-
ening it for effects of tension and hostility:

> Or sit, the doors being shut,
> 'Twixt coffee and the fruit,
> Touching, decline to hear
> Sounds of conclusive war.   (*EA*, 24)

Or he reduces the language to simple, epic phrases: "But he is defeated; let the son/Sell the farm lest the mountain fall:/His mother and her mother won" (*EA*, 17). The strong syntax shows particularly in impressive last lines: "Enough to have lightly touched the unworthy thing" (*EA*, 15); "Ears poise before decision, scenting danger" (*EA*, 22); "Rocks shutting out the sky, the old life done" (*EA*, 12).

Aside from the occasionally pretentious tone, the most notable weakness is imagery that seems unfocused, blurred, confused. But the successful imagery is the book's triumph. Almost every poem, despite the often admonitory tone, implies some full human situation, from the foggy context of which the poem's utterance emerges. Auden gives us glimpses of individuals involved in the predicaments common in adventure novels or sagas; but the predicaments are weighted with what would be for a novel (though not for an epic) a more than usual moral gravity: "Go home now, stranger, proud of your young stock;/Stranger, turn back again, frustrate and vexed" (*EA*, 22); "Travellers may meet at inns but not attach./They sleep one night together, not asked to touch . . ." (*EA*, 12).

Indeed, every landscape no matter how vague and every situation no matter how blurred seem to focus some moral choice or moral failure. The whole book suggests that being human, especially now, is hard work because there are so many ways to fail. It is true that even in the midst of all the moral dangers one may still experience satisfying hours of repose and love (*EA*, 26, 14), but ordinarily the war goes on. It is a subtle and perplexing war because it is largely internal, and the people engaged in it know themselves so slightly that they may at any moment lose their bearings—by misreading their natures, by being dishonest, by consenting to be misled by the ignorance or dishonesty of others ("lies about the cost of a night's lodging"—*EA*, 12), or by underestimating the difficulties:

> Nights come bringing the snow; and the dead howl
> Under the headlands in their windy dwelling,
> Because the Adversary put too easy questions
> On lonely roads. (*EA*, 26)

II Paid on Both Sides

Six of these early poems were incorporated in *Paid on Both*

Sides, a short dramatic sketch about two feuding communities, Lintzgarth and Nattrass. The setting is in some ways modern, with talk about mills, docks, maps, private flats, Scotland Yard, employers, and pulleys; the characters sail to the "Colonies," send wires, drink sidecars. But Auden's language, starkly elliptical and reminiscent of Old English, transforms the events into a modern-dress Norse saga. As in the sagas, the feud takes its own course, and there is no modern law; the suggestion is clear that in our own day national wars are carried on as senselessly and wastefully as were family feuds a thousand years ago. The verse is sometimes too close to its Old English models, amusingly so:

> Then watchers saw They were attacked
> Shouted in fear A night alarm
> To men asleep Doomed men awoke
> Felt for their guns Ran to the doors
> Would wake their master Who lay with woman
> Upstairs together Tired after love.   (*EA*, 6)

But the piece has great vigor. In writing it, Auden gave his extravagance free rein and achieved a humor that is absent from *Poems* (1928). Although the basic situation is tragic, and most of the poetry elegiac, there are funny passages, notably the scene in which the Doctor takes from his bag "circular saws, bicycle pumps, etc." and "extracts an enormous tooth from the body" of a character recently shot. Through such mischievous touches, which give the charade diversity if not coherence, Auden reveals an easy playfulness that he has exploited throughout his career.

III   Poems (*1930*)

Poems (1930) returns to the serious tone of the earlier collection. Indeed, nine of its thirty untitled poems are taken from the 1928 volume; and the general mood of the new book is not strikingly different, although the poems are more accomplished and less surrealistically disconnected. There are still some private love poems, but the chief thematic innovation in this volume is that the poems as a group compose an urgent diagnosis of

England's condition and an appeal, even a warning, in behalf
of a change of heart. The Norse imagery is found chiefly in the
poems retained from 1928; the new pieces that use the imagery
of war, enemies, and the two sides seem more immediate in time
and place.[1] The situations may still be blurred, but the patient
is unmistakably modern England.

More sharply than in 1928, these poems contrast the mythical
and the commonplace. As Barbara Everett writes, Auden's myth
"combines an elusive generality with a startling particularity of
detail. As in a dream, random details are invested with enormous
emotional or psychological importance, though the meaning of
the whole is never absolutely explicit."[2] Poem XXIX, for example,
gives new significance to such ordinary details as a "cigarette-end
smouldering on a border/At the first garden party of the year."
The same poem presents commonplace features of English life
("The leisurely conversation in the bar/Within a stone's throw
of the sunlit water/ . . . those women/ . . . in the country
parishes"—*EA*, 46–47) as strategic elements in a mammoth conspiracy. In one poem after another the ordinary is thus suddenly
and peculiarly freighted with meaning. The mysterious signifi-
cances of Mortmere, of John Buchan, or of detective stories are
surprisingly and brilliantly used to light up the pervasive guilt,
the radical anxiety, of England.

At the same time, it is a mistake to see Auden's criticism as
Marxist. Monroe Spears is surely right in stating that the new
poems "imply more clearly a social-political theme," but he is
surely wrong in considering that, together with the old, they
"form an analysis of bourgeois society, of capitalist England"
(31). These phrases suggest that Auden is coming to think in
economic terms, which is not yet true. Other critics, too, have
written as if they thought Auden had been a Marxist in 1932,
or 1930, or even 1928.[3] A sounder view is that of Justin Replogle,[4]
who holds that Auden's interest until about 1933 is in individual
illness or in such illness as a widespread phenomenon and, therefore, as a social problem.

For, even when Auden shows us rich people in this volume—
and he does so very little—he does not condemn them for their
moral-economic vices of waste or idleness or exploitation of
others; he condemns them, as usual, for their inner sickness. The

"nonchalant pauses" of the wealthy man-about-town (not a "prosperous capitalist," as Spears says [32]) in Poem IV give a false impression of assurance; but inside he is torn apart, "poised between shocking falls on razor-edge." And the candidate for secret agent who is being tested in Poem I (*EA*, 35–36) must be willing to "interrogate" the "poises" of the rich: their sickness, not their injustice, disturbs Auden.

What *Poems* (1930) shows is that the whole country, all of Western civilization, is constantly growing more ill, and that the proper cure is a redistribution not of wealth but of health. Such hopes for a new world as appear in the volume are the ordinary ones that young men have of reworking the social institutions they have inherited. Such reform may require surgery, and much that seems attractive will have to go: "We know it, we know that love/. . . Needs death, death of the grain, our death,/Death of the old gang . . ." (*EA*, 40). There will have to be a *social* revolution. But Auden is not yet thinking (if he ever seriously did) in terms of bourgeoisie and proletariat; the war imagery is a metaphor for cultural illness, not a literal description of a political reality to come.

Of course, the imagery *sounds* political; and its very obscurity reinforces the impression that it must *be* political. Decision and action; understanding one's choices and making them; choosing between the old, corrupt life and the new, hopeful one, between death and life—such alternatives fitted the political realm even more obviously than the psychological. Ironically, by the time Auden was ready to write poems announcing a *literal* revolution, he had entirely abandoned the war-poem style that seemed so eminently suited to it.

Nevertheless, Auden's 1930 volume does clearly call on Englishmen to change their world. Poem after poem focuses on psychological illness as a ruinous social fact. Again and again Auden explains (even with a certain glee, as Barbara Everett has pointed out[5]) that there is no escaping the choice of health or illness, the human condition: "Do not imagine you can abdicate;/Before you reach the frontier you are caught . . ." (*EA*, 45). And he keeps asserting that the moment has come for change: "It is time for the destruction of error" (*EA*, 40). This clear certainty, the unmistakable tone of challenge ("Will you turn a deaf

ear . . . ?" is the first poem's first line) rings through the whole
book and makes a strong contrast with the relative confusion of
Poems (1928).

But most surprising in this volume is a new sophistication,
both of technical skill and of tone. Despite their obscurity, most
of the 1928 poems are fairly plain in manner, usually iambic
without complication, and declarative if elliptical in syntax; the
rhyming and stanza arrangements are fairly simple, the versification conservative. Some more elaborate rhetorical devices occur
in the poems later used in *Paid on Both Sides;* and there are
some interesting experiments with slant-rhymed quatrains that
remind us of Emily Dickinson and with consonance-rhyme (after
Wilfred Owen); but there is nothing technically striking or
original.

The 1930 volume shows an extraordinary increase in deftness.
A number of poems, written in short lines after the manner of
John Skelton,[6] reveal for the first time Auden's remarkable skill
in manipulating sound and form:

> This lunar beauty
> Has no history
> Is complete and early;
> If beauty later
> Bear any feature
> It had a lover
> And is another.   (*EA*, 52)

This first appearance of the now familiar Auden elegance is
accompanied and consolidated by a new grandness of manner.
If the 1928 *Poems* sometimes pointed the finger at the guilty
reader, the 1930 persona is more magisterial still: "Since you are
going to begin to-day/Let us consider what it is you do" (*EA*,
44). Sometimes the point is insisted on with mock pedantry:
"Love by ambition/Of definition/Suffers partition/And cannot
go/From yes to no/For no is not love; no is no ..." (*EA*, 30).
The tone is that of a schoolmaster pointing out a lesson with a
stick; the wit, not exactly funny, is that of the master of whom
we are a little afraid. Many of the new pieces are surprisingly
abstract, but the abstractness is guarded from possible dullness
by the verbal wit, the versifying skill, and the quickness with

which the abstract passages or poems are followed by the saga-like landscape imagery.

That imagery is so powerful in several of the new poems that, in giving texture to the whole volume, it obscures the nature of Auden's development since his 1928 *Poems*. Certainly the imagery is surer; of the ability to endow the commonplace with significance, Auden has become an assured master. But, along with this development of his imagery, the 1930 *Poems* moves clearly in a very different direction—toward wit, abstraction, elegance of manner.

Even the seven new poems which Auden added to the 1933 edition (to replace seven he discarded) show this new elegance. Only one is Norse in manner; only one is Skeltonic and abstract; three effectively combine the new verbal or stanzaic wit with the older symbolic landscape of war and crisis. But thereafter Auden abandoned the Norse saga-style, with its epic tone and its ambiguous myth of a public-private war. The other two fresh poems in the 1933 edition are in a new vein entirely: they ironically exploit the rhythms and idioms of popular songs ("What's in your mind, my dove, my coney?"). Auden thus begins that virtually unlimited mining of the colloquial resources of our time that has been one of his principal trademarks.[7]

IV   The Orators

In general, then, *Poems* (1930) is much more poised, more articulate, than its predecessor; the poet is much more aware of the possibilities of both form and fun. *The Orators* (1932) explores these possibilities further. Startling and exciting to his contemporaries, it has been interpreted variously by readers and disparaged by Auden himself.[8] Despite its obscurity, *The Orators* has great exuberance. If the hallmark of the 1930 *Poems* is its movement toward form and elegance, that of *The Orators* is its explosive cleverness, especially its display of Auden's newfound skill at parody.

The Orators: An English Study is a deliberately disjointed series of *tours de force* in prose and verse. The major theme of all the pieces is the sickness of modern society. In these years, as I have indicated, society's illness did not to Auden mean economic injustice or political tyranny so much as the psychological warping of the young. Auden consequently took a strong interest in educational methods and practices, and in the public school system in particular where England's leaders supposedly were trained, where he himself was teaching after his return from Germany, and where one could find all the rhetorical modes, phrases, and systems which were to keep the new leaders as sick as the old. The book, as its title suggests, attempts to expose the national rhetorical structure; to make clear that it is upon this crumbling structure of false ideals, empty phrases, rationalizations and self-excuses that English life is built; and to demonstrate how even the best men, even "revolutionists" in the service of more valid beliefs, may be fatally infected by the insidious poison of the system and destroy themselves rather than it.

In addition to a Prologue and an Epilogue (the first exhibiting the disparity between public performance and private anxiety,[9] the second asserting that action is possible and necessary), the work consists of three sections. Book I, "The Initiates," is a series of prose pieces cast in different rhetorical modes: the address; the prose poem (after St.-Jean Perse); the litany ("O Bulldog Drummond, deliver us . . . Fair Maid of Kent, hear us"); Gertrude Stein's abstract prose ("An old one is beginning to be two new ones. Two new ones are beginning to be two old ones. . . ."); and the informal letter. The parodies are often delightful; the meanings are not always plain. Still, it is evident that Auden is sympathizing with those who seek a way out of this Babel; but, at the same time, he is showing how hard it is, how all the ordinary verbal routes to clarity and sense are blocked by the ludicrous debris of adult humbug and schoolboy ineffectuality.

In the opening section a jaunty speaker at a prize-day ceremony speaks to the boys in the style of an energetic "old boy"; he uses Dante's analysis of excessive, defective, or perverted lovers to focus his images of "England, this country of ours where nobody is well," and he finally calls for "some pretty stiff changes"—which are to begin right away with the boys stuffing their most conventional masters down a stoke-hole "under the floor of this hall, the Black Hole we called it in my day." Scholars have sometimes wondered whether we should admire or be horrified at this speaker, but he is obviously, like many characters in Auden, a figure of fun, an absurd speaker, who yet voices some very sensible or penetrating ideas.

Sections II ("Argument") and III ("Statement") are more mysterious. If Section I has, in its eccentric way, proclaimed the revolution, these sections, each divided into three parts, evidently present a revolutionary consciousness at a later stage of conspiracy. "Argument," mainly concerned with an unnamed leader who seems almost divine and is always referred to with a capital letter ("He" or "Him"), shows the readiness of followers to treat a leader as a god. If there is anything in *The Orators* that seems authentically Fascist, it is that this readiness is too little rebuked. The emphasis of "Statement" is more social. Here a similar consciousness makes abstract observations about individual people and their talents and fortunes: "One is obeyed by dogs, one can bring down snipe on the wing. . . . One drinks alone in another country. . . . One discovers in middle age his talent for painting" (*EA*, 69–70).

The final section of Book I, "Letter to a Wound," appears to be written not by a revolutionary but by an excessive lover of self, who nurses his wound lovingly until, of course, it will kill him: "Nothing will ever part us. Good-night and God bless you, my dear." The point is obvious enough: the consciousness, or the society, that falls in love with its own disease is sure to die of it. As always in Auden, the death wish is a real temptation. The old life is attractive; its comforts make us feel good.

Book II, "Journal of an Airman," shows us a more individuated member of the revolutionary conspiracy. The miscellaneous entries in his journal include genetic charts, symbolic alphabets, descriptions of dreams, bits of verse, and cryptic notes on friends and colleagues ("Percy is not to be trusted and should be watched"). From this assortment we make out vaguely not only the progress of the revolutionary plot but also the Airman's continuous struggle against such weaknesses in himself as kleptomania, epilepsy, homosexualism, and masturbation. But readers have frequently felt confused as to whether the Airman is to be regarded as a revolutionary who successfully copes with his difficulties ("Hands in perfect order" is the last line of Book

II) or as one who finally commits suicide. Since death may be a metaphor for a changed life, a death to *this* life—as in "1929" Auden calls for "death, death of the grain, our death,/ Death of the old gang" (*EA*, 40)—it is hard to be sure.

Another question often raised about the Airman is whether or not it is fair to see him as partly a Fascist and the revolution as rather Fascist than Marxist. Stephen Spender observes that the Airman is "the man of action, flying, planning Fascist (?) coups, circulating leaflets."[10] In the context of Auden's and his friends' later Marxist allegiances, the Airman's position as both artist and Fascist is especially perplexing; but again it must be remembered that up to this time in England it was the Fascists, not the Communists, who were demonstrating in public, disseminating their propaganda, and forming what looked like private armies. On the other hand, the Airman seemed in those days a natural symbol of freedom and heroic action. Lindbergh's flight across the Atlantic in 1927 was still fresh in memory, and T. E. Lawrence, after his remarkable adventures in the Middle East, had become an airman. Something of Lawrence's odd mixture of heroism and neurosis (he joined the air force as a private in an apparent effort to repudiate his fame and begin a new life) is certainly present in this work of Auden's.

But Auden is also dealing in metaphors—the metaphor of flight, and the metaphor of conspiracy that is prominent elsewhere in *The Orators* as well. As usual in Auden, these metaphors work on two levels: the Airman functions as a combatant in Auden's fiction about a conspiracy directed against the government of a mythic yet modern country, another version of Mortmere; but the conspiracy seems also, in part, a daydream of the Airman's, a means (along with his vocation of Airman) of projecting his own efforts to understand and cope with that psychic illness which is at once peculiar to him and shared with all his contemporaries. Auden's method—one of his favorites throughout his career—is to magnify the inner condition as if it were an outer world, with its own geography, social events, flora and fauna. But such a world, only a metaphor to begin with, is developed so fully and with such near-coherence that we find ourselves wanting it to be wholly coherent. We want to understand the significance of different details of the Airman's war, to know where we should share his views and where we should see him as going wrong. Above all, to judge from what critics have written on *The Orators*, we want to know whether, in his fiction, he functions as a Fascist.

But only to the extent that the Airman's world is a literal country is this question legitimate. To the extent that it is a daydream, a projection of his inner struggle for health, it is beside the point. The inner life is no parliamentary democracy, and the war Auden presents is a suitable symbol of its wayward, chaotic, embattled feeling. What we see in the Airman's journal is a psyche at war, rebelling against its condition. Auden is extraordinarily inventive in bringing this revolt to life through a thousand imagined details, but they are all, in a sense, jokes—some grim, some restrained, but all enlisted in the service of the same absurd premise: that what we call the war within is literally a war.

But why an Airman? Flight, in Freud's dream system, connotes sex; in Auden's psychosomatic catalogue, it is connected with epilepsy (see above, p. 47). But both of these meanings, as Peter E. Firchow has shown, derive, for Auden, from John Layard's studies of the sorcerers of Malekula: the Bwili, or "flying tricksters" (a poem in "Journal of an Airman" uses this phrase), who resemble the Airman in several important respects, including a "predisposition toward homosexuality."[11] And this element in the symbolism is essential to an understanding not only of the Airman but of all the mythology of conspiracy used by Auden and by some of his friends in the 1930s. To be a homosexual in this period was to stand outside the system, which was heterosexual as well as bourgeois. It required one to hide one's sexual preferences, as a spy has to hide his allegiances. The tale of espionage, of unspecified political conspiracy, is a suitable metaphor for the acceptance, by the usual homosexual of the period, of a lifelong commitment to a secret order. It also turns out to be a suitable image for the more general quest for psychological health, a quest threatened by external opposition and by inner self-deception. That the conspiracy figure was used as well by heterosexual writers in the Auden circle does not diminish its special significance for those who, like Auden, could use it to express the poignancy of sexual stigma and exile.[12]

Once we become alert to the homosexual content of this imagery, the search for leaders also takes on a different meaning. The leaders who appear as potential saviors in Auden's early poetry are almost always single men; they belong to a different order from the normal middle-class family man. It is understandable, then, that the band of brothers in "Journal to an Airman," for example, or more generally in *The Orators*, these young men formed by their education in British public schools (Auden later described his own school as "a Fascist state"[13]), should look to strong male leaders and to a discipline or ethic as far as possible from the muddle of middle-class normalcy. But the metaphors in *The Orators* (and generally in Auden's early verse) do not serve a political doctrine. Any reader may hear authoritarian cries in the background—Auden, as always in this period, makes us aware of contemporary political forces just offstage—but the Airman is more of a flying trickster than a Fascist. A young man struggling to accept his condition, "a unit of life, needing water and salt, that looks for a sign" (*EA*, 93), he seems at the end to have prepared himself for some crucial showing, some test, which has no equivalent in the realm of ordinary life and which, as Auden and Isherwood already realized, the Truly Strong Man doesn't need (see below, page 76).

Book III consists of six odes, experimental in form, mostly celebrating or exploring aspects of the present emptiness and the hope of improvement; but these poems are arresting for their exclamatory utterance, their grim humor, and their private allusions. Spears has noted (35) that, whereas in the 1928 *Poems* the poet speaks always in his own person, in the 1930 volume he uses several personae. In doing so, Auden reveals an immense talent for parody, for catching the tones of virtually any kind of verbal life. *The Orators* shows Auden apparently going wild over this discovery; the book is all parody, of one kind of false rhetoric or another. And the odes in Book III are all extravagant in style as they burlesque their putative models— the dream-vision ("Lo, a dream met me in middle night..."); the birthday ode; "The Battle of Maldon"; Pindar; Hopkins; hymns.

In some of these odes and in other parts of *The Orators*, Auden not only parodies a manner but uses it to express his own views. This complex, Swiftian technique, with which Auden has experimented from time to time and which frequently baffles resentful single-minded critics, Auden has employed with great success, notably in the Caliban section of *The Sea and the Mirror*. The double perspective, as it reflects accurately the contradictions of human feeling, makes for an engaging design. "One expects the argument to be ironic," says Spears; "but, with double irony, it isn't" (48). Yet this device does make it difficult for the reader to disentangle what is mocked from what is affirmed.

The difficulties of perspective are especially acute in Ode V (*EA*, 106–109), which gives a new turn to the usual war in Auden. Ordinarily, that war has two aspects—the young English rebel fights against the Establishment conceived both as a set of external institutions and as a set of responses conditioned by them. That is, both the external enemy and that enemy *internalized* are presented as external enemies in a war. This procedure accounts largely for our sense of profound ambiguity in these early poems.

Ode V, however, shows us a slightly different war, not that of the rebel against *his* enemies, but that of the Enemy against his —the struggle of the conventional, the Conscious, to repress the Instinctive. The battle is hopeless, for the repression of Instinct only results in the conversion of healthy impulses into unhealthy ones: Love becomes Lust; the natural feelings become deadly sins. The effort to avoid this situation, to behave in conformity to one's nature instead of damming it up so that it resorts to violence and perversion, is the basic theme of *The Orators* as a whole. The exuberance of the athletes' ode and the birthday ode; the call for help, bizarre though it is, of Ode VI; the decision of the rider in the Epilogue to go "Out of this house"—all provide partial alternatives to the terrifying self-destruction that accompanies conventional dishonest feeling. It is hard for the crooked to become straight, but nothing less will do.[14]

CHAPTER 5

Hawk and Marx

I As the Hawk Sees It

BY 1933 AUDEN, at twenty-six, was an important poet. His work, though admirably various, was marked by certain distinctive features: a recognizable imagery, elliptical syntax, the schoolmaster's tone, the schoolboy's fun. His career for the next decade or so, long misunderstood, amounts to a rejection of the notion of personal style, a refusal to be limited to a few tones, a few forms, a characteristic manner. In fact, as I have shown, this refusal began even earlier, for each of his first volumes explored a new direction. Throughout the 1930s and 1940s his stylistic experiments continued, to the despair of critics who hold that poets should commit themselves to styles as well as doctrines.

Actually, Auden chose what seemed to him the more difficult way—not to recline among the cushions of a comfortable style, but to knock on as many poetic doors as possible, to try out new forms, tones, vocabularies, imageries, approaches, patterns. The flexibility and the range of contemporary poetry consequently owe more to Auden than to anyone else. We instinctively suspect such a poet of having failed to probe deeply enough the implications of some single style; but, although some of Auden's work was marred by carelessness and haste, most of his experiments were serious, intelligent explorations of poetic modes new or long discussed. Some styles, too, and some techniques he returned to again and again; but he varied them, used them for different purposes or in conjunction with different accompanying elements. And, finally, it must be said that although poets, especially Romantic ones, usually do develop distinctive styles, there is no rule that requires a poet to do so; that the implications of

63

diversity in style are as profound as the implications of narrow-
ness; and that the personal style to which a poet eventually submits may be stronger for having been long resisted.

Auden's chief reason for avoiding the kind of style that we
recognize at a glance—"Oh, yes, that's Browning" or "Obviously
Swinburne"—is his lifelong suspicion of Romanticism. The Romantic poet, in Auden's view, thrusts himself into the center of
his work, exhibits his private "dementia," makes a virtue of
personal confession, and values his own subjectivity not because
it tells him the truth but because it is his.[1] The typical techniques
of the Romantic poet are self-revelation and symbolism—not the
responsible symbolism that we find in allegory, in which symbols
are strung together and the suggestions of each symbol are therefore limited to what will go with the rest, but disconnected symbols that are deliberately blurred and left loose to pick up like
magnets all possible stray content. Auden admired the unconscious, but not such misuse of it.

In general, therefore, Auden tried to keep his own poetry from
being autobiographical in content and from using loose symbols
that give us the *feeling* of significance without establishing any
precise intellectual connection. These avoidances are by no means
absolute, for Auden tried almost everything. The problem he
set his poetry, however, was very largely that of remaining force-
ful and impressive even without these two cornerstones of Romantic technique. By 1933 he must have felt that his poems
were often admired for the wrong reasons—for their strangeness
and their atmosphere, qualities uncomfortably Romantic. So,
rejecting his early symbolic imagery as too charged with un-
located meaning (however allegorical in actual content), he
began to search for other techniques to give scope and generality
to his work. This search for generality, for largeness arrived
at fairly without Romantic cheating (for poetry is always a game
and a ritual), animates much of Auden's work after 1933.

Throughout the rest of the 1930s Auden's writing burst forth
in all directions. He wrote satire, ballads, songs, verse of all
kinds; he contributed articles and reviews to learned and popular
journals; he wrote chapters for books on education, psychology,
and literature. He helped to found the experimental Group

Theatre, wrote plays for it with Isherwood, and gave it its political direction. Two new journals, *New Verse* and *New Writing*, were founded largely to print his and his friends' work, and one issue of *New Verse* was entirely devoted to poems and essays about Auden. Until 1935 he taught school, first at Helensburgh in Scotland, later at Malvern; giving it up, he went into film work for six months, then traveled—to Iceland, Spain, China— and based two travel books and a political poem on his experiences. By the end of the 1930s, a literary man who had to publish to make a living, he was a journalist as well as a poet; he edited two anthologies of poetry; he taught in New York and wrote as voluminously as ever—books, essays, reviews, poems, a pamphlet on education, a radio play, an opera libretto. His energy was prodigious, and his work sometimes too hurried to be good.

Good or not, its constant aim is scope. Auden struggled to master the largest issues, to understand himself and his times, to see Western civilization in perspective.. His prose was therefore full of generalizations about man, art, Christianity; his articles and reviews relentlessly established the contributions of this or that period, poet, or thinker. His liberal-humanist eye increasingly scanned the whole history of mankind and especially that part he knew well—Europe, the West. In 1940 the stance changed but not the large perspective. "What I valued most in Hardy, then, as I still do," he wrote in that year about his boyhood admiration, "was his hawk's vision, his way of looking at life from a very great height. . . ." No one who has had this large perspective "can ever accept either an egocentric, overrational Humanism which fondly imagines that it is willing its own life, nor a pseudo-Marxism which rejects individual free-will but claims instead that a human society can be autonomous." For, to the hawk's eye, "the difference between the individual and society is . . . slight, since both are . . . insignificant. . . ."[2]

But while the hawk's perspective may confer distance, Auden wished also to stress matters that are within the individual. His art, therefore, continually changes its focus. Like a camera, it moves in from an aerial view to a close-up, moves even up to and through the skin until we see spread out within the self an interior landscape that seems the Platonic source of the one

outside. For such quick changes the self often *has* to be generalized—to be not an individual person but a silhouette darkened
by the characteristic anxieties of mankind:

> And within the indigenous figure on horseback
> On the bridle path down by the lake
>
> The blood moves also by crooked and furtive inches,
> Asks all our questions: "Where is the homage? When
> Shall justice be done? O who is against me?
> Why am I always alone?" (*EA*, 203–204)

Virtually all of Auden's poems look at generalized particulars
of human life *sub specie aeternitatis* or, if not of eternity, at
least of a very long time. The standard may be that of Evolution
or of History as well as of the Christian Eternity. But what is
constant is the contrasting focus, moving from inner to social to
cosmic framework, from personal to public, from tiny contemporary man to the universal patterns against which man's life
makes what sense it does.

II *The Marxist Perspective*

This search for scope, for perspectives on contemporary
anxiety, is basic to Auden's work of the 1930s. The Marxist view
is merely one such perspective; Auden's devotion to it was never
wholehearted and frequently seemed forced and false. The urge
to see Marxism as central, to read the early Auden as a social
propagandist and the later Auden either as a religious propagandist or as a kind of Grand Duke of Political Poetry in exile,
corrupted criticism of his work for a long while. Still, he did
unquestionably for a time accept the view that, although the
main illness of the age is psychological, a political revolution
must precede the psychological cure:

What is the use of trying to remove complexes from individuals when
the society into which they will go demands that they should have
them? It is no time to talk of educating the young until you can guaran-
tee them security of livelihood, interesting work, and a rational amount
of leisure. Goodness knows these alone are not enough. . . . But educa-

tion succeeds social revolution, not precedes. You cannot train children to be good citizens of a state which you despise.[3]

Justin Replogle has shown convincingly[4] that from 1933 to 1938 some of Auden's poems and plays show two kinds of Marxist influence. The first is that of "Marx the political economist," whose views Auden presents seriously in the 1938 play *On the Frontier* (written with Isherwood) but elsewhere often burlesques. From "Marx the philosopher," on the other hand, Auden derived "the only new intellectual element to appear in his work during the 1930s" (595): "a theory of human nature" according to which freedom consists not "in the dream of independence of natural laws, but in the knowledge of these laws" (587). As man comes to understand the laws of his environment, he can use such knowledge to control it; and *this* kind of control can result in authentic freedom: "But along with freedom goes a heavy burden, the responsibility of choice. Men must choose to learn and choose to control. And at every stage of this process they must choose to act" (593–94). To bring about this new freedom, internal changes in individuals are not enough; spontaneous love is not enough: "Love must be guided by reason" (589).

Aside from a handful of poems, including the impressive *Spain*, only two main works by Auden are, according to Replogle, fully Marxist in idea: *On the Frontier* and "In Time of War," his sonnet sequence in *Journey to a War*. "Most of Auden's works [in this supposedly Marxist period] are not Marxist in any sense of the word" (595). Even the poems that sound like Marxist rallying cries are usually mixed with deliberate or inadvertent skepticism; Auden seems to be trying on, like a hat, doctrinaire arguments, shrill accusations, and arrogantly portentous diagnoses and predictions. In *Spain*, for example, we find an uneasy blend of apocalyptic utopian vision and mischievous playfulness, as Auden hails a future that includes "the enlarging of consciousness by diet and breathing./. . . the rediscovery of romantic love; /The photographing of ravens . . ./[and] for the young the poets exploding like bombs" (*EA*, 212).

Furthermore, his sympathy for the proletariat was always abstract and remote. Incurably the psychologist, he preferred to probe the inner weaknesses of revolutionists and capitalists alike rather than to describe the happy proletarian world of the future. Incurably the artist, Auden had by 1935 firmly refused to see art as propaganda: "those who come to poetry for a message, for calendar thoughts ... have come to the wrong door. ..."[5] Incurably middle class, he tended to think of revolution in terms of its effects on himself and his friends. As he wrote many years later: "Looking back, it seems to me that the interest taken by myself and my friends ... was more psychological than political; we were interested in Marx in the same way that we were interested in Freud, as a technique of unmasking middle class ideologies, not with the intention of repudiating our class, but with the hope of becoming better bourgeois. ..."[6]

As the 1930s proceeded, all hope deteriorated of improving the middle class, of preventing war, of finding an answer in communism. Spain as an idea might be inspiring, but the reality —not merely of Fascist but of Communist practices—was shocking: "Nobody I know who went to Spain during the Civil War who was not a dyed-in-the-wool stalinist came back with his illusions intact."[7]

The increasing grimness of the world situation gradually altered the buoyant tone of discovery that had characterized Auden's work of the early 1930s. Even in the mid-1930s Auden's books—*The Dog Beneath the Skin, On This Island,* and *Letters from Iceland*—are full of life and fun, rich in experiment with forms and phrasing. But his style toward the end of the decade often seems strangely constricted. The later plays, the later travel book *Journey to a War,* and the later collection of poems *Another Time* are more somber than their earlier counterparts. The imagery becomes abstract, the tone impersonal; the writing, though still vigorous, has turned grim and pale. Personifications multiply; persons disappear. A forbidding verse, on the whole—that which Auden wrote in the year or two before his move to America, a period in which, after his extended travels, he had clearly begun to despair of the Marxist answer to human unhappiness.

A more pervasive influence on Auden's work of the 1930s than his Marxism, then, is this increasing skepticism about the power of secular reform to change the world. His verse takes on a new quality—becomes dry, wooden, brittle. But as Europe's immediate prospect grows darker, Auden's perspective becomes more lofty, too lofty to be dominated by any single thinker like Freud or Marx, whom even by 1935 he sees as partial critics:

Both Marx and Freud start from the failures of civilisation, one from the poor, one from the ill. Both see human behaviour determined, not consciously, but by instinctive needs, hunger and love. Both desire a world where rational choice and self-determination are possible. The difference between them is the inevitable difference between the man who studies crowds in the street, and the man who sees the patient, or at most the family, in the consulting-room. Marx sees the direction of the relations between outer and inner world from without inwards, Freud vice versa. Both are therefore suspicious of each other. The socialist accuses the psychologist of caving in to the status quo, trying to adapt the neurotic to the system, thus depriving him of a potential revolutionary: the psychologist retorts that the socialist is trying to lift himself by his own boot tags, that he fails to understand himself, or the fact that the lust for money is only one form of the lust for power; and so that after he has won his power by revolution he will recreate the same conditions. Both are right. As long as civilisation remains as it is, the number of patients the psychologist can cure are very few, and as soon as socialism attains power, it must learn to direct its own interior energy and will need the psychologist.[8]

During this period Auden's poetry, like his prose, increasingly aims at depicting the total human situation, on which each great thinker throws his partial light. It achieves this generality through various techniques, the most permanent and pervasive of which is that of dislocation, of suddenly shifted perspectives. Auden dislocates us because he wants us to see something we would miss in its ordinary context, and what he wants us to see is a general truth about life or man or ourselves—perhaps Freud's truth or Marx's but other truths as well, and especially truths that relate one sphere in which we live to others; the public to the personal, the interior to the cosmic or social.

The techniques of dislocation are already at work in the early poetry, and critics have often discussed them. But in the 1930s Auden consciously developed other procedures for achieving generality in his poems. The next four chapters consider the main methods he explored during his search for a poetry that could be large and significant without being self-centered or loosely symbolic.

CHAPTER 6

Plain Speech

B Y THE END of 1931, Auden had begun to write poems with more definite settings, more explicit subjects, and a more continuous line of narration or argument. The first of these, "Now from my window-sill I watch the night" (February 1932—EA, 115–16), sets the prevailing tone of the new period. From this point on, although Auden is as experimental as always and tries out many different poetic modes and voices, his poems come to be characterized by a much greater openness and clarity than his readers had previously found in his work. The private jokes and riddles, the puzzling ellipses, and the unexplained wars and enmities did not entirely vanish; visionary pieces, too, are frequent in this period of transition; but other kinds of poems came to look central in his repertoire—notably, the song, the satirical ballad, and the casual, personal, reflective poem.

For, under the influence of Marxist social philosophy, Auden was trying to make his poems more accessible to a wide public. The search for largeness began as a search for clearness. Although Auden never quite subscribed to the view of art as propaganda—and after 1935 was consistently hostile to the idea—by 1932 his poems nevertheless began not only to explore Marxist themes but to speak more directly and openly.

Even *The Orators,* completed in 1931, obscure as it is, contains some plain, blurt writing, including coarse invective: "Benthameer, Benthameer, bully of Britain,/With your face as fat as a farmer's bum" (EA, 86). One poem of August 1932 is plainly titled, "A Communist to Others" (EA, 120–23). Another, composed in February of that year, presents through a dream-vision a satiric portrait of contemporary England and includes such lines as these: "Ramsay MacDonald was rubbing his seat:/

At last he'd been invited to a Leicestershire Meet" (*EA*, 447).

These poems all show Auden working toward a more accessible style, with which to appeal to a more general audience. But another notable work of this period gives us clues to the nature of this development. This is his long, unfinished poem, "In the year of my youth. . . ." Begun late in 1932, in the four-stress alliterative style of William Langland's medieval poem *Piers Plowman*, and abandoned by the poet a few months later (though he drew on it for some passages in *The Dog Beneath the Skin* and for other works of the 1930s), it seems an important transitional piece. Rough and unpolished as it is, its 1,235 lines show Auden pretty well emerged from the cryptic and hermetic style of his earlier verse and trying to present more distinctly, though still with considerable obliqueness, the contemporary situation of England. The poem shows us a dream, in which the events and characters are sometimes puzzling, but the narrative is continuous and easy to follow; the language is compressed and witty, but not obscure.

> In the year of my youth when yoyos came in
> The carriage was sunny and the Clyde was bright
> As I hastened from Helensburgh in the height of summer
> Leaving for home in a lounge suit.
> . . . .
> 'The car is waiting.' The wind blew in.
> Framed in the doorway in flying kit
> Liebig stood with an electric torch.
> 'So kind of you both to come. Good-night.'
> Titt and Tool bowed both together,
> Lifting their nightcaps with their left hands.[1]

Essentially, "In the year of my youth . . ." shows Auden trying to move from the relatively unstructured subjective style of his earlier lyrics to some more defining framework—the dream-vision of Langland (and Dante)—within which his own controlled, appraising voice can survey representative images of modern civilization and assess its chances of survival.[2]

If this is the general programme of Auden's verse during the 1930s, it is carried out variously in different poems and plays—most successfully, as we shall see, in songs, in ballads, and in

lyric poems written in a casual style. It leads him now and again
to be coarse, vulgar, garrulous, and banal—as people often are
in their ordinary talk. Auden, always inventive, his mind abstract
but prolific of details, begins in this period (or in some parts
of *The Orators*) to appear at times to be chattering on and on.
The stanzas unroll across the page—increasingly regular in form,
increasingly informal in manner—and the impression is conveyed
of an irrepressibly clever performer, an impression notably different from that conveyed by the clipped and guarded lyrics of his
earlier years.

Among the devices he uses to make his language more direct
is the mimicking—part parody, part serious—of colloquial idioms
and clichés. Taking his hint from Eliot's "Sweeney Agonistes,"
Auden learned to explore, partly for amusement and partly as a
path to illuminating perceptions, the literal implications of ordinary phrases whose full significance we usually fail to notice.
A brilliant early example is the song from *The Ascent of F6*
in which such common phrases as "Still waters run deep," "there's
never smoke without fire," and "there is more than meets the eye"
are weighted with Freudian content (*EA*, 287). A brilliant later
example is the *"God only knows"* that ends "The Willow-Wren
and the Stare" (*CP*, 439).

In most of Auden's poems the banal occurs, if at all, in company with more elevated diction, so that the reader is jolted by
the apparent inappropriateness. In "September 1, 1939," for example, when Auden writes, "The unmentionable odour of death/
Offends the September night" (*EA*, 245), he refers with deliberate
vulgarity to the then current advertisement for a soap that would
protect its user from offensive body odor. Such appearances of
the banal in nonbanal contexts constitute another kind of dis-
locating technique: by juxtaposing spheres and attitudes we
ordinarily keep separate, they require us, at their most effective,
to look more closely at the categorizing habits with which we
protect ourselves. As we shall see in Chapter 8, Auden's ballads
exploit the banal in similar fashion by using it in a traditional
form already loaded with ironic significance. But what about
the banal by itself? Can it form the basis of a style? Can it, with
its great advantage of clarity, stand alone or almost alone?

I   *The Plays:* The Dance of Death

For answer we must turn to Auden's plays where, more than
anywhere else, the banal is given extended work to do. The
short play *The Dance of Death* (1933) and the three full-length
pieces by Auden and Isherwood—all produced during the 1930s
by the Group Theatre—are strongly, if decreasingly, influenced
by the German experimental theater of Bertolt Brecht. Brecht's
"epic theatre" keeps the audience at a distance, forbids it to relax
into an easy, irresponsible identification, and aims at inciting it
to thought and action. His drama uses popular songs with political content; scenes shift abruptly; characters address the audience directly; and moods change quickly from harsh to soft,
pathetic to bitter. Brecht's drama is thus episodic, stylized,
didactic; it uses surrealistic dialogue sometimes; and its emphasis is on the social significance of each action rather than on
character, plot, or atmosphere. Auden and Isherwood have more
fun; but, especially to begin with, their techniques are Brecht's.
   The Dance of Death (by Auden alone) is an animated but
trivial masque that treats modern society's death wish. The
characters are undifferentiated (most are called merely A, B, C,
etc.), and they participate in a series of disjointed skits in which
the early psychological analysis of social illness seems at last to
give way to Marx's social analysis.[3] In this play the banal receives
its fullest test as Auden employs it throughout. The result is
disastrous. In trying to milk the commonest idioms for their
symbolic suggestions, he is often amusing; but the language is
too flat and dry to yield much significance. Thus:

> You are responsible,
> You are impossible,
> Out you go.
> We will liquidate,
> The capitalist state
> Overthrow.[4]

In the full-length plays the flat idioms and the beginner's
rhymes ("The bus is leaving in a minute:/Those who are coming must step in it"—*Dog*, [32] are increasingly subordinated
to other styles that range from prose realism to the poetic

sublime. For the more modest tasks assigned to it, therefore—patter and chatter and mock self-revelation—the simple colloquial style is not too unsatisfactory. But Auden does make fewer demands on it; he evidently realizes that, by itself, the loaded colloquialism, even if everyone can understand it, is too weak to support much intellectual substance.

II   The Dog Beneath the Skin

In *The Dog Beneath the Skin* (1935) the Brechtian influence can be felt in the abrupt transitions, but the play's make-believe air largely deprives it of Brecht's single-minded bitterness. Characters and action have almost no realistic foundation. The play seems hardly intended for actual production, with its cast of thirty-three distinct individuals, plus Chorus Girls, Courtiers, Diners, Doctors, Dressers, Invalids, Lunatics, Nurses, Police, Priests, Procurers, Prostitutes, Students, Waiters, and Villagers. There is also an obviously unactable dialogue between the hero's right foot, which "speaks in a cultured voice," and his Cockney left foot. Through stylized situations and type-characters Auden and Isherwood survey elements of political reality in the 1930s, especially the hypocrisy and stupidity of bourgeois society, and the difficulties of the exile-hero who seeks something better.

Every year, according to the fairy-tale plot, a questing hero leaves his village in search of the late squire's missing son. The present quester, Alan, wanders rather aimlessly around Europe and inadvertently encounters one kind of corruption after another. The modern world is, in effect, shown successively as Red Light District, Lunatic Asylum, Hospital, and Luxury Hotel. A kind of Boy Scout hero, Alan manages to remain innocent and conscientious throughout all his tests by avoiding or surviving the various dangers which are represented by other characters: cynical journalists, superpatriotic lunatics, power-mad magnates, solipsistic poets, the rich who applaud destruction of the beautiful, the lovers who seal themselves off from the rest of the world, and a mannequin that offers empty heterosexual love. As Alan survives his ordeals, the missing son gratuitously declares himself (an act which anticipates Auden's later view of the Incarnation); and they return to the village, where Alan refuses his reward and voluntarily seeks further significant exile in the company of other men of good will.

The banal style is still central in this play, the norm to which the dialogue and incidental songs continually return: "Speak to me, please, just one little word,/I don't understand you! Oh, this is absurd!" (149). But there is also a great deal of prose dialogue, and prose is used as well for some long set pieces of considerable substance. In addition, lengthy choruses take a hawk's-eye view of contemporary civilization and give dignity and loftiness to what might otherwise seem mere fooling:

> The Summer holds: upon its glittering lake
> Lie Europe and the islands; many rivers
> Wrinkling its surface like a ploughman's palm.   (11)
>
> . . . .
>
> A man and a dog are entering a city: They are
>   approaching a centre of culture:
> First the suburban dormitories spreading over fields. . . .   (117)

The grandness of the choruses makes an extremely effective framework for the commonplace dialogue. But, even so supported, and reinforced by the good prose passages, the dialogue cannot avoid seeming silly much of the time. *Every* banal phrase does not have a deeper significance; much is mere playful nonsense, as when a waiter directs Alan to the Roof Garden: "Take the lift on the right, sir./At the Fifth you alight, sir" (153). And even the choruses lose their elevation in bathetic or prosy propagandizing:

> Mourn rather for yourselves; and your inability
>   to make up your minds. . . .   (179)
>
> . . . .
>
> You have wonderful hospitals and a few good schools:
> Repent.
> The precision of your instruments and the skill of
>   your designers is unparalleled:
> Unite.
> Your knowledge and your power are capable of infinite
>   extension:
> Act.   (157)

Aside from the lyrical choruses, the best bits of verse are set pieces (the song of the 1st Mad Lady and "You who return tonight to a narrow bed") in which the diction is also rather literary than colloquial. In fact, in this play Auden, though not encumbering himself with an overstated theory, is in the position of Wordsworth in *Lyrical Ballads*—trying to center his poetry in really ordinary diction, he does his best work in a grander style.

III   The Ascent of F6

The Ascent of F6 (1936) is more realistic and more dominated by Isherwood's prose. Instead of a fairy-tale quest, the basic story is a psychological fable, an exemplum about a question that had long interested the two authors: what constitutes real strength in a man? Isherwood argues in *Lions and Shadows* (207–208) that "the truly strong man" does not need to prove himself by heroic conquests of mountains or jungles. On the contrary, it is "the Truly Weak Man" who requires such proofs of his strength, and for him no proofs will ever be sufficient. Michael Ransom, the hero of *The Ascent of F6*, is clearly such a figure. A man of great gifts, a scholar and adventurer, he *appears* strong but actually suffers from a hopeless oedipal problem. This weakness leads him to attempt the ascent of F6, a strategic mountain whose conquest by a British team will improve England's position in its pointless rivalry with Ostnia.

In agreeing to make the ascent, Ransom plays into the hands of the hypocritical forces that govern modern countries. And, as the leader of his own team, he faces the tragic dilemma of all honest leaders: should he allow his followers to choose their own lives, in which case they will be lost; or should he choose *for* them, in which case they are no longer free and he as a governor will become corrupt? For all government is evil since it "requires the exercise of the human will," which is "from the Demon" (74).

The play is thus extremely pessimistic in its view of society. Someone has to govern, but all who do are corrupt. In the modern world as it is—and no better one is heralded in this play— heroes, and the public that needs them, are equally flawed and equally used and betrayed by their empty governors.

In F6 the part of the banal style is further reduced. The stylistic norm of the play is realistic prose, and it is mainly the departures from realism that tend to break out into verse—the confrontations (essentially interior) between Ransom and his mother, a few songs, one hawk's-eye chorus, and, most notably, the choral subplot in which Mr. and Mrs. A., representing ordinary people, review public events and private emptiness, often in the familiar banal style: "Home to supper and to bed./It'll be like this till we are dead" (180). Since the ordinary development of this play is accomplished in prose dialogue, the flat style can be used sparingly and for special effects—for example, to underscore points about cultural drought.

But the implication is that flatness, in this form at least, can serve no larger purposes. When Mr. and Mrs. A. become really eloquent, they do so by leaving their average characters behind them, and their average diction as well. The stylistic separation of powers—prose for development, poetry for distance and innerness—fails because the different perspectives are not fused or focused, as they are to a greater extent in *Dog*. Auden's early imagery (and his later imagery as well) keeps looking two ways at once; in *F6* the modes of speech merely follow one another, blankly. And the flat and simple style fails to achieve largeness because it can say only one thing at a time.

IV   On the Frontier

In *On the Frontier* (1938) the verse has still less to do. Neither fairy tale nor fable, this play is a Shavian (and Marxist) investigation of the dynamics of public opinion and ignorance that leads to war. Ostnia and Westland (read, no doubt, Waste Land) are the two countries in question, and in each country we see one family of "ordinary decent people" brought by propaganda to hate the rival country. As Replogle puts it, the play shows how everyone—leaders and people alike—"misunderstands what is happening because each sees the world in terms of the conventional cultural framework which created his view in the first place" (591).

As in *F6*, we oscillate between a set of public figures and the ordinary people, but this time *both* groups are developed realistically (except for the device of dividing the stage and showing

both families simultaneously). Furthermore, both groups speak
prose. Verse occurs only between the scenes, in a few songs, and
in the speeches of the two young people, one from each family,
whose love affair is frustrated by the foolish war between their
countries. Except for the ballads (see Chapter 8), the verse
seems perfunctory—as if, with Isherwood's prose realism taking
over, Auden had lost interest in the project. The result is, at
times, bathos:

> But I was wrong. We cannot choose our world,
> Our time, our class. None are innocent, none.
> Causes of violence lie so deep in all our lives
> It touches every act.
> Certain it is for all we do
> We shall pay dearly.   (120–21)

Certain it is, indeed. Since the play seems to show almost
everyone's stupidity or shortsightedness, the lovers lack conviction when they suggest that, under Marxism, "the will of love"
(122) would be done. Like the other plays and like most of the
propaganda poetry of the 1930s, including Auden's, the play is
effective when it attacks and caricatures, but not when it presents as a political possibility a never-never land of happy lovers
and workers.

Thus Auden's extended attempts to use ordinary language in
all its flatness are not very successful. Amusing lines and even
some faintly moving passages—these are the best the style can
offer. The concern to attract an audience leads Auden and Isherwood to write more and more realistically and more and more
prose. To be sure, Auden cast some later poems in flat language,
some of them quite successfully. A notable example is "Law
Like Love," from *Another Time* (1940):

> Others say, Law is our Fate;
> Others say, Law is our State;
> Others say, others say
> Law is no more,
> Law has gone away.   (*CP*, 208)

But this language is really more than flat; it has a childish ring to it, yet the concepts summed up in the childish tone are abstract and complex. "Law is our State" is not the way ordinary people who believe it would actually put it. On the whole, Auden's experiments with very plain language taught him that plainness by itself is not enough; that prose, on the whole, can do the plain job better; and that other poetic ways of achieving largeness promised more.

CHAPTER 7

The Casual Style

I   On This Island

OF ALL the styles Auden developed in the 1930s, the casual, open style was perhaps the most attractive. It is also central in Auden's *oeuvre* as no other style is, for in one form or another he continued to use it throughout his career. As it begins, in 1932, it is buoyant, clear, and surprisingly personal:

> Now from my window-sill I watch the night.
> The church clock's yellow face, the green pier light
> Burn for a new imprudent year;
> The silence buzzes in my ear;
> The jets in both the dormitories are out.   (*EA*, 115)

By 1936, when he put together his next collection, *Look, Stranger!* (American edition: *On This Island*, 1937), he could include some eight or ten poems written in this style, which, together with the dozen songs, dominate the volume of thirty-two poems and give it an entirely different feeling from the earlier collections. The Nordic mask has disappeared, and there is only one poem in the Skeltonic style. Auden is now a public poet, a man speaking with relative clarity of contemporary events and choices, sometimes writing quite directly of himself and his friends and the historical crisis:

> Now North and South and East and West
> Those I love lie down to rest. . . .   (*EA*, 137)

> And I, each meal-time with the families,
> The animal brother and his serious sister,

Or after breakfast on the urned steps watching
The defeated and disfigured marching by,
Have thought of you, Christopher, and wished beside me
Your squat spruce body and enormous head.   (*EA*, 156)

In such poems the setting is often specified, the old elliptical
speech gives way to a more traditional sentence structure, and
the ideas are clearer and more accessible. Even in poems less
personal and less clear the discussion of contemporary events is
warmed by the sense we have of a worried man talking, trying to
figure things out.

The style reflects Auden's search in these years for "lightness,"
for the kind of verse in which the poet can talk to an audience
easily about things that he and they are both interested in. The
alternative, as he tells us in his introduction to *The Oxford Book
of Light Verse* (1938), is that Romantic verse in which the poet
is "acutely aware of himself as the poet" (ix) and consequently
cannot talk easily with his readers. In their progressive alienation
from common humanity, the Romantics followed Milton, who
was probably "the first to make a myth out of his personal experience, and to invent a language of his own remote from the
spoken word" (xi)—as Auden himself had done in his early
verse. "Lightness" is preferable to that, but it often requires a
personal voice. It poses to Auden, therefore, some crucial questions: How personal can one be in a light poem without indulg-
ing in Romantic autobiography? And can one be light and still
profound, still deal with complex ideas?

The first question is a delicate one, indeed. Above all, Auden
wants to avoid the kind of verse in which the poet says in effect,
"Look at me! Isn't my illness fascinating?" and proceeds to describe the symptoms. Can one use oneself in poems at all without
falling into this trap? Well, Yeats did so, and many of the poems
in *On This Island* recall his casual reflective style. The essential
thing, though, for Yeats and for Auden, is to pass from the
immediate personal situation to the more general, to *use* the personal as a way of getting to what is *really* important. In the
gross particulars out of which one's own life is made, one dis-
cerns general principles, general truths and patterns.

So in the poem that begins, "Now from my window-sill . . ."

Auden quickly moves, in the second stanza, to the town and beyond, and, in the third, both farther out to a cosmic perspective and further in, to the inner human being—not himself but anyone. His own personal life does not quite get into the poem, only the life of the town and the school: "Preserve our Provost, Piermaster, Police/ . . . To these players of badminton to-night,/ To Favel, Holland, sprightly Alexis give."[1] Auden is trying to establish his speaker in an actual human environment, as Yeats often surrounds himself with cultural or country figures.

But, even after writing such lines, Auden is suspicious of them: the first of the three lines above appeared in *New Country* but did not survive even until *On This Island;* the last two got that far but no farther. The original eighteen-stanza poem, in fact, was cut to eight in later collections, and the stanzas lost include all of those which once contained local details. The resulting poem is far more austere and impersonal than the earlier versions.

Much of Auden's later verse, nevertheless, continued to be written out of his personal situations, although the poet's self rarely intrudes very far and serves mainly as a characteristic self. The situations he writes about are those in which the poet can function as "anybody"—waking up, feeling lazy, being tempted, falling in love. What he explores in such situations are not the respects in which W. H. Auden's reactions are different from everyone else's, and more intriguing, but the respects in which his perceptions and responses are normal, are human, and tell us something about man in general. The speaker of the personal poems is, therefore, a man, an intelligent man, who yet makes no extravagant claims. He is a man speaking to men, but not, as in the Wordsworthian version, a better and more sensitive man than his listeners. He is just someone who knows how to talk in verse.

But can he, while speaking easily, say anything important? Auden's practice suggests both that he can and that he can't. The casual poems of *On This Island* frequently make points that are not at all easy to grasp. Even the relatively popular verse form of "Now from my window-sill" or of "Out on the lawn I lie in bed,/Vega conspicuous overhead/In the windless nights of June . . ." (*EA*, 136) gives way, in later poems of the same group, to more complex forms that present more elusive ideas:

Your portrait hangs before me on the wall
And there what view I wish for, I shall find,
The wooded or the stony—though not all
The painter's gifts can make its flatness round—
Through the blue irises the heaven of failures,
The mirror world where logic is reversed,
Where age becomes the handsome child at last,
The glass sea parted for the country sailors.   (*EA*, 145)

There seems to be too much to say for *very* plain speech; irony
and indirection are too valuable to do without, even when one
knows that with every use of them the audience is dwindling,
the light style gaining perhaps not the right kind of weight.

In *On This Island* Auden wishes, after all, to discuss some
complex questions. The volume places before us the choice between the crooked, private, solipsistic love that is a death wish
in disguise and the disciplined love that leads to action, knowledge, control of the world, and freedom. So one casual poem,
in not so casual English, states:

'Yours is the choice, to whom the gods awarded
The language of learning and the language of love,
Crooked to move as a moneybug or a cancer
    Or straight as a dove.'   (*EA*, 154)

The two loves are not always easy to tell apart; but when the
terms are political, the forces of death are those of the status
quo; the forces of life call for a new world, condemn dictators
and militarists, and resist those who love death.

If these ideas are not extraordinarily hard to grasp, they are
nevertheless developed with considerable ingenuity. Auden's
poetic intelligence—consistently juxtaposing and superimposing
disparate elements, shifting perspectives, and providing new contexts (linguistic, physical, and social) for familiar objects, persons, and practices—tries to show us the world in which we live,
a complex world further complicated by changes in our own
ways of seeing it. The plainest English is simply not up to the
job of showing all this. What seem like clear ideas get awfully
intricate when we look at them closely. For the poet's material
consists not only of life as we lead it but of life as we watch our-

selves leading it; and this extra dimension, a gift of Romanticism
which we cannot ignore, makes authentic simplicity impossible.

So in Auden's practice the poems that retain the casual manner
are often not easy to read. The warm, personal speech is balanced
by the complexity of the perception that we see the persona
working out. The syntax becomes playful—"Easily, my dear, you
move, easily your head" (EA, 152)—or ambiguous: "Looking and
loving our behaviours pass/The stones, the steels, and the
polished glass . . ." (EA, 152). And the most powerful images
are often those that escape rigid adherence to logical categories,
that mix metaphors boldly:

> In the houses
> The little pianos are closed, and a clock strikes.
> And all sway forward on the dangerous flood
> Of history, that never sleeps or dies,
> And, held one moment, burns the hand.   (EA, 157)

This is plain enough in its way, but surrealistic; as usual in
Auden, the poem looks two ways at once—toward the rational
imperatives of history and toward the irrational impulses of the
unconscious.

Thus, the poems in *On This Island* are often less clear than
they at first seem, and perhaps intentionally so. For, since Auden
is trying to fuse the rational and the instinctive, if the poem were
too clear it would be false to this double source of modern life.
So the imagery is often elusive, the abstractions confusing; key
words, recurring often, seem to have private meanings. The
riddling Rilkean sonnets, and the sestina, "Hearing of harvests,"
with their surface clarity and their hidden significance, carry
further this curious tendency to give and to withhold, to expose
and to conceal, to speak distinctly but in code. The casual style
is casual only in tone; as with Yeats's poems in the same genre,
the warm and winning manner turns out to belong to a highly
developed intellect, and what may be casual for him is hard work
for the reader.

In fact, the combination of casual tone with diction a little
elevated is characteristic of Auden's poems throughout the 1930s.
One of their strengths is the ease with which the casual manner

gives way to the prophetic, thereby suggesting that absolute and apocalyptic reality which lies just beneath our ordinary life. Anything can happen and probably will—so Auden's poetry continually tells us with its styles as well as with its words. Some poems of the 1930s are completely prophetic in manner, like the "Prologue" to *On This Island* (*EA*, 118–19); others, often written in a kind of Latin Alcaic meter (usually four lines, the first two longer than the last two), use conversational expressions but maintain some distance from the casual tone—"Journey to Iceland" or "Epilogue" (*EA*, 203–204; 165–66). And this technique, developed throughout the 1930's, leads Auden to his main stylistic solution of the problem: the syllabic poems that dominate his later work and that drench exceedingly complex speech in disarmingly casual tones. The agreeably chatty poems of *On This Island* prepare us for the openly cryptic style of the last two decades (see Chapter 17).

II Letters from Iceland

It would be ungrateful, however, to overlook the last and most impressive monument of the pure casual style, the charming *Letters from Iceland*. This miscellany tries to avoid the dull repetitiousness of most travel books in which "the actual events are all extremely like each other—meals—sleeping accommodation—fleas—dangers, etc." (142). Instead, the book is an engaging hodgepodge of letters in prose and verse, photographs, travel tips, amusing quotations from former visitors, and a poetic "Last Will and Testament" in joint doggerel by Auden and his collaborator, Louis MacNeice. Most of the writing, however, is Auden's; and though it includes some fine serious poems, its general mood is lively and witty. In particular, the "Letter to Lord Byron," its parts scattered throughout the volume, is brilliantly Byronic, full of absurd polysyllabic rhymes and delightful chat—more about books and authors and Auden and England than about Iceland. Here Auden writes about Jane Austen:

> You could not shock her more than she shocks me;
>   Beside her Joyce seems innocent as grass.
> It makes me most uncomfortable to see

An English spinster of the middle-class
Describe the amorous effects of "brass,"
Reveal so frankly and with such sobriety
The economic basis of society. (*EA*, 171)

This is charming verse, and it abounds in "Letter to Lord Byron."
But the form was too loose for Auden to continue using it; it encouraged laxness and empty facility. And Auden's genius depends
on his continuing to explore increasingly subtle forms.

The whole book, however, is more subtle in form than it appears. It is a collage,[2] loosely strung together on the thread of
the "Letter to Lord Byron," which Auden conceived as "a description of an effect of travelling in distant places which is to
make one reflect on one's past and one's culture from the outside" (141). As in Brechtian epic theater, the audience as well
as the poet is supposed to think, instead of passively receiving
picturesque descriptions. So the book shifts from one kind of
writing to another, from one persona to another, from one author
to another, with the abruptness of fantasies or dreams. And, as
Auden makes clear, the journey to Iceland would not have taken
place without the elaborate saga-fantasies that had been so important to his boyhood.

Furthermore, there is considerable reference to dreams, nightmares, riddles, séances. One poem asks: "O who can paint the
vivid tree/And grass of phantasy?" (*EA*, 205). Auden, of course,
tries to do so and cares much less about painting the actual
tree and grass of Iceland. The Auden who had used Norse
imagery in England turns, in Iceland, to fantasy, fairy tale,
detective story, and Lord Byron; and the connections of this
travel book are as whimsical as the connections of dreams—
except that everything fantastic points to the actual, everything
in Iceland relates to Europe, and the very letter form suggests
that the meaning of the experience is not complete until it is
sent back home.

Continuous narration is, of course, impossible for Auden.
Always hostile to realism, he prefers notions of gratuitous grace,
sudden confrontations not earned but granted. For sequence
and significance have little correlation; in remembering a trip
(to Iceland, for example), we do not recall the events in chron-

ological order but jump from one high point to another, exhibiting what Auden later praised Byron for capturing: "the motion of life" (*DH*, 405). Auden captures it here. The journey's meaning—so the structure of the book implies—is not so much in the place visited as in the rhythms of feeling, the mental connections, the insights, that the journey arouses in the travelers.

How successful is the collage? More so, I think, than most critics have been willing to say. And the book has a special interest in relation to Auden's other extended works. *Letters from Iceland* belongs to what we might call, in respect to his longer works (at least), his messy period. It begins with *The Orators* (if not with *Paid on Both Sides*) and reaches its messiest with *Dog* and *Iceland*. The other plays retreat from this extreme of untidy design, as do the longer works of the decade's end, "In Time of War" and "The Quest." But what follows then is remarkable and unexpected: first, the scrupulous couplets of "New Year Letter"; next, the careful arrangement of tableaux in *For the Time Being*; and then the spectacular craftsmanship of *The Sea and the Mirror* and *The Age of Anxiety*. In these longer works Auden has moved far from the cheerful, honest, plain disorder of *Letters from Iceland* to sophisticated artifice, from the random collage to orderly structure, from Romantic trust in whatever comes into the head to classical restraint, from Byron perhaps to Jane Austen or even to Shakespeare and Spenser. And much as we enjoy reading *Letters from Iceland*, much as we may lament the years of abstraction it cost Auden to move beyond it, we know the later work is the finer.

It appears, then, that all of Auden's excursions into casual talk either are qualified or are qualified successes. Plainness may do much, but to do all that Auden wants poetry to do, other techniques must be added: irony, obliqueness, surrealism, ambiguity. And these intimidate the audience. But plainness does not jolt enough; in fact, it may succeed best in contexts where to be plain seems odd. In a poetry where perspective matters so much, the poem's effect often depends on the relation between detail and formal context, between what the words seem to be saying and what the form implies. If the poet's *language* cannot be as simple as he would like, he may yet engage an audience by using traditional public *forms*.

CHAPTER 8

Public Forms

I *Songs and Ballads*

MONROE SPEARS, in his book on Auden, has dealt so fully with Auden's songs (105–23) that I need not speak of them at length. Auden wrote many in the 1930s, and a number have been set to music. These songs usually achieve a simple and clean clarity of form and feeling, the quiet elegance common to the melodious tradition of Campion, Shakespeare, Jonson, Dryden, Tennyson, and Housman, all of whom Auden sometimes echoes. In these "art songs" (as distinguished from his ballads, which Spears calls "popular songs"), the poet may at times be ironic, but the irony is veiled by a certain blandness, an evenness of texture, which makes them more suitable for setting but which also encourages readers or listeners to tune out the meaning. The gist tends to escape through the multiple abstractions:

> Bells that toll across the meadows
>   From the sombre spire,
> Toll for those unloving shadows
>   Love does not require.
> All that lives may love; why longer
>   Bow to loss
>   With arms across?
> Strike and you shall conquer. (*EA*, 161)

Words like "shadows" and "loss" come at crucial junctures where we hope for concrete words to fix meaning clearly.

From the point of view of Auden's search for generality, the songs are important. For the song is a public form; to write a song is to write for the public. Even if the songs are art songs, they are still something to sing; and vast numbers of people like to sing or to hear new songs. If the songs have good tunes, people may learn the words before they understand them, as a child learns hymns. Even without tunes at all, if the verse is rhythmic or insistent, or suggests certain attractive moods, lines of the song may sink into the mind before it quite sees what they mean. After the song is familiar, the very fact that one knows it, that its lines keep haunting one, gives it a special value, a kind of sacredness of its own; and the sacredness may be extended in part or entirely to the ideas expressed in the song. Thus the song achieves its purposes mainly through nonverbal means, through its hypnotic musical properties. And to these anyone may be susceptible.

Auden's ballads are, of course, different. There may be something of charm and hypnotic power in repeated rhythms or in certain verse formulas, but the strength of the ballad is usually in its ironies of statement or situation. And there is a kind of hovering irony in the ballad form that perhaps derives from its having been traditionally used to celebrate the ironic disproportion between public event and private feeling. The ballad strikes an immediate note of community among all those who are aware, perhaps without saying so, that the public world is not what one could wish it to be.

To be sure, the modern popular song—a "ballad" in Spears's classification—often says nothing about the public world but, by allowing the private world to become all that there is, makes a point. Thus Auden frequently parodies the phrases and attitudes of popular love songs: "He was my North, my South, my East and West,/My working week and my Sunday rest" (*EA*, 163)/"O but he was as fair as a garden in flower,/As slender and tall as the great Eiffel Tower . . ." (*EA*, 213). But the parody is not unsympathetic. Such elegies, for all their extravagance, are moving expressions of how it feels to lose a lover. Auden's treatment shows that the extravagance of the modern popular song, if pursued with tact, can be made to yield very delicate effects.

But his more usual ballad makes a social protest and, instead of exaggerating, proceeds by understatement. Typically, his ballads show us victims of social injustice or of psychological warping. In spite of ellipsis, the situations and their significance are

almost always clear. Most of them present ghastly situations—
the horror of the modern world—through ordinary language,
ordinary tones of voice, and ordinary imagery, so that what is
principally conveyed is the impact of an impersonal society or of
lunatic public policy (and the madmen who direct it) on the
private life. For example, the song of the soldiers in *On the
Frontier*: "The biscuits are hard and the beef is high,/The
weather is wet and the drinks are dry,/We sit in the mud and
wonder why" (*EA*, 288). Or, from the best of the poems in this
vein, "Roman Wall Blues": "Over the heather the wet wind
blows,/I've lice in my tunic and a cold in my nose" (*EA*, 289).
Auden catches well in such songs the attempt of ordinary people
to keep their lives intact in the face of the horrifying facts of
military or industrial impersonality. Other ballads use similar
techniques to attack totalitarian barbarism. Several narrative
ballads ("Miss Gee," "Victor," "James Honeyman") show representative lost souls produced by modern society.

The most remarkable ballad of all, "As I walked out one evening," which has been analyzed extensively,[1] shows Auden so
complete a master of the ballad style that he boldly exceeds its
usual limits by interweaving moral generalizations with the ordinary imagery in a way that the traditional ballad does not
dare to do: "The glacier knocks in the cupboard,/The desert
sighs in the bed,/And the crack in the tea-cup opens/A lane
to the land of the dead" (*EA*, 228). Puzzling connections and
abstract imagery help to convey Auden's main perception in this
poem—that the Romantic habit of expecting too much of life
makes disappointment and despair likely. Ballads are usually not
asked to say so much. But Auden's intensity of phrase, aptness
of detail, and mastery of the ballad feeling succeed in pushing
back the normal limits of the form.

And perhaps it is not merely the union of abstract and concrete that accounts for the strange force of this poem. The personification of Time and Justice, the supernatural effect of Time's
speech, the odd fairy-tale archetypes (Jack and Jill, the Giant),
and even the quasi-religious imperatives and confrontations
("Stare, stare . . . look, look . . . stand, stand . . .") add to the
already public form of the ballad the still more extensive generalizing powers of myth.

II *Myth*

Myth, in fact, seems an inevitable resource for a poet who wishes to reach a wider audience, especially when Eliot and Pound had made such significant use of myths in their work. Auden's early imagery, as we have seen, amounts to a developed mythology. It is tempting, therefore . . . But what about Romantic vagueness? That is the danger, and the poet must be careful. By trying to say too much, he risks saying nothing distinct.

During the middle 1930s, to avoid this danger, Auden stayed as close as he could either to plain speaking or to highly stylized forms in which the significance of each element tended to be quite clear. In *The Dog Beneath the Skin,* for example, the fairy-tale plot might encourage us to feel a loose identification with the hero; but the banal language and the hero's lack of innerness make any such identification unrewarding. *The Ascent of F6* plays more dangerously both with myth and with Romantic identification: Ransom is an attractive hero, and his quest is epic. But the playwrights' attitude is severely antiheroic: the hero is tainted, his enterprise corrupt, and the need that Mr. and Mrs. A. feel for public heroes is part of their illness. One of the play's shortcomings is exactly this: that it fails to make us feel antiheroic, fails to make us want to solve our own problems, personal or national, in their own contexts, without recourse to futile dreams of ourselves or others as heroes.

But with his interest in the unconscious, Auden cannot entirely eschew the mythical. The myth of the hero may be harmful, but all myths are not so, and art may sometimes make good use of folk material. The songs and ballads exploit hypnotic effects or unstated assumptions. The open, casual style, too, is often, even typically, haunted by dreams, nightmares, the unconscious. In many of Auden's more rhetorical, high-style poems of the 1930s, especially in conjunction with his hawk's-eye imagery, there is an incantatory quality that has something of the grand, priestly air he dislikes in Milton and in the Romantics.[2] One thinks of the pageant of Yesterdays, Todays, and Tomorrows in *Spain,* or this, from a poem of 1932:

Some possible dream, long coiled in the ammonite's slumber
Is uncurling, prepared to lay on our talk and kindness
Its military silence, its surgeon's idea of pain;

And out of the Future into actual History,
As when Merlin, tamer of horses, and his lords to whom
Stonehenge was still a thought, the Pillars passed

And into the undared ocean swung north their prow,
Drives through the night and star-concealing dawn
For the virgin roadsteads of our hearts an unwavering
keel.   (*EA*, 119)

If prophecy, nightmare, and balladry all use tones we know
and feelings we have but are not always aware of, the same is true
of fairy tales. During the 1930s Auden used fairy-tale structure
and motifs most extensively in *The Dog Beneath the Skin*; and
in such songs as "Now the leaves are falling fast" and " 'O for
doors to be open,' " the imagery is drawn from childish proverbs
or situations. Auden's fuller use of fairy tales came during the
1940s, when the fables and imperatives of fairy-tale lore seemed
especially appropriate to his exploration of Kierkegaardian Christianity. In *The Age of Anxiety* (1947) and in the libretto for *The
Rake's Progress* (1951), we can see later, sophisticated uses of
fairy-tale atmospheres and situations.

But there were several long works at the end of this period in
which Auden pursued further his interest in myths. His sonnet
sequence, "The Quest" (1940), uses a theme that, as he himself
says, "occurs in fairy tales, legends like The Golden Fleece and
The Holy Grail, boys' adventure stories and detective novels."[3]
Indeed, the quest motif is a permanent one in Auden's work—
understandably so, for it offers not a random series of loose
symbols but a symbolic structure in which every detail may have
a precise signification.

A second lengthy work of this time, the libretto for Benjamin
Britten's opera *Paul Bunyan* (presented at Columbia University
in 1941 and thereafter suppressed by its creators—see pp. 182–83,
below), is also based on a popular myth. And *The Dark Valley*,
a one-act radio play commissioned by the Columbia Broadcasting
Company and produced on June 2, 1940, is full of what seems

like highly Romantic symbolism. Although printed in prose, much of it is actually in four-stress alliterative verse reminiscent of Auden's early poems and anticipating *The Age of Anxiety* (the line-divisions are mine): "The gold was gone; they got nothing;/they lost heart, gave up their drilling;/it paid no longer; they departed poor./And none remained but mother and I [*sic*]/on this stony farm in a stony silence./She never loved me. I knew it from the first./She was prim and pious and praying always/for father's soul and shuddered at his songs/and thought him wicked and wept much."[4]

The play concerns an old woman almost totally isolated in a dark valley, her only companion a goose whom she now, without regret, is making plans to kill, and to whom she talks about her own past, about the wretched world, and about their meager future. Mythical overtones abound: the golden age has passed; the old woman's powerful, miracle-performing father is dead. Her mother represents conventional society; the old woman is both an observer of the modern world and that world itself. The goose, perhaps, is life; in killing it, the woman destroys herself.

To go further, the situation of the old woman, impelled to kill the goose ("I'm sorry, but it has to be done"), gruesomely parodies that of Abraham sacrificing Isaac. Auden seems to be suggesting that, in the darkness of the contemporary world, Kierkegaardian despair and resignation may be appropriate; but there is no indication at the play's end that the God who halted Abraham's sacrifice will intervene to save this old woman from a violence that will involve her own destruction.

The Dark Valley, with its bizarre image of the world's self-destruction, indicates the direction of Auden's concerns at the end of the decade. It may be said very generally that his early work through *The Orators* focuses on England; that for the next few years, perhaps through 1937, his poems and plays and his first travel book *Letters from Iceland* take Europe for their subject; but that from 1938 on, and rather grandly from 1938 to 1941, his subject is Man. This interest does not start overnight, but by 1938 the enlargement of perspective is clear and pervasive. His visit to China may have helped to widen his view. But, under the stress of the frightening events of Europe, he is rethinking his positions in the light of extensive reading in sociology, anthropology, and even theology. His interest in myth, therefore, reflects his wish to write about the nature of man in general.

But most of his work of this period *discusses* man and makes little effort to involve the general reader. It thus avoids Romantic reliance on the unconscious, whereas myth is a little suspect and, except in some secondary role, is rarely used by the later, more scrupulous Auden. The issues are subtle here: for Auden the seductive, hypnotic virtues of sound and form are perfectly acceptable in poetry; but art as magic, as propaganda, is not. Anything that draws the reader in is fair means; but it is foul to trick him into assenting to propositions, as an unrestrained symbolic art may do. Hence his gingerly use, from now on, of myth and symbol, and his feeling that the poet has the right to make his patterns of meaning cryptic but not vague. Symbols must designate, not merely suggest. Largeness is still his aim, and public forms may still help him achieve it; but after 1940 no loose emotion, no idle incantation, is tolerable. All symbolic detail must be submitted to classical design.

CHAPTER 9

The Life of Man

W HAT IS MAN?" had by 1938 become the fundamental question for Auden, and his work for the next few years keeps trying to work out an answer. His early studies in Freudian psychology and his continued curiosity about how animals differ from human beings reflect his permanent wish to describe the species Man. But his early psychological perspective had, since about 1930, been dominated by a social perspective: man is sick, but he is sick in groups, sick largely *because* of his groups. Hence it is social problems that in this period first take up Auden's attention: how can social institutions be organized so that man need no longer be ill? Education, politics, government, the press—these are the subjects that for a while engross him.

His view is thus that of the liberal humanist, wanting to re-make society so that people can be happier in it. The events of the 1930s, however, were enough to shake any man's faith in human ability to improve the world: the men who seemed to have most power to change it were rapidly making it worse. Perhaps, then, Auden's position was basically at fault. It seemed so simple a process, to examine social institutions and to improve them. But human societies do not work that way, not just because this or that institution resists reform, but because man is deeper than his institutions.

Auden's contribution to *Journey to a War* (1939) is the first large work that exhibits this perspective and the style that goes with it, neither of them entirely new but both now newly dominant. *Letters from Iceland* having proved moderately successful, Auden was commissioned with Isherwood to travel to China and to report on the war then in progress against the invading Japanese. *Journey to a War,* the result, is dominated by Isherwood's extended account of their journey from Hong Kong to the interior and eventually to Shanghai, a prose report characterized by Isherwood's usual narrative expertness—amusing, absorbing, and wonderfully clear. Auden's contribution—diminished in this second travel book as it was in the later plays —consists of the dedicatory sonnet to E. M. Forster, a short poem, "The Voyage," and five sonnets, all of which precede Isherwood's long narrative, and "In Time of War," which comes after and comprises a sonnet sequence and a verse commentary.

The introductory sonnets, several of which reflect on the meaning of journeys in general, get us by stages to China. Since Isherwood's prose takes care of their activities *in* China, the sonnet sequence and its verse commentary show us the *meaning* of their journey. "In Time of War" actually tries to do more: its highly abstract and impersonal sonnets formulate the nature of man—troubled, weak, yet capable of love and free to choose it. The opening sonnets survey human history, each from a different point of view, so that the history is not at all continuous; each angle of vision is independent of the others and allows us to see only a part of the total picture. There is even a sort of Jamesian technique at work here: in each sonnet we see what the subject sees (the poet, the peasant, etc.); and we also see that which can be seen by looking at him, by taking him for the moment as the center of things.

The same shifting technique continues throughout the sequence, but the more omniscient sonnets, XII and XIII, make a bridge to a group directly concerned with the Chinese War. Again each one studies a different aspect of the war—the planes, the Japanese pilots, the soldiers planning, wounded or dead—and its meaning. Then gradually the sonnets become more general ("The life of man is never quite completed"—XXI), and Auden leaves China to comment even more abstractly on the nature of human history: "We have no destiny assigned us ... we are articled to error ... We live in freedom by necessity ..." (XXV, XXVII).[1]

That self-inclusive "we" does not obscure the fundamental detachment of the speaker. In earlier volumes Auden's diagnosis of the significance of gestures, habits, diseases, and actions had usually been supported by a vividly sketched landscape or by a warmly casual tone; but here the tone and imagery have become remote and strained. The observer is no longer a full person but an objective commentator, a stylish surgeon dispassionately feeling out the malignant lump: "Wandering lost upon the mountains of our choice,/Again and again we sigh for an ancient South . . ." (XXVII). The mountains are symbolic, not actual; so is the South; all the situations are generalized; and objects, persons, and places seem useful to the speaker only as illustrations. But the abstraction does give the verse an impressive dignity and implies that the situation is now so appalling that mere vividness would be trivial. The Rilkean style intensifies the detachment of the sonnets; the unspecified perspectives and un-located third-person pronouns make each sonnet partly a riddle and encourage the reader to go through the same figuring-out process that the poet is himself engaged in.

The metallic tonelessness of these sonnets approximates that of some war correspondents' reports—taut, tense, tough, like a more intellectual and abstract Hemingway in the avoidance of obvious emotion, the eye for the revealing detail, the unsmiling amusement at passing ironies. Indeed, this detail and these ironies, though always quietly observed, seem to burst out, like sudden shots in a quiet place, from the general abstraction. Usually these bursts occur when the poet sees something in a new way: "A telephone is speaking to a man . . ." (XVI); or, of the wounded: "A bandage hides the place where each is living . . ." (XVII).

Lines like these dispassionately call attention to the divergence between what one can observe and what is actually happening. Muted similes often compare things of different dimensions: "Here war is simple like a monument . . ." (XVI) or "The cities hold his feeling like a fan;/And crowds make room for him without a murmur,/As the earth has patience with the life of man" (*EA*, 234). Often, external things are likened to internal or intellectual ones. The attacking Japanese airplanes, for example, "take us by surprise/Like ugly long-forgotten memories,/And like a conscience all the guns resist" (XIV). In the hospital the wounded "lie apart like epochs from each other" (XVII).

Indeed, the whole poem draws together the world of external event, the world of inner event, and the conceptual world, by exposing their mutual alienation. And alienation is the major theme here. The poem works in smaller syntactical units than Auden ordinarily uses: as the above quotations suggest, he aims at the effective single line. Even the tercets and quatrains seem curt, on guard. Connections between events are consecutive, not casual; the poems are full of *and*'s, which isolate events and actions, and of *the*'s, which isolate things and people. Each sonnet is detached and separate; they, too, "lie apart like epochs from each other." It seems likely that Auden meant his poem to be like the war he is reporting—direct, impersonal, measured, yet capable of sporadic human outbursts.

The Commentary (a dozen pages of unrhymed iambic triplets, varying from five to eight stresses but so conversational in rhythm that we may easily ignore the iambic beat) explains more straightforwardly, and in more extended periods, the significance, in the whole history of mankind, of the Chinese war, for it "Is but the local variant of a struggle in which all/ ... In all their living are profoundly implicated" (*EA*, 264). Using much variation and corroborative imagery, Auden names the enemies of this struggle: "All the great conquerors" and such other assorted villains as Plato, Macchiavelli, Hobbes, and Hegel. But still, the poet goes on, we also have our leaders who tell us how to build "*a world united*" (*EA*, 268). It may yet be possible to "*construct at last a human justice*" (*EA*, 270).

Some of the Commentary is stiff and prosy. Of goodness he says: "... even to exist, it must be shared as truth,/ As freedom or as happiness. (For what is happiness/If not to witness joy upon the features of another?)"(*EA*, 268). Some of it is deadly quiet, as in mechanical iambs it speaks of mechanical horror:

> Now in a world that has no localised events,
> Where not a tribe exists without its dossier,
> And the machine has taught us how, to the Non-Human,
>
> That unprogressive blind society that knows
> No argument except the absolute and violent veto,
> Our colours, creeds and sexes are identical,
>
> The issue is the same.   (*EA*, 264)

At other moments the verse is very grand, in the hawk's-eye manner:

Night falls on China; the great arc of travelling shadow
Moves over land and ocean, altering life:
Thibet already silent, the packed Indias cooling,

Inert in the paralysis of caste. And though in Africa ... (*EA*, 269)

This passage, which extends its sublime imagery for another seventeen lines, shows the broadness of Auden's perspective. Beyond the constrictions of tone, the occasional prosiness, the dryness everywhere, he tries to lead us to this large view of man. It is still a humanist view, a view of man in society. But now, as it broadens, it withdraws not only from the immediacies of England and Europe but from those of the sensory world itself. If, for Auden, the fundamental realities had always been hidden from view, the outer symptoms had at least been fascinating, and fun to depict and to interpret. But now the situation is too grim. The diseases and weaknesses which through the early poetry could have their charming and attractive aspects have now turned into unambiguous horrors; the life to avoid is not merely that of pleasant self-indulgence but the ghastly Death-in-Life of the machine:

"*Man can have Unity if Man will give up Freedom.*

The State is real, the Individual is wicked;
Violence shall synchronise your movements like a tune,
And Terror like a frost shall halt the flood of thinking."   (*EA*, 266)

Thus, as beneath the telephone's apparent action and the bandage's concealment something desperate is really happening, Auden tries to discern the hidden currents operating within man and within civilizations, forces that have brought mankind to its present appalling predicament. In the poet's search for the large patterns underlying modern history, he almost forgets for a while the visible world, or he uses it only as a source of illustrations or of points of departure for his large statements. That this practice, in a sense, reinforces the life-draining powers that he detests is one of the ironies of this period for Auden; but it appears that he could not rest in his confusion, he *had* to live among abstractions for a time—even if this meant temporarily abandoning clarity and the possibly wide audience—in order to find his way back to the actual world again.

CHAPTER 10

Toward Agape

I *Eros, Logos, Kairos, Agape*

AT THE END of the 1930s Auden slowly makes his intellectual way from liberal humanism to Kierkegaardian Christianity. Ironically, as he deplores the mechanization of modern society, his own poems become more removed from ordinary sensuous existence. Cities and great men, parading before him, submit to his examination; but too often the life they must once have possessed is reduced to an idea. If many such poems have a fineness of intellectual outline, we still miss the warmth of his more personal poems: this enlarged perspective treats even inwardness from outside. Convinced of the value of the instinctive life, but distrusting such wayward manifestations of the irrational as Nazism, the increasingly rationalist Auden detaches himself from his subject: inwardness is not a sea to dream in and drown in, but a realm of existence whose laws the intelligent man must seek to understand without distortion or destruction.

Gradually, in this period, as we can see in Auden's reviews and articles, his political militancy declines: the Marxism withers; the faith in social democracy, which in December 1938 is to be defended, "if necessary, at the cost of our lives,"[1] is no longer sufficient a year later when the war has broken out: "When the ship catches fire, it seems only natural to rush importantly to the pumps, but perhaps one is only adding to the general confusion and panic: to sit still and pray seems selfish and unheroic, but may be the wisest and most helpful course."[2]

Early in 1939 Auden could sympathize with Voltaire's view of the Catholic Church as one of the "three great enemies" of democracy and freedom.[3] But as the year proceeds, he begins to bring into his reviews such terms as "mortal sins," "damnation," "pride," "repentance," "faith." Economic solutions are not enough: "there is not the slightest reason to suppose that owning the means of production will create for the people a sudden traditional source of value."[4]

For, granted the unconscious is a dangerous guide, we still cannot count on man to be reasonable. Besides, while his social organization ought to be rationally arranged, the irrational remains the source of much that is important and valuable. What we must do is not to oppose these forces against each other, but to use them both, to recognize that both work together to produce the whole man.[5] As Auden discusses these matters, theological terms soon replace the secular ones. He had long used Eros in Freud's sense to mean Love or the forces of life. Now it becomes a term for the purely irrational, the disordered energy of uncontrolled life, even the rather lunatic Id. And opposed to Eros is Logos, the form, the outline, which gives shape, meaning, order, to the random force of Eros. Eros is admirable insofar as it represents honest feeling, love, "the basic will to self-actualization without which no creature can exist."[6] But too often it is perverted and becomes a destructive force. Such destruction can be prevented by order and reason, especially with the aid of science, whose method is still "the only way of asking questions to obtain valid knowledge."[7] This order is not, therefore, the kind that tyrannizes, against which Auden is always strong, but the kind that liberates for constructive activity, the routine that allows work to get done, the method that makes for progress.

In actual life, order (the human expression of the divine Logos) tends to be provided by attention to the immediate, to the present moment and its concerns, to whatever is before one or whatever activity the moment seems best fitted for. The Greeks had a word, "Kairos," for this moment—"the propitious moment for doing something" (DH, 140n.)—and it is one of Auden's favorite terms in these years. Thus, although in one sense Logos (as form and order) is opposed to Eros (force and energy), from another point of view Logos (as eternal) is opposed to Kairos (the immediate moment), or, rather, distinct

from it. For between Logos and Kairos, eternal law and immediate moment, there is a metaphysical but not an ethical distinction. We reach Logos through Kairos.

Eros, on the other hand, is dangerous. In fact, the history of
Western Europe is dominated by two equally treacherous here-
sies—"isotypes of Eros"—each of which is, of course, best summed
up in parabolical figures: Tristan and Don Giovanni. The Tristan
myth derives from "Manicheism, a dualistic heresy introduced
into Europe from the East, which held matter to be the creation
of the Evil One and therefore incapable of salvation. From this
it follows that all human institutions like marriage are corrupt,
and perfection can be reached only by death, in which the limitations of matter are finally transcended and the soul is merged
into the infinite nothingness of the Logos."[8]

For Tristan and Iseult love is predestined, they have no responsibility for it, and it "can exist in the world of time only
so long as there are obstacles to its physical consummation; only
after death can they be at last eternally identified in the Infinite" (756). In Don Giovanni, on the other hand, "it is the
flesh that is asserted and the spirit that is denied; the present
moment is all, the eternal future nothing. Tristan sees time as
something evil to be passively endured; Don Juan sees time as
something evil to be aggressively destroyed: the former is a
suicide, the latter a murderer" (757).

Unlike animals, who live only among actualities, human beings
live amid the actual and the possible. But Don Giovanni's
actual is undermined by his sense of the possibilities (all the
women who are not yet on his list), and Tristan's "myth of
passion ... that is, that only perfection is worthy to be loved,"
is undermined when the actual "physical world invades and
destroys his consciousness" (757). What each man needs to do
is to accept the fact that every moment limits the formerly
infinite number of possibilities, to have faith in his choices even
though he knows that he may have chosen wrongly.

If these two myths show the wrong kinds of love, the right
kind is Agape, which is "Eros mutated by Grace, a conversion,
not an addition" (757). The Divine Love, which breathes life
into form, makes the Word incarnate in the Flesh, reconciles
Eros and Logos. For ordinary human beings in a society that

has been gradually split into smaller and smaller units where real community is difficult, where "men no longer have neighbors tied to them by geography, only a far-flung association of personal friends kept in touch with by machinery,"[9] the problem is somehow "to seek *Agape* in the everyday world,"[10] not in an other-worldly abstraction and asceticism. For Auden, in his Christian phase just as in his earlier work, one of the worst human offenses is to hide, to fail to deal with the facts—the outer world of social corruption, the inner world of anxiety, guilt, and love. Hence, while we must be aware of the eternal, the setting for action and choice is here and now. And only Agape can reconcile eternity and time, the Love to Whom Auden appeals in the poem, "Kairos and Logos," to help the world: "O Thou who lovest, set its love in order" (*CP*, 239).

II The Leap of Faith

We might expect an inveterate rationalist like Auden to pause on the edge of so mystical a faith. It did take him several years to accept it, as he relates in his contribution to *Modern Canterbury Pilgrims*.[11] According to this report, the progress of Auden's conversion was far less intellectual than his reviews of the time suggest. After a childhood of close familiarity with church services and the Bible, he proceeded to the liberal humanism which seemed the only sensible outlook for "civilized people." The Communist attack on Christianity encouraged him to be anti-Christian, but the Nazi attack on it made him think again.

In this state of mind he found, on his visit to Spain, that churches meant something to him, after all; later he met Charles Williams "and for the first time in my life felt myself in the presence of personal sanctity" (41); and as he began to read Kierkegaard and other theological works, "I was forced to know in person what it is like to feel oneself the prey of demonic powers, in both the Greek and the Christian sense, stripped of self-control and self-respect, behaving like a ham actor in a Strindberg play" (41). By the autumn of 1940 he had taken the leap of faith and become a Christian.

In fact, Auden had already experienced an intense moment

of religious consciousness. As he wrote about it thirty years later:

One fine summer night in June 1933 I was sitting on a lawn after dinner with three colleagues, two women and one man. We liked each other well enough but we were certainly not intimate friends, nor had any one of us a sexual interest in another. Incidentally, we had not drunk any alcohol. We were talking casually about everyday matters when, quite suddenly and unexpectedly, something happened. I felt myself invaded by a power which, though I consented to it, was irresistible and certainly not mine. For the first time in my life I knew exactly—because, thanks to the power, I was doing it—what it means to love one's neighbor as oneself. . . .

. . . Among the various factors which several years later brought me back to the Christian faith in which I had been brought up, the memory of this experience and asking myself what it could mean was one of the most crucial, though, at the time it occurred, I thought I had done with Christianity for good. (*F&A*, 69–70)

This experience undoubtedly lies behind Auden's efforts in the 1930s to understand and expound the nature of Love, and it served the new convert as a firsthand encounter with Agape.

Even from a severely intellectual point of view, it is clear enough what attractions Christianity possessed for a man of Auden's temperament. Where liberal humanism insisted that the conditions of life must inevitably improve, although anyone in the late 1930s could see them getting worse and worse, Christian faith, with its longer perspective, could interpret present reverses as part of a more complex pattern. Christianity could thus provide what was indispensable to Auden: a ground of acceptance of the world in all its apparent evil. It could also shift the ground of acceptance from such a shaky future as, in his occasional utopian visions, Auden had never been at ease with—to the present moment seen in the light of eternity. Thus the Christian perspective opened two doors of hope, one metaphysical, one ethical: first, if the world seemed nasty now, it could yet be good in the long run; second, no matter how depressing its nastiness, a man's business was not to judge it (God would do that) or to wish to change it miraculously (the

Romantics had wished that) but to work quietly at his own limited tasks.

Furthermore, the Christian view of reality fitted perfectly Auden's symbolic (or allegorical) habits of thought. From his earliest work the phenomenal world had served him principally as a reservoir of symbols. He never denies its actuality and often insists on it, but he insists also on seeing beneath its surfaces, on subjecting it to different perspectives which have the effect of showing it always to be not quite what we had thought. In a sense, Auden, whose way of thinking seems at times remarkably Platonic, has always aimed at finding the right underlying pattern, the magic formula, that would validate the actual world. If in the late 1930s his poetry seems to lose touch with that world, it is because for him existence without meaning is a contradiction in terms; and the meanings that had been warming his world were turning cold. Christianity renews them, gives them life.

Perhaps most congenial to Auden in the Christian framework are certain basic patterns on which he later laid great stress. As in his poetry the chief characteristic is surprise, its chief technique the sudden dislocation of perspective, so his theology emphasizes the unexpected. Of the finite universe whose conditions are mainly knowable by reason, God is the unconditional creator. And, as He is beyond conditions, so is one's choice of Him. One believes not because one is convinced, nor in hope of being convinced, but in despair and resignation. And then, as with Abraham, as with the fairy-tale hero (a third son, like Auden) who in defeat gives away his last coin to the beggar woman, the miracle occurs and one gets everything back—the world, light, hope, meaning. Not of one's own doing, nor even of one's own deserving, for Agape is a gift not earned but conferred by Grace.

It is all very Kierkegaardian; Auden's Protestantism is profoundly influenced by the Danish philosopher and borrows his insights, distinctions, terms. For both men are interested in the rational analysis, from a Christian point of view, of an inner life driven by a logic all its own. Auden refers especially often to Kierkegaard's division of perspectives into the Aesthetic, the Ethical, and the Religious; and he frequently explains and extends this classification, which he finds most useful for proving that the only acceptable view of life is the one he has chosen. The Aesthetic attitude (or even religion) honors passionate existence; its divinity (epitomized in the Greek gods of Homer)—what it regards as the source of human effectiveness—is identified with external and unpredictable powers (luck), who impose their will from outside the human being. The Ethical attitude honors knowledge, reason; its divinity (epitomized in the God of Greek philosophy) is the knowledge of good and evil. The weakness of both attitudes is, in effect, that nothing guarantees existence when no one is there, when passion or the Greek gods absent themselves or when reason is asleep.

But existence, one's relation to the ground of being, cannot be intermittent; and one must therefore find a more reliable ground —something which is essentially outside consciousness and therefore more objective than passion or reason: God. "God is not present as an object of consciousness. ... God is not knowable as an object."[12] The Christian God for Auden is something to which one cannot *not* be related: "there is only a question of the right relation."[13] And the right relation quite neatly synthesizes the Necessity of the Aesthetic and the Freedom of the Ethical views: "The commands of God are neither the aesthetic fiat, 'Do what you must' nor the ethical instruction, 'These are the things which you may or must not do,' but the call of duty, 'Choose to do what at this moment in this context I am telling you to do.' "[14]

The Aesthetic and the Ethical are not precisely congruent with Auden's early terms, the "Unconscious" and "Reason," nor certainly with "Eros" and "Logos"; but his readers ought to be aware of a certain continuity in the patterns of these favorite oppositions. Kierkegaard supplies Auden with what his thought has hitherto lacked—a synthesizing third term (the Religious category, and Agape[15]) which satisfactorily resolves the opposition between the other two. Now, with a standard of value outside the private psychological life, and coming from beyond either reason or feeling, a poet ought to be able to make poems that are neither too Romantic nor too abstract but that reproduce in their form the patterns that exist in the world—specifically, the pattern in which such opposed polarities as reason and feeling do not struggle for mastery but give to man what they have to give, in the service of an enabling higher source. All his later work will try to realize this situation.

The value of this work does not exactly depend on the validity of the poet's religious beliefs, but his portrait of life owes much to his view of its sources. Without convictions, without a philosophic framework of belief, his craft suffers: "Art is not metaphysics any more than it is conduct, and the artist is usually unwise to insist too directly in his art upon his beliefs; but without an adequate and conscious metaphysics in the background, art's imitation of life inevitably becomes, either a photostatic copy of the accidental details of life without pattern or significance, or a personal allegory of the artist's individual dementia, of interest primarily to the psychologist and the historian."[16]

From the point of view of his art, Auden's devotion to abstraction during these years was necessary to the elaboration of an intellectual structure that could serve as the basis for all his subsequent work. If, in the later 1930s, his poetry went consistently in the direction of greater generality, it was only through his developed framework of ideas that he came to write at last with this generality beneath him, assumed, a part of every poem, so pervasively present that he could in time return to the personal and give it genuine largeness.

CHAPTER 11

Down Among the Lost People

I Another Time: *Chronology*

FOR ANYONE who wants to understand Auden's development as a poet, his third main collection *Another Time* (1940) is a confusing and miscellaneous volume—inevitably so, when we consider how fast his ideas were changing and how variously he was trying to achieve largeness without Romantic sublimity. If his early work takes its character from Nordic imagery and the elliptical manner, and if *On This Island* is dominated by a developing musical verve and elegance, *Another Time* seems marked by its abstraction, by the poet's disposition to discuss, to comment on, and to fix the value of men, cities, civilizations, events, aspects of life.

But the fifty poems of this book are very diverse in their styles, and Auden's arrangement of them seems calculated (as in his collections of the next decade) to disguise the current of his thinking: the reader is invited to take each poem as a poem, not as a chapter in the personal history of the poet. Still, it is just this development, the unity in his diversity, that his early critics commonly misread. And since Auden himself in his poems (especially those in this volume) and reviews often followed the changes in other eminent men, his objection was rather to the poet's stressing his own development than to the critic's piecing it together. For most scholars, understanding a poem involves seeing it in relation to other poems by the same poet.

The poems of *Another Time*, therefore, can be read in two ways: first, as Auden has arranged them, in three groups divided on a basis that, though rough, is formal. The book opens with a long section of thirty-one poems ("People and Places"); continues with a second section ("Lighter Poems") of eight parts,

which in fact include thirteen poems (mainly songs and ballads);
and concludes with a third section ("Occasional Poems") made
up of six more ambitious poems—five elegies (the poems on
Spain, Yeats, Freud, and Ernst Toller, and "September 1, 1939")
and one epithalamion. A plausible and even helpful division,
it obscures Auden's development in this period; and in some ways
the volume becomes more coherent if we see it as composed of
chronological and stylistic layers, if we look at it not logically,
as a democracy of forms, but historically, as a succession of
dynasties.

Thus, to begin with, most of the songs and ballads of the
second section, and some other poems as well, are, in a sense,
left over from the energetic musical period of the middle 1930s:
"Orpheus," "Danse Macabre," "Lay your sleeping head," "O
lurcher-loving collier" (from a movie Auden worked on in 1935),
"O the valley in the summer," "Stop all the clocks" (from *The
Ascent of F6*), "Miss Gee," "Victor," and "Wrapped in a yielding
air." These poems share many qualities with the poems in *On
This Island*: the elegant polished expression of longing, the
deliberate flatness of colloquial language used to heighten the
ballad's impersonal pathos, and celebration in song of the differences between man and the rest of the universe. All these poems
were written no later than 1937.

By 1937, however, the more discursive of Auden's poems
begin to show signs of stress. His visit to Spain from January to
March no doubt had much to do with the change. I have already
suggested that *Spain* rings false, that the verse in the latter plays
loses its life, and that Auden's contributions to "In Time of War"
are strong, but in a tight, tense way. The same quiet constriction
is to be noted in most of the topical poems Auden wrote in 1937
and 1938: "Schoolchildren," "Dover," "Oxford," "Brussels in
Winter," "The Capital," "Rimbaud," "The Novelist," "The Composer," "Gare du Midi," "A E. Housman."

Effective as some of these poems are—they all have a certain
force—they share a bleakness of outlook. The speaker in all of
them describes, formulates, interprets; but he never steps into
the life he peers at. The streets, the railway stations, the restau-
rants of the modern world become the focus of an intellectual
despair:

In unlighted streets you hide away the appalling;
Factories where lives are made for a temporary use
Like collars or chairs, rooms where the lonely are battered
Slowly like pebbles into fortuitous shapes.   (*EA*, 236)

The improper word
Scribbled upon the fountain, is that all the rebellion?   (*EA*, 217)

The quiet irony, the defeated tone, the sense of pervasive horror
evenly noted, justify our thinking of these poems, along perhaps
with "In Time of War," as Auden's Inferno; and the comparison
with Dante, whom Auden soon after this period in "New Year
Letter" considered his chief mentor, might well be pursued
further.[1]

Then early in 1939 Auden moved to the United States, and
we can see almost at once a resurgence of spirit. Perhaps it
begins before his emigration, with the relaxed and affirmative
"Musée des Beaux Arts," a product of his sojourn in Brussels in
late 1938. Along with his reading in sociology, history, and
anthropology, he has begun to look at works on theology, especially at Kierkegaard and at Charles Williams's masterly account
of the history of Christianity, *The Descent of the Dove*. From the
impasse of the contemporary world—the defeat of Spain, the
increasing power of Hitler, the hypocrisy of England and France
—Christianity seems to offer a way out, at first doubtful and
improbable; by mid-1939 conceivable if mistaken; then admissi-
ble at least as a hypothesis; and at last, sometime in 1940, accepted as the truth.

It is a disturbed but fruitful period; and the poems begin, in
1939, to shake off, little by little, the mood of despair. If "Musée
des Beaux Arts" (December 1938) is the first of these poems to
speak easily and freely again, it is followed by the impressive
elegies on Yeats and Freud, by the fine ballad "Refugee Blues,"
the satirical "The Unknown Citizen," and the surprisingly personal "The Prophets" and "September 1, 1939." None of these
poems slights the seriousness of the world situation, but some of
them recover grounds for hope, affirmation, and ease. Although
poetry is said in the Yeats poem to make nothing happen in any
large way (poets are not unacknowledged legislators), it can
help us singly. The poet can "Still persuade us to rejoice," start

"the healing fountain" in "the deserts of the heart," and "Teach
the free man how to praise" (*EA*, 243). Freud, too, has helped
to make us more free: "he quietly surrounds all our habits of
growth;/he extends, till the tired in even/the remotest
miserable duchy/have felt the change in their bones and are
cheered . . ." (*CP*, 217). The speaker of "September 1, 1939,"
though he recognizes the seriousness of the times, does so in
rhythms at times almost blithe, and ends by seeking to "Show
an affirming flame" (*EA*, 247).

As these poems are generally brighter in outlook, they also
achieve an openness of manner, a fullness of tone (muted, of
course, in the satirical pieces) that had been lacking in Auden's
work since his "Letter to Lord Byron." The speaker is still a
shrewd observer and acute analyst of the world around him; but
now, instead of the cold formulations of the controlled scientist,
we find the warmer tones, the more natural rhythms, and the
more casual locutions of ordinary good conversation: "About
suffering they were never wrong,/The Old Masters . . ./In
Brueghel's *Icarus*, for instance: how everything turns away/
Quite leisurely from the disaster . . ." (*EA*, 237); "You were silly
like us . . ." (*EA*, 242); "Perhaps I always knew what they were
saying . . ." (*CP*, 203). Even the satiric poems swing along in a
relaxed way: "Say this city has ten million souls,/Some are living
in mansions, some are living in holes . . ." (*CP*, 210).

Not that all the poems of this time are relaxed and genial:
these satiric poems are aimed at very somber actualities, and
Auden never wrote a poem that breathes more despair than
"Where do They come from," with its nightmare vision of
demonic forces within us that match (and have produced) the
horrors of the contemporary world: "For the barren must wish
to bear though the Spring/Punish; and the crooked that dreads
to be straight/Cannot alter its prayer but summons/Out of the
dark a horrible rector" (*EA*, 244). The period is a transitional
one, hovering between hope and horror, yet even this poem
returns to a richer imagery and more natural phrasing and
rhythm (it is one of his first syllabic poems) than we find in his
earlier, stiff sonnets.

II *Four Key Poems*

Auden's uncertainty during 1939 and his gradual progress from liberal humanism toward Christianity can be seen with particular clarity in one set of four poems which, though Auden separates them in *Another Time,* he may have intended to be taken together. These four are all concerned with representative thinkers (Voltaire, Arnold, Melville, and Pascal); all have essentially the same meter (regular iambic lines usually of varying lengths, usually arranged in stanzas); and the first two poems rhyme.

"Voltaire at Ferney" (first published in March 1939) shows the secular reformer, committed to "civilise," to make society more decent, more humane, by "Cajoling, scolding, scheming" (*EA,* 240). "The night was full of wrong,/Earthquakes and executions," and he goes on struggling against them, mainly with his poetry: "Only his verses/Perhaps could stop them." Of this hope, though, Auden, who once thought poetry could "make action urgent and its nature clear" (*EA,* 157), has grown more skeptical; for in his Yeats elegy, published the day before the poem on Voltaire, he asserts that "poetry makes nothing happen." Voltaire is much more hopeful: he "never doubted, like D'Alembert, he would win." The poem stresses this sureness of Voltaire, his confidence in a cause that to us appears so dark. Less sanguine, its verse moving fast, Auden's poem gives us a sense of Voltaire's activity; but we see him from a distance, a gaunt, irascible old man, fighting tirelessly what seems a losing battle.[2]

"Matthew Arnold," published in September 1939, presents another secular reformer, one more decisively defeated. Arnold is shown as having betrayed the poetry in him, which might have expressed creatively his interior "disorder." Instead, he lectured his contemporaries on their faults—a mistake, says Auden, who had not yet disencumbered his own criticism of the "jailor's voice" that he deplores in the poem (*EA,* 241).

Indeed, the poems of 1939, as their more open style suggests, often work vaguely toward a renewed personalism of the kind Auden had entertained before his Marxist phase. Personal love teaches us much: "Bless you, darling," he can say to one lover,

"I have/Found myself in you" (*CP*, 207). His "Epithalamion" suggests that the physical experience of love may symbolically "justify/Life on earth" (*EA*, 455). And he praises Yeats and Freud not for their commitment to any noble social ideal—for Yeats, quite the contrary—but for what their achievement may mean for the personal life. Clearly, in this phase, though one does well to be on the right side, political and social problems have to await the resolution of inner disorder.

The last two poems of the set of four show something different—not so much resignation as actual hope. Both were published in the Autumn, 1939, *Southern Review*. "Herman Melville" concentrates not on the years of rebellion or of silence but on Melville's reconciliation with the cosmos and his approach to something like blessedness: "Towards the end he sailed into an extraordinary mildness . . ." (*CP*, 200). He has insights into the nature of Evil and Good and realizes that "all the time he had been carried on his father's breast." The result of this final "exultation and surrender" (Melville is more like Simeon than is the Simeon of *For the Time Being*) is, of course, *Billy Budd*, in which Melville at last accepts and affirms things as they are.

The series is completed in "Pascal" (*EA*, 451–53), which purports to describe and explain that thinker's religious history. This poem, the most triumphant of the four, appears most clearly to affirm the Christianity which, in fact, Auden had not yet come to. The triumph is, unfortunately, more religious than poetic; for the poem, though linked firmly to the three just discussed, is also the first of a series (the rest will appear in book form for the first time in 1945 in *Collected Poetry*) of highly abstract, symbolic, difficult, polished stanzaic poems in which impact is fatally sacrificed to metaphysical and formal subtlety ("Kairos and Logos," "In Sickness and in Health," and "Canzone"). It is too much to assume that Auden in "Pascal," or in "Melville," describes experiences of his own, but he is feeling his way into such inward dramas as he knows have touched the lives of other men of letters; and he is thinking about the nature and shape of the experience of conversion.

In "The Prophets" he even tries out this experience; in "New Year Letter" (1941) he goes the whole way. But, before we come to that work, we should notice one other kind of poem that

appears in *Another Time*. This final group shows convincingly
that the problem of abstraction in his verse is by no means
shunted aside; for these poems, written late in 1939, are studies
of such abstract themes as Hell, Law, and Time. Four in number ("Law Like Love," "Hell," "Our Bias," and "Another Time"),
they are all exceedingly well turned (all of them are included
in his 1958 selection); and, in spite of their abstraction, some
of them have an odd warmth, even a muted joy, very different
from the more usual abstraction of the late 1930s. "Law Like
Love," for example, revives in a new form the old Auden playfulness:

> Law, says the judge as he looks down his nose,
> Speaking clearly and most severely,
> Law is as I've told you before,
> . Law is as you know I suppose,
> Law is but let me explain it once more,
> Law is The Law.   (*CP*, 208)

And the poem's conclusion, spoken to some loved person, has
a disarming gentleness—the first sign of that smiling benevolence
which, to the outrage of his socially conscious critics, continued
to mark his work throughout its Christian phases: "If we, dear,
know we know no more/Than they about the law,/If I no more
than you/Know what we should and should not do. . . ."

Apparently, one solution to the problem of reconciling the
abstract and the concrete is to present the ordinary man's feeling
response to ideas, as the ideas are made real in the world around
him. Auden has used this technique before; but from this point
on, his performance is assured because of his own fuller certainty about what he is doing, about his aesthetic, about his
metaphysics, and about the relationship between them.

To be sure, for a poet as much given to generalizing as Auden
is, and to saying large things about man without saying large
things about himself, abstraction is always a danger. Through
his poems of the next few years he continues to discuss the
world, often in abstract terms and often with too little of the
personal voice. Still, it is clear that for Auden the nadir of his
despair had come in 1938 and that in 1939, though yet uncer-

tainly, new lights had begun to edge away the darkness. When in 1940, a year of apprehension for everyone else, Auden resolved his metaphysical dilemmas, he acquired the means by which, not all at once but in different ways here and there, he could leave his abstract Olympus (or Hades) and revisit the life to which its laws referred.

CHAPTER 12

Thing and Meaning

I *Abstraction*

BUT THE PROBLEM of abstraction requires further comment. Impersonal, detached, its imagery serving to illustrate general ideas, not to show us the abundant life of the world, the poetry of this transitional period is weak in Eros, strong in Logos. The techniques of personification and psychological landscape become automatic and careless ("the deserts of the heart," "the mountains of my fear," "the ponds of apperception"). Epigrammatist that he is, Auden can often sustain his verse for a considerable time by direct statement alone; but even when he slips into imagery, it is abstract and often quietly bizarre.

For example, the elegy on Yeats contains several images so odd, or so far extended, as to parody the metaphysical conceit:

> The provinces of his body revolted,
> The squares of his mind were empty,
> Silence invaded the suburbs,
> The current of his feeling failed . . .

Earlier we are told:

> The mercury sank in the mouth of the dying day.
>
> . . . .
>
> The peasant river was untempted by the fashionable quays;
> By mourning tongues
> The death of the poet was kept from his poems.   (*EA*, 241)

I suspect that most admirers of the poem fail to see how far its

118 W. H. AUDEN

little jokes are carried. The most extended of all is the comparison of poetry to a river:

> it survives
> In the valley of its saying where executives
> Would never want to tamper; it flows south
> From ranches of isolation and the busy griefs,
> Raw towns that we believe and die in; it survives,
> A way of happening, a mouth.   (*EA*, 242)

How many readers actually see that pun on "mouth"? But it matters very much to the dignity and seriousness of the poem that we should be aware of the clowning imagery that guards against sentimentality by echoing the childish impulse to laugh at funerals, and so manages to present, more completely than it otherwise could, the whole feeling of a mourner.

But all these abstract poems do not have this emotional range. And, characteristically in Auden's work of this time, there is no poetry of objects, of sensory experience. He is *always* writing of abstract ideas, so that it almost never happens that one sensory object is compared with another. To portray the concepts, he invents landscapes; but these, instead of being developed for their own sake, function only as allegorical topographies that point back to concepts. Reality, as always for Auden, is beyond the actual; the actual is merely a parable for the real. Intrigued as he is by classifications and schemes, distinctions and categories, feeling at home with highly articulated structures of thought, he exploits whatever imageries can represent reality's most basic arrangements: war, quests, landscapes, dreams, fairy tales. These are "sacred" realms; our imaginations respond to their presence with awe. They can, therefore, in theory provide his drier abstractions with life. Although the abstraction is here more real than the thing, Logos more basic than Eros, both need each other; and they need as well to be not so much joined as fused, the Logos made incarnate through some artistic equivalent of Agape.

For a while this fusion does not happen often enough in Auden's abstract verse—not until the first impact of his theological zeal is over and the doctrines begin (in the poetry) to be assimilated to, instead of seeming to dominate and impoverish, the personal life. For if Agape has a poetic equivalent in this heavenly geometry of Auden, it is surely the sense of the man in the poem—poet, hero, or protagonist, someone whose feeling, as it changes and develops, reconciles abstraction and image.

Abstraction in itself, though dangerous for a poet, is not, however, all villain. To abstract a thing is to take it out of its context in order to have a good look at its nature. In intellectual affairs, to abstract something is, in effect, to make a separate entity of it—to make it into a thing in itself, a thing in its own right—so that we can talk about it as something independent of, or in formal relation to, all those other things among which in actual experience it is always found. Hence the personification, the hypostasizing of aspects and elements of reality, so that people, places, ideas, and forces can be spread out on the operating table like maps and their parts inspected and pointed out as if they were elements of a landscape.

This practice is an ancient one; all analyses of emotion, spirit, mental faculties (imagination, ego, feeling), proceed in this convenient fashion. So do modern physicists and chemists, as they construct models (allegories, really) to depict events they cannot see. So do myths, in their choosing to personify cosmic forces or aspects of the self. And so, in more obscure ways, do dreams and fairy tales. When Auden operates on any of these landscapes, he is expert at isolating the symbolic tissue, but, in this period, much less effective at restoring its flesh and blood.

II Dinge *and Names*

The model for this abstract technique is clearly Rilke. Auden's first "Rilkean sonnet" appears in his 1928 volume, there are several in *On This Island*, but they multiply in the later 1930s when he produces more than sixty of them. Rilke, like Auden, is concerned with interior anxieties, pressures, urgencies; and, as in the following passages from the Third Duino Elegy, he fills the inner life with abstractions and personifications:

> his tall cloaked destiny stepped
> behind the chest of drawers, and his restless future

> that easily got out of place, conformed to the
>   folds of the curtain.
>
>   .   .   .   .
>
>   Descended,
> lovingly, into the older blood, the ravines
> where Frightfulness lurked, still gorged with his
>   fathers. And every
> terror knew him, and winked, and quite understood.
> Yes, Horror smiled at him . . .[1]

Auden was rereading Rilke in 1939–40 and discussing him at
length in reviews. In one especially illuminating passage he
praises Rilke for having found "a fresh solution" to the problem
of expressing "abstract ideas in concrete terms":

> . . . Rilke thinks of the human in terms of the non-human, of what he
> calls Things (*Dinge*), a way of thought which, as he himself pointed
> out, is more characteristic of the child than of the adult. To the for-
> mer, tables, dolls, houses, trees, dogs, etc., have a life which is just as
> real as their own or that of their parents. Indeed, as a rule children
> think of life in terms of things and animals rather than in terms of
> people: a conscious interest in people does not commonly begin until
> adolescence.[2]

In Auden's view, to see "the human in terms of the non-
human" does not necessarily deprive it of its humanity but
throws a fresh light on it that keeps us from pursuing blindly our
ordinary, uncriticized life of sensation. Abstraction of this kind—
not the usual bland abstraction of intellectual discourse, but
the introduction of surprising allegorical perspectives (people
as countrysides, internal conflicts as military strategies)—is not
cold and remote but suffused with feeling. For the child the
things, the *Dinge* of which Rilke speaks, are "sacred," filled
with mana and meaning, and not only the things but their
names, so that a mispronunciation (like the *pirrits* of Auden's
aunt) seems blasphemous. On the other hand, it was not
blasphemous for the aunt; since she did not share his idea of
the sacred, she could not blaspheme against it: "One cannot
be taught to recognize a sacred being, one has to be converted"
(*DH*, 56). This problem is precisely the poet's—to make what

is sacred to him sacred to the reader, or, by praising his own sacred objects, to remind the reader of his.

The first course presents obvious difficulties: if any particular being or event is sacred to A and not to B, how can they share the verbal rite of poetry, which, says Auden, "pays homage by naming?" (*DH*, 57). Is naming enough? The moon or darkness or death may, as he says, be sacred to us all; but their *names* are not necessarily so. It would appear that what the poet must therefore do—if he wants to pay homage, say, to the moon—is not to pronounce the word but to find images, phrases, and rhythms that will make us somehow feel the sacredness of his own encounter with the moon.

Since the moon, he says, is sacred to us all, his presentation of his encounter with it justifies itself. But, if his encounter is with some more special object whose sacredness the rest of us do not feel (lead mines, for example), then what must come through for us (or the poem fails) is some quality or pattern of feeling common to sacred encounters generally (or to certain kinds of them), so that we recognize in the poet's awe for lead mines the same sense of significance that for us is located, say, in attics.

Thus, even though Auden's *Dinge* are different from ours, his *naming* of them is a rite of homage that we can share, for naming—apostrophe, invocation, celebration—is a universal human impulse. And how he loves to name! Anyone acquainted with his verse knows his passion for lists: "Newman, Ciddy, Plato, Fronny, Pascal, Bowdler, Baudelaire,/Doctor Frommer, Mrs. Allom, Freud, the Baron, and Flaubert . . ." (*EA*, 48); "The child, the waterfall, the fire, the stone . . ." (*CP*, 243); "The nights, the railway-arches, the bad sky . . ." (*EA*, 237); and even for repetitive syntactical devices: appositives, variations, and parallel sentence structure. One example should suffice—one in which every new phrase picks up and varies an earlier phrase, with the effect almost of a ritual dance, whose slow progress forward even mimics the speaker's reluctance to give up the society dying around him:

> You whom I gladly walk with, touch,
> Or wait for as one certain of good,

> We know it, we know that love
> Needs more than the admiring excitement of union,
> More than the abrupt self-confident farewell,
> The heel on the finishing blade of grass,
> The self-confidence of the falling root,
> Needs death, death of the grain, our death,
> Death of the old gang. . . . (EA, 40)

Auden seems to take, even for a poet, an extraordinary delight in such significant repetition (witness his gluttonous appetite for rhyme-schemes and verse forms). To say something's name and then to say it again satisfies his invocational passion. Indeed, his poems, religious or not, are full of invocations, explicit and implied, invocations to various figures—God, famous writers, abstract ideas, the superego, the life instincts, any felt source of power. Before he believes in a God to call on, he turns naturally to prayers, litanies, choruses, hymns. Isherwood writes in 1937: "When we collaborate, I have to keep a sharp eye on him—or down flop the characters on their knees. . . . If Auden had his way, he would turn every play into a cross between grand opera and high mass."[3]

If to call on a man's name is to secure his power for one's own side, how much more effective to possess his style or his stanza! Thus, another form of invocation is the imitation or parody, for even Auden's parody is usually affectionate. Its extent, too, is almost bizarre. Surely no English poet—Eliot nor Pope nor Jonson—echoes so many sources. And Auden not only acknowledges this feature of his own work but recommends to young poets that they choose masters, one at a time, and learn to do recognizable imitations of each, which involves "attending to every detail of his diction, rhythms and habits of sensibility" (DH, 38). Even a passage like the long one just quoted from the poem Auden later called "1929," though original in most respects, echoes in its repetitive syntax, in the very syntactical motions described on the last page, Yeats's similarly titled poem, "Nineteen Hundred and Nineteen":

> That image can bring wildness, bring a rage
> To end all things, to end

> What my laborious life imagined, even
> The half-imagined, the half-written page. . . .[4]

The English language itself in all its forms sometimes seems the chief theme of Auden's praise. As he puts it much later: "Whatever else it may or may not be, I want every poem I write to be a hymn in praise of the English language: hence my fascination with certain speech-rhythms which can only occur in an uninflected language rich in monosyllables, my fondness for peculiar words with no equivalents in other tongues, and my deliberate avoidance of that kind of visual imagery which has no basis in verbal experience and can therefore be translated without loss."[5] Hence, too, his imitations of the diction of jukebox love songs, political speeches, the Book of Common Prayer, officialese, sermons, letters, diaries, wills, hymns, petitions, reveries, and curses. It seems sometimes as if Auden had set himself the task of imitating any kind of English speech, any use of English words.

As for his verse forms, they are far too numerous to list because almost every poem Auden writes is original in form. Even when he repeats a form, as in his sonnets or his syllabic verse, something is altered from poem to poem—the rhyme scheme or the pattern of stresses or syllables. Every poem, therefore, is a new ceremony, its form springing out of the new material, or even shaping that material—Logos and Eros again fusing (if successful, if watched over by Agape) to celebrate something, to say its name.

III *Realm and Realm*

To say the name of something, to pay homage to it—that is what Auden's poetry tries to do. The thing itself can never exist on the page, or in the voice; but if the words are right, they can become to others, too, a *name* for the thing, or for things of its kind. Invocation is a sacred process, by which Auden's feeling for *his* things may parallel our feeling for ours, his celebration be shared by us. These sacred forms of appeal, basic in his work, also dramatize his sense of reality as issuing out of significant confrontations between different levels of experience—inner and outer, psychological and social, the world of ordinary surfaces and the inner, anxious, stricken soul, Myself and the Other.

Almost all his poetry pits one such realm against another, not to show the superiority of one but to emphasize the constant unexpectedness of life, the way one world has of opening up to reveal another: it is only through such confrontations that we see things in a new light, and new light is all the light there is. Wherever life is most ordinary, there the miracle is most likely to happen, the conditional world to be surprised by the Unconditional. Beneath the surfaces of life lies the Freudian id, or the Marxist pattern of history, or the Incarnation; the ordinary and the miraculous, time and eternity, Eros and Agape, are different sides of the flashing, surprising world, where the chief events are these changes in perspective. In such circumstances naming and invoking are means of opening doors to this more real realm where the meanings are at play.

His poetry is always most successful, therefore, when the changes of perspective are most skillfully managed. In all his best work the structure of dislocation is implicit in the poem's form, or in the ironic disproportion of form to situation. In his later poems, as we shall see, he builds these ironic structures with special care. The abstract poems, on the other hand, often fail to reach us, I think, because their structures lack perspectival variety. The mutual illumination of realm and realm, abstract and concrete, is intermittent. The straightforward discussion dips down too little into "the ponds of apperception"; and the subtle observations on human life are not reinforced by our sense of some significant relation between the observer and his occasions—that is, by tone.

Certainly there are moments when Auden's abstract poems do exhibit that sudden accession of "the world's body," when the actual rises out of the surrounding plateau of abstraction, as in the dramatic finale of "In Time of War": ". . . night's tiny noises/Will echo vivid in the owl's developed ear . . ." (EA, 269); or, from "The Quest" (1940): "The nights came padding after him like wild/Beasts that meant harm, and all the doors cried Thief . . ." (CP, 226). But too often the poems remain in the one realm; references to the actual world do not quite carry us to it; the objects do not get through to us as objects, but only as words for objects: "The hour-glass whispers to the lion's roar,/The clock-towers tell the gardens day and night/How many errors Time has patience for,/How wrong they are in being always right" (*CP*, 218).

Despite the sly humor, we are not at all moved; we feel no encounter with anything important; we do not really get into the world of lions and gardens, whereas when Destiny steals behind the chest of drawers in Rilke's poem, the effect is startling. For in Rilke the discussion of the inner life in abstract terms is balanced by the extraordinarily urgent tone, often agonized, always supremely warm, quivering with a humanity we feel he shares with us. Auden's tone, on the other hand, in the very poems that owe most to Rilke, is detached, unruffled, observant. And even his few successful invasions of the actual are not sustained, as Rilke's are, through a whole Rilkean poem.

Thus, statement is not enough; abstraction is not enough. For Auden's poetry has as its central action the process of exchange (disguise, hostility, conversion) between realms of existence, usually between the actual and some more significant and fundamental but abstract realm. In his successful poems this exchange is dramatized (named) variously, the abstract realm being conveyed through allegorical imagery or by intellectual formulation, the actual through concrete imagery and personal tone. But the poems fail when, however clever the abstract formulation, the realm of the actual is presented too weakly to serve as a fitting antagonist to the abstract, when the shifts in perspective show us nothing important.

John G. Blair, in his fine book on Auden, maintains that virtually all of Auden's principal poetic techniques are allegorical, that they deliberately prevent us from paying excessive attention to particular objects, scenes, persons, even feelings, in order to direct our attention always to the general case. Hence the lists, the skipping imagery, the suppression of articles, the allegorized landscape, and similar devices that encourage us to look for the general principle that links a series of actualities.[6] It may be added that, instead of allowing us to identify smugly with some speaker who is feeling deeply but vaguely and irresponsibly, Auden permits identification only with speakers who are quietly and unpretentiously becoming aware of truths. Learning, beginning to see something—this is almost the only pattern of feeling which Auden judges his poetry has a right to ask the reader to share—except, of course, the joy that follows such insight, the pleasure of seeing the world in a new perspective. Since Auden in his later work is at pains not to overstate any emotion in which he wants his reader to participate, this joy and pleasure are never accompanied by the grandiose orchestration with which almost all Romantic poets, even Eliot and Yeats, often overwhelm the reader.

Throughout the late 1930s and early 1940s Auden is still working out just how poetry can be written that may move and urge and yet not drown. Much of it, at first, in its caution not to drown, seems to move too little and to urge too much. The search for generality leads to a forbidding abstraction; even where we can accept a language almost entirely conceptual, we still wish for some hint of a human person in the tone. But it should be clear by now, as we watch Auden explore the possibilities open to him in the years following the formulation of his mature ethics and aesthetic, that, far from being the uncommitted, frivolous, trivial poet that hostile critics have found him because they misunderstand his political and religious ideas and his assertions about the "frivolity" of art, Auden in his later career was unfailingly constant and serious in his pursuit of an honest poetic and of poems that reach the reader without victimizing him.[7]

CHAPTER 13

The American Auden

I *Voluntary Exile*

EARLY IN 1939, Auden and Isherwood sailed to the United States with the intention of settling there permanently. They had traveled through much of the American continent on their way home from China in the previous year, and they had been attracted by certain qualities they thought they discerned in American life. Isherwood eventually made his home in southern California; Auden found the energy and vitality of the New York intellectual scene more congenial. In any case, the decision to leave England and become a professional New York writer was a momentous one for Auden and for his reputation. When, a few months later, the Second World War broke out, he, Isherwood, Aldous Huxley, and others were reviled in the British daily press and even in literary periodicals for what seemed like a desertion in time of crisis.

This accusation against Auden later was conflated with two connected but separate charges of desertion. When Auden became an Anglican shortly afterward, it seemed to many of his former admirers that he was turning his back on the political commitment that had made his poetry in the 1930s so exciting. Furthermore, the poetry he wrote in the United States, as it shied away from political subjects and ceased to refer directly to European war, outrage, and power, seemed to many readers to have become trivial and thin. Many of Auden's British readers have felt that his poetic career from this point on went continuously downhill, that his later work was one long embarrassing failure, that he never wrote so well after he "abandoned" England, and even that his moral cowardice was a major cause of his diminished art.

These are serious charges, even when presented in a more moderate form, and they need to be discussed at some length. In effect, Auden is accused of having deserted his country, his politics, and his muse. In addition, these desertions have led critics and readers to think of Auden generally as a poet who gave up, who made a great refusal of his poetic gift, and who frittered away his remarkable talent for thirty shameful years in America. Readers who see Auden in this light are likely to find all his later work (and even some of the earlier) dishonest.

But this view is surely wrong. The evidence shows clearly that Auden was an unusually honest poet. If he changed his country, his political views, and his style, he did so in response to his altered understanding of the human condition and his own personal situation. He did so also at great personal cost. But each of these cases needs to be taken up in turn.

First, his abandonment of England. Auden and Isherwood actually emigrated to America in January 1939, eight months before the outbreak of war. They were not merely on an extended visit; they had decided to uproot themselves from their country of birth and become citizens of another country. The reasons for which they did so will, of course, not seem convincing to those who decided to stay. If, when the war began, they had gone back to England to fight, what would then have been said about the strength of their commitment to emigrate? But in 1939, Auden's critics will continue, anyone could see that the war was coming. Again a reply can be made: Yes, but does that imply that the only possible correct action was to wait around till it did?

Auden's intellectual history during this period, and the development of his thought from liberal humanism, or Marxist doctrine, to a kind of Kierkegaardian Christianity have been treated already in earlier chapters. The thoroughness with which Auden studied and meditated on these matters leaves no room for doubt as to the earnestness of his quest for a view of life he could accept. Again, those who prefer a different view may see his quest as wrongheaded and its conclusion as regrettable. But Auden's passage from one view to another during this period came out of deeply troubled questionings and anxious testing of alternatives. Few intellectuals go through so searching an inquiry before settling down comfortably with the beliefs that are to last them through life.

As for Auden's desertion of his early manner, we have already seen how in the 1930s his changes in style proceed out of changes in his view of poetry and of society. The same is true of his later changes; the major style of his late poetry is consistent with his late-adopted views of the world: his perception of human beings as flawed and limited, of poets as making fantastic structures that tell us the truth, of poetry as making nothing happen except to individual persons. The comic style of his later work, far from originating in Auden's more trivial and trivializing attitudes, springs authentically from his anti-Romantic understanding of life, his rejection of the grandiose except as a comic resource, his disgust with "poets who, to wow an / audience, utter some resonant lie" (*CP*, 609).

II *The Poet in New York*

Several features of Auden's personality have made it more difficult to see how serious a writer he is, or have tempted readers to regard his earnestness as spurious. His amazingly quick wit, his habit of turning almost everything into a joke, his gift for hyperbole, his readiness to try out opinions (or hats) that are not yet quite his (and perhaps never will be)—all these, along with his personal untidiness, his addiction to strong dry martinis, and his reported sexual adventures make it hard for some readers to see him as the ascetic poet, intent on his work, obedient to the clock, fanatical about form and order, that he also was.

Certainly Auden's life in New York created for his readers, over the years, a different portrait of the poet from that of the gangling genius of the 1930s. After a few years of teaching in the provinces (as New Yorkers are likely to think of them), notably at Swarthmore and Bryn Mawr Colleges near Philadelphia, Auden became a permanent New York resident. His entire life up to this time had been spent in schools here and there, as a pupil or teacher, or in wandering about—to Berlin, to Iceland, to China, or on other brief trips and tours. Now, for the first time, in his middle thirties, Auden settled down. His habits of work, and especially his attention to the clock, had always been rigorous, even eccentric. For the next twenty-five years, while he continued to live in small apartments in Greenwich Village, his routine became increasingly fixed. Though the turns his poems took remained as unpredictable as ever, the *enfant terrible* of the 1930s would become almost unbelievably set in his ways.

Auden had always written copiously, but some of his writing had certainly been undisciplined. Now in New York he became a hard-working professional writer. "I have never written nor read so much," he wrote to a friend late in 1939 (*EA*, xx), and for more than thirty years—the more comfortably after 1947, when he could afford to teach less—he continued to work steadily. By the end of his career he had produced a body of work that must exceed in variety and volume the output of any other modern English or American poet. The routine he adopted undoubtedly made this possible. He would rise early, work for many hours every day (except Sunday), then give over the late afternoon and evening to drinking, talking, and dining with friends and going to the theater, concert, or opera. But at nine or so he would announce that it was past his bedtime. He never worked at night: that was only for the "Hitlers of the world."[1] He almost never, in his later years, took vacations or traveled for pleasure. It is clear that Auden understood that the only way to continue to develop as a poet was to work hard at it, and he meant to be a great poet.

In the United States also his love life became more orderly. Having come to terms early with his homosexuality, he had never been reticent about seeking lovers. But most of his sexual affairs were of short duration, and his love poems are normally addressed to lovers who are asleep, away, or otherwise unresponsive. His role, apparently, in any love-relation was that of "The More Loving One" (see *CP*, 445), though one can imagine how Auden's mercurial manner must have astonished some casual lovers. By the end of the decade, in any case, the strain of sustaining an active but irregular sex life had begun to tell on him. Isherwood reports Auden's state of mind as they completed their journey home from China in 1938: "Then, in New York and on the Atlantic crossing, we had these extraordinary scenes—

Wystan in tears, telling me that no one would ever love him, that he would never have my sexual success."[2]

In New York the following year he met Chester Kallman, and they began the long friendship that lasted until Auden's death. Kallman was eighteen when they met, Auden thirty-two. They lived together for many years, first in New York, later (for half the year) in Ischia, still later (for the same half-year) in Austria. Although Kallman from the beginning had other lovers besides Auden and in the late 1950s took to spending the other half of the year in Athens with a Greek lover while Auden remained alone—and lonely—in New York, his affection and companionship clearly meant a great deal to Auden. It is not too much to claim that he, and the establishments which he and Auden shared, provided a stability that had been missing from Auden's earlier life and that now he badly needed. In addition, Kallman's intense interest in opera, and his considerable knowledge of it, changed the direction of Auden's later career. The two friends collaborated on several important operatic libretti, and their work in this medium can undoubtedly be felt in Auden's later poems, where certain devices of style strike a distinctly operatic note.

What not even Kallman could change was Auden's personal untidiness. "I'm very disorderly myself," Auden once told an interviewer, "but that doesn't mean I like being disorderly. I don't. I would just prefer servants of my own."[3] Almost everyone who has left an account of Auden's later life has remarked on his astonishing neglect of his appearance, and of all the appearances around him. Hannah Arendt recalls occasions when it seemed that

he could not cope any more, when his slum apartment was so cold that the water no longer functioned and he had to use the toilet in the liquor store at the corner, when his suit—no one could convince him that a man needed at least two suits so that one could go to the cleaner or two pairs of shoes so that one pair could be repaired . . .— was covered with spots or worn so thin that his trousers would suddenly split from top to bottom. . . .[4]

This side of Auden made so strong an impression even on friends who loved the man that it is worthwhile, before going on

to consider Auden's fastidiously composed later poems, to quote
one more passage that depicts the personal neglect that characterized Auden's (and Kallman's) residence. In December 1952
they gave a Christmas party for Igor and Vera Stravinsky and
Robert Craft. Craft's ironic account follows:

The apartment is imaginatively decorated for the Yuletide, with
empty bottles, used martini glasses, books, papers, phonograph rec-
ords, all realistically strewn about to create a marvelously lifelike
impression of randomness. And the decorators have achieved other,
subtle touches of picturesqueness as well, such as, in lieu of
frankincense, filling the flat with stale, boozy air. We compete for the
most recently occupied, and hence dusted, chairs—the furniture
looks as if it had been purchased with Green Stamps—then choose
drinks, tipping out cigarette butts and ashes, dregs of earlier drinks
and other detritus from the glasses in which they seem most likely to
be served. But, shortly before dinner, the fine line between decor and
reality momentarily confuses V[era]. Visiting the lavatory and finding
shaving utensils and other matter in the sink, a glass containing a set
of snappers (store teeth), a mirror in which it would be impossible
even to *recognize* oneself, a towel that would oblige the user to start
over again, and a basin of dirty fluid on the floor, she unthinkingly
empties the basin and fills it with fresh water. Not until dessert time
do we discover, with mixed emotions, that she has flushed away Chester's chocolate pudding.[5]

Even Auden's face in his later years looked as if it had been
let go. Youthful-looking and smooth-skinned even into his for-
ties, his face became deeply lined over the next decade. But
anyone who has seen a photograph of the older Auden knows
at once how much "deeply lined" understates the condition. The
lines in his face were like crevasses; its whole surface looked
cracked and ridged. When Auden posed for photographs with
people like T. S. Eliot or Marianne Moore, poets twenty years
his senior, he seemed at least their age. He himself said that
his face looked like "a wedding cake which had been left out in
the rain."[6] Stravinsky, a quarter-century older than Auden,
warned: "Soon we will have to smooth him out to see who
it is."[7]

This extraordinarily rapid aging—it is not just joking to say so—seems connected with Auden's personal carelessness. "He showed almost no interest in possessions," writes Louis Kronenberger,[8] and other friends confirm the fact. Craft suggests that "With Auden the senses seemed to be of negligible importance," and he points out that Auden cared little for painting or for natural beauty. Even "the idea of music appealed to him more than music itself," for he was "a conceptualizer in quest of intellectual order."[9]

This judgment seems very accurate, and it goes far to explain Auden's almost colossal indifference to his physical surroundings. He registered them with remarkable accuracy and had a gift for selecting the salient detail in any scene, but his main interest in such details was in the intellectual and formal order they composed. He took no pleasure in wine, in flowers, in clothing, in the visual arts, in any of the usual sensuous experiences—or so it appears—except, as Craft suggests, as they have *meanings*. What his later poetry does to an extraordinary degree is to isolate these meanings, to strip them of their sensuous clothing, and to fit them into the not excessively sensuous forms of his poems. Perhaps more than any other poet of the century, Auden did indeed create "secondary worlds," as he later came to call them, constructions made out of primary-world materials but having their own rules, order, and joys—better worlds than the troubling one we face every day, more complete, more satisfactory, more perfect.

To a large extent, then, Auden conducted his life in the mind. He stands almost alone as a striking example of the artist who lives so intensely among concepts and abstractions that the sensory world is shut out much of the time. In his later poems Auden frequently praises the senses and praises life. The physical self we are is constantly with us; like Yeats's "rag-and-bone shop of the heart," it provides us with all the material for our own creations. But such praise is often reluctant; the mind's (or soul's) coexistence with the body is cause for regret:

> Really, must you,
> Over-familiar
> Dense companion,
> Be there always? (*CP*, 543)

If we cannot really be abstracted from the body, that is at least the direction of our wishes.

Still, given Auden's unusual degree of abstraction, his detachment from things of this world, he seems to have known exactly what he was and to have kept to the end, despite all his eccentricities, his balanced and relatively illusionless view of human life. Hannah Arendt wrote of him:

There was nothing more admirable in him than his complete sanity and his firm belief in the sanity of the mind; all kinds of madness were in his eyes lack of discipline—'naughty, naughty,' as he used to say. The main thing was to have no illusions and to accept no thoughts, no theoretical systems that would blind you against reality.[10]

A clear-minded, rational, unchaste ascetic, he never forgot how good the life was that had made him at times so unhappy.

It had also given him friends. Toward the end of his life he fell into the habit of saying that he was proud of two things—his knowledge of prosody, and his friends. Many of those who have written about him say that Auden was the most vivid and amazing person they had ever known, and they praise his capacity for warmth and affection, his generosity in helping them with their problems, in giving advice or in leading them to see their own situations clearly. Some of his university friends remained friends for life; as he moved from circle to circle he acquired friends constantly; he clearly had a gift for intimate and fascinating talk, which could make him a valued and important person in one's life, quite apart from the interest of his being a literary celebrity. The various collections of essays written about Auden, especially the memorial volume edited by Spender, attest to the feelings of affection and love that his friends felt for him. "And say my glory was I had such friends," Yeats wrote at the end of his life,[11] and Auden, even in his lonely last years, often felt so, too.

CHAPTER 14

A Place to Stand

AUDEN'S PRINCIPAL WORK between 1940 and 1947 consists of four long poems: "New Year Letter," *For the Time Being, The Sea and the Mirror*, and *The Age of Anxiety*. Although critics differ in their preferences, most agree that at least one of these poems is brilliant and at least one is painfully bad; opinions about "New Year Letter" and *The Age of Anxiety* have been particularly mixed. All four poems continue the progression I have noted in *Another Time* from cosmic, detached abstraction toward the warmth of closer engagement in ordinary life. The issues are still very large, but the tone is often more personal: we find people before us who breathe their hopes and regrets. The general outlook, too, is much brighter than in the despairing works of the later 1930s. And the verse achieves unprecedented elegance; while the tones of the speakers become more informal, even colloquial, their verse settings grow more operatic. At their worst, these poems are distinguished by a glossy, brittle quality; at their best, by a radiant splendor. Auden's treatment of the *ordinary* life of man is either grandly offhand or deftly grave.

Auden is able to take such stances, accurately reflecting the ambiguities and contradictions of our complex life, because of the elaborate stylized structures that the poems present. Simple as some of them seem in design, all of them are supported by extensive scaffoldings of philosophical irony. Each work presents a multiplicity of contradictory attitudes; one basic contradiction is that between the ordinary human desire for simplicity, directness, and clarity and the intelligent man's awareness of the need for irony and qualification. Human truth is the product of incongruities, of distorted perspectives, of surprising analogies— Caliban as Henry James, St. Joseph as a character out of Saroyan, the Faerie Queene in a Third Avenue bar.

135

What Auden basically does—here as elsewhere—is to construct a bizarre situation, composed of elements we do not expect to see in each other's company, and then allow the characters (or the speaker) to behave normally, taking for granted what is odd in their situations or in their own styles, and within these limitations carrying on with relative simplicity. In effect, Auden's personages, provided with apparently inappropriate styles by their apparently whimsical creator, accept the necessity of the Kierkegaardian leap of faith. As human life is absurd but can only be affirmed and embraced, so too the provisional life of these characters is accepted by them as inexplicable but given; their verse forms, their dictions, are modes which, like the social and physical conditions of our own life, cannot be evaded but must be used as the medium of each man's salvation.

Throughout these poems, too, it *is* the working out of one's own salvation that is most often central. Auden no longer sees any likelihood that socialism or any secular solution or, indeed, any foreseeable religious transformation will shortly redeem the whole world. Hence his poetry no longer urges the reader to the disciplined love and concerted action that seemed desirable in his more Marxist frame of mind. Secular reform is not now *un*desirable, but Auden's emphasis has returned to where it was in his early poems and to where it had always been straining to return: to the individual anxiety, to the progress of the ordinary human soul toward health or God. Now, however, his presentation of this ordinary soul is strengthened by his having arrived at a mature and consistent view of life and art, a complex and yet flexible point of view from which he may survey, describe, and interpret the patterns of everyday behavior—patterns of outer activity and of inner *malaise*.

Where Auden's early poetry badgered the reader to choose between normal illness and healthy rebellion, or later between conventional evil and Socialist community, and still later simply faced him with the ghastly spectre of a dead world, the poetry of the 1940s and after urges upon the reader the possibility of becoming himself, the person he is capable of being. There is little or nothing of the schoolmaster's tone in these later works; instead of the direct plea or the pointed presentation that accuses the reader and requires him to renounce and choose (as in much of the work down to 1934 or so), and instead even of the logical analysis that implicitly tells the reader what side to take (as in the 1937-38 period), the later poems tactfully limit themselves to exposure of certain speakers' positions. When the accusing finger makes its appearance now, it is only as part of an ironic pose. As the character or speaker on view explains his position or arrives at a new one, we are invited to be present at his artistic apotheosis and to let its brilliance, its meaning, illuminate our lives. But all this is carried on now with elaborate discretion, with a classical concern for our delicate sensibilities, as if the poet were at pains not to let it be seen too baldly that the lives whose mistakes and weakness he permits to appear before us are, in fact, emblems of our own.

This new tact is largely due to Auden's having found new principles of construction for his longer works. The Brechtian challenge to the audience has given way to the Kierkegaardian exposure of the truth: for any man whom poetry is likely to reach, truth is sufficient challenge. In any case, the method is appropriate to the poetry of a man who believes in the voluntary penitential way. Grace is something conferred from outside, yet one must will to be ready to receive it. Hence the poetry is not to be read without a certain effort; its riddles are sometimes difficult; its language, its syntax, its references, even its rhymes, may have to be worked at a bit. When all is done, illumination may or may not reward the effort. Poetry can only, at most, present "An abstract model of events/Derived from dead experience,/And each life must itself decide/To what and how it be applied."[1] Interpretations may differ; still, the symbols are tied, not loosely suggestive; the structures are systematic; the "abstract model" yields its meanings to methodical study.

The Kierkegaardian attitude is supported, furthermore, by the formal structures Auden used in these four poems—structures which owe much, as Edward Callan has shown,[2] to Kierkegaardian categories of thought, especially to the triad of attitudes already discussed: the Aesthetic, Ethical, and Religious. In conjunction with other organizing frameworks, this dynamic scheme —in which the first two categories, insufficient but necessary ingredients of the modern whole man, are reconciled and made fruitful only upon the acceptance of the third—provides a solid basis not merely for these four poems but for most of Auden's later verse.

In particular, this scheme gives to this work a unity lacking in the earlier, for the earlier establishes no consistent ground of value; it keeps observing the patterns of twentieth-century human reality, but from constantly shifting positions that are strongest when they condemn and assail but that often become blurred and false in feeling when they propose. Auden, running in his early years from mentor to mentor, from country to country, from style to style, from hat to hat, becomes emblematic himself of a certain cultural displacement: a visitor everywhere, nowhere quite at home, Auden the uprooted, the Wanderer, the refugee. Christianity gives him a place to stand. Once it is his, the verse becomes more sure even as it becomes less cocksure.

Thus, where the old, attacking, exposing poetry was constantly faced with the unspoken question, "All right, if that is evil, what is good?" and could devise only relatively unconvincing or negative replies ("Love!" or "Don't be Romantic, don't be dishonest" —good advice as far as it went), now, far from hedging at these crucial junctures, Auden's poetry, as it moves to its conclusions, begins to do so with a kind of triumphant joy. As the end approaches and the art gets ready to release us again into life, we are invited to share a double pleasure—pleasure in the fineness of the work itself, so elegantly contrived and richly developed, and pleasure, too, in the splendor of life, with all its marvelous patterns, and especially with its art and its intelligence crowned, improbably but absolutely, by its religious coherence.

We need not even, it seems to me, accept Auden's religious views in order to share the pleasure he takes in life, for his view does not minimize evil: he is aware of it, he writes about it, he finds it in himself as in others. But as submission to the Unconscious was urged by his early verse, and submission to History by his verse of the 1930s, what he advises now is submission to our own time and place and possibilities—to the limitations inherent in our being human. Given such submission to the Necessity of life's conditions, we are then free to observe, to use our senses, to play with art, to exercise our intellect, even to perform our civic duty. We are free to do what, in fact, we must do: to love our neighbor. Auden's old convictions are by no means all discarded; the basic ones remain, only to be given new meaning by a new framework. The Christian setting amplifies echoes of Homer Lane: "If a man does not love mankind and the universe, he is not true to his nature. Man does not choose to love; he *must* love."[3]

CHAPTER 15

Person and Quest

I "New Year Letter"

T HE FIRST of these four long poems, "New Year Letter"
(1941), seems, after *Another Time*, remarkably hopeful.
The simple diction, the melodic ease, and the quietly cheerful
outlook of the last poems in *Another Time* are developed and
deepened here. Affirmative, relaxed, urbane, loyal always to its
colloquial base of the chatty, ranging, witty letter, this survey of
contemporary feeling and thought is still intensely serious, sometimes solemn. The verse itself (octosyllabic couplets) is a modern
marvel: the phrasing and rhyming are almost always easy and
natural; the danger of monotony is reduced not only by Auden's
epigrammatic ingenuity but by the long and complex sentences
that, together with the occasional difficulty of ideas or allusions,
guard against the possible feeling that art, history, and life are
being oversimplified. Frequent changes of pace, style, or mood
quicken the poem again and again, and so does the constant
shift from personal to public concerns. If the values of such
verse—its dazzling clarities of sound and sense—are nowadays
subordinated to our taste for irregular rhythms and images that
explode from inside, it still seems likely that "New Year Letter"
will one day seem a classic of our time.

According to Edward Callan's analysis,[1] the three sections of
the poem correspond to Kierkegaard's Aesthetic, Ethical, and
Religious categories; as Auden reviews the metaphysical limitations of Art and Reason in the face of contemporary troubles, and
shows at last how nothing can save us but knowledge of ourselves, humility, confession of our sins, and acceptance of what
God gives, the poem marks out the stages of conversion. Part
III, in particular, as it ponders Auden's own relation to English
140

landscape and the history of man since the Renaissance, seems to turn finally both to a rational recognition of the necessity of dispensing with pride and to that impulse to invoke which is never far from Auden and which here embodies the imperative of the leap of faith: *O da quod jubes, Domine.*

The poem is dated January 1, 1940, but was not published until early in 1941; in that time Auden was converted, so that the poem's movement from its relatively jaunty and secular tone at the beginning to Christian injunctions and Christian invocation at the end seems entirely appropriate. What gives particular life to the poem is the personal tone that keeps warming the abstractions and the learned tour of history and literature. We feel always that the intellectuality is swept with feeling, that the search for meaning, for ground, is a suffering, human search, and that even the speaker's leap of faith at the end is validated by the seriousness and honesty, even by the air of exhaustiveness (he has really looked everywhere), which, beneath the urbanity, have throughout characterized his quest.

It is difficult to illustrate this personal warmth, for it is something we feel as we read through long passages which, however abstract they become, almost always return to the personal note. The abstract complexities are not just fascinating puzzles but truths that distress or encourage a human being. We see him turning in various directions as he seeks guidance in the good life, or we see the results of his having so turned. Art, he shows us first, can do much, can offer us a model of the way things are; but "Art is not life and cannot be/A midwife to society" (*CP*, 162). The "great masters" of the past "have shown mankind/An order it has yet to find" (*CP*, 163), but they cannot reorganize our lives for us; at best, the poet now can show us our own disorder.

Reason, too, as we see in the second section, has severe limitations; still, it has its uses. The instinctive life certainly offers us much, but we cannot trust it entirely. We should be aware that life as we actually experience it emotionally is different from the measuring order of time, that "all our intuitions mock/The formal logic of the clock./All real perception, it would seem,/Has shifting contours like a dream..." (*CP*, 169). But we are mistaken if we therefore "throw away intelligence" and give ourselves over to instinct. Indeed, this is the greater danger. Modern man suffers from the double lie of Plato and Rousseau (cf. "September 1, 1939")—the "lie of intellect" that resigns authority and responsibility to the philosopher-kings, and the "falsehood of the flesh" by virtue of which we think we are all equal because we have equal access to the world of feeling.

Both lies, in Auden's view, encourage us to do as we please, to embrace any or all experience, and to forfeit the standards by which we might evaluate and choose. The result is Wagner and his Tristan, an operatic, unredeeming nightmare from which nothing can release us but submission to the facts of life, acceptance of human limitations. In human experience, art can give us a foretaste of the perfection of Heaven, but it is Hell to expect life to be like that. Ordinary life is, rather, Purgatory, a constant struggle in which we are tested, through which we may be *really* redeemed.

Through all these truths and "half-truths we can synthesize" (*CP*, 176) the human speaker seeks to "Ascend the penitential way" (*CP*, 179), to reconcile all those doublenesses and multiplicities in himself which, like intelligence and feeling, exert rival claims upon him. The original American edition of the poem was, in fact, called *The Double Man*, and the doubleness refers not only to the Aesthetic and Ethical realms and to the opposition of thought and feeling, but to other polarities inherent in being human. As this discussion has already indicated, the poem moves continually between the abstract and the personal; it jogs back and forth as well between personal and public life. We all live, Auden tells us, in two worlds:

> There are two atlases: the one
> The public space where acts are done,
> In theory common to us all,
> Where we are needed and feel small
>
> . . . .
>
> The other is the inner space
> Of private ownership, the place
> That each of us is forced to own,
> Like his own life from which it's grown . . . (*CP*, 180–81)

The poem tries to balance this doubleness, too, as it discusses matters important to Auden personally—as a poet, a friend, an

Englishman come to America—and affairs in the public world: Europe as it is now and as it has been since the Renaissance. In treating this various material, Auden adopts the tone of the civilized man of letters, an Englishman writing in America to a German woman about culture, history, and art. He alludes casually to such literary works and authors and to such ideas and historical events as educated people presumably are familiar with; and he drops words and phrases in French, German, Latin, Italian, and Greek. His perspective—that of the European tradition—inevitably imposes order on the diverse matters that he takes up. The "*civitas* of sound" that results from playing Buxtehude, the *polis* that is made up of friends (*CP*, 162, 180)—these are the images that European civilization can provide of the good life—and the octosyllabic couplets are a fitting measure to order his perceptions and insights.

The final acceptance of a Western history given to error but ultimately overseen by a Christian God is one of the central doublenesses of this poem, in which Auden seems to have been thinking of himself as sharing that "belief-in-disbelief" that Charles Williams attributes to Montaigne.[2] Indeed, Montaigne provides the volume's epigraph: "We are, I know not how, double in ourselves, so that what we believe we disbelieve, and cannot rid ourselves of what we condemn." By the end of the poem it has become clear to the speaker that the "situation of our time" (*CP*, 165) can be resolved only in belief, belief that "every day in sleep and labour/Our life and death are with our neighbour,/And love illuminates again/The city and the lion's den,/The world's great rage, the travel of young men" (*CP*, 193).

For the poem, always controlled by the personal tone, has been fundamentally an account, logical rather than chronological, of the speaker's travels, especially of his intellectual travels through the past and present, the Europe and America of feeling and thought. With all the elegant motions of a chivalric romance, "New Year Letter" reports his quest—its adventures and its success.

II *Addenda*

The poem is most effective by itself, but it appeared in *The Double Man* (British edition: *New Year Letter*), in company with certain other writing that presumably was meant to locate or explain or reinforce it:

1) A Prologue (*EA*, 457–58) and an Epilogue (*CP*, 222–23), both in rather prosy syllabic verse. The Prologue can only lament the present trouble, but the Epilogue arrives at the possibility of prayer.

2) Notes—and not just a few explanatory observations, but a jumble of quotations, citations, comments, poetic jottings, sonnets—altogether a messy assortment of random effluvia on most of the subjects dealt with so neatly in the "Letter." Here again, perhaps, is a doubleness, the wild disorder lurking behind the stately scene. But the disorder quite overwhelms the stage; the "Letter's" sixty-two pages fall away before eighty-four pages of Notes. Where in *Letters from Iceland* mess and order were all thrown together, here they are side by side; in the later long works the disorder will be invisible, a realm of existence to be conveyed not by disorder itself but elegantly: we know what Caliban is even while he talks like Henry James.

3) "The Quest," a sequence of twenty sonnets, first published in November 1940, which means that Auden probably began it later than "New Year Letter" and finished it earlier. Very different in tone, feeling, and approach, this group of poems touches more explicitly on the same quest-motif that is fundamental to "New Year Letter," and it is closely concerned with the same ethical problems: how to live a good life, a life successful in the deepest sense, how to avoid the wrong kinds of commitment, what one can learn from those who had great gifts and yet failed, what part luck plays in one's success, and so on. As is typical in Auden, the heroic quest becomes a metaphor for ordinary life and its crucial but inconspicuous choices; it is one of his frequent themes that the heroic event, or the experience of significant suffering, occurs "nowhere particularly unusual" (*CP*, 204), "While someone else is eating or opening a window or just walking dully along . . . (*EA*, 237).

So, as the couplets of "New Year Letter" swing from the personal to the public atlas in an attempt to survey Auden's own important relationships (to art, to England and America, to European civilization, to intellect, and to friends), the Rilkean sonnets of "The Quest," both less personal and less public, generalize the various patterns of relationship that may exist among such elements of a man's life as temperament, talent, training, and desires on the one hand, and, on the other, the immediate conditions. It becomes clear that every man's quest is different, and its chances of success depend on the adaptation of his gifts to the particular situations that confront him (or that he *is* from time to time).

We are told differently in our childhoods, of course; we are given lists of virtues that everyone is to acquire:

> In villages from which their childhoods came
> Seeking Necessity, they had been taught
> Necessity by nature is the same,
> No matter how or by whom it be sought.

The city of adulthood, on the contrary, "welcomed each as if he came alone,/The nature of Necessity like grief/Exactly corresponding to his own" (*CP*, 225). If there is in this series, as in "In Time of War," a certain disjunctiveness—so that no sonnet seems quite to begin where the last has left off, and all are in different forms—it is because in life we all pursue our own journeys simultaneously, in sight of one another yet alone. The abstract arrangement corresponds, therefore, to the obscurity and isolation of the individual quest.

Still, it *is* abstract; the tone stays even and without urgency; the dispassionate diagnostician observes the diagrammatic configurations of the inner, anxious world and of its encounters with outer conditions—observes and epigrammatically reports, and the result, though often witty, is also chilling. The classical externality of "New Year Letter" is balanced by the warmth of feeling throughout, by our sense of the man at the center of the poem who moves from his intellectual formulations to remarks about his own life, fears, worries, friends. Like so many other poems of this era in Auden's career, "The Quest" proceeds from a nameless expositor who seems not to share the life he describes.

"The Quest" is the last extended work to use this disembodied speaker, and "New Year Letter" clearly shows us why. From now on Auden characteristically locates his abstractions within a feeling frame so that they are felt as occasions of feeling, as affective elements in a structure of feelings. Not the poet himself but his securely dramatized speaker experiences these abstractions, and we watch what happens. This dramatic structure occurs in earlier poems, of course, but in no consistent way; in the ballads and in certain poems with dramatized personae, the dynamic relationship between the speaker and his situation, which he often misreads, fascinates us. Auden's best poems—and the best effects in other poems—tend to be of this kind. But only around the time of "New Year Letter" does he seem consciously to center his poetry in the dramatized reception of new understanding. Not simply truth, but *a man seeing a truth*, is henceforth the central situation in his work.

Does this development involve a radical shift from Auden's old anti-Romantic position? Not necessarily: the poet still need not present his own private life, and even the details that he does present may be chosen for their effectiveness in exhibiting some *general* truth. But it is nonetheless true that the example of man most familiar to the poet is himself; and, as we shall see—not in the long works of the 1940s but increasingly in the more ambitious shorter poems—Auden opens his life and his mind more and more to public view. For the moment, in other long poems, he sees what can be done with less personal forms, but even in these highly stylized works the movement toward personal illumination (Kierkegaardian and Jamesian) remains the characteristic mode.

CHAPTER 16

Three Pageants

IF "NEW YEAR LETTER" dramatizes its speaker and his quest, the three other long poems of the 1940s are even more fully and more formally dramatic. Variously mannered, suggesting analogies with other arts, especially with opera, they are, in Blair's term, "semi-dramas—longer works which assume stage conventions but are intended primarily for reading."[1] Each semi-drama is constructed as a series of tableaux which we feel as both static and dynamic: the juxtaposition of the panels pleases us, but we sense as we proceed that the issues are deepening, and that between the beginning and the end a significant development has taken place. Just how this progress occurs varies with the form: For the Time Being is, Auden tells us, a "Christmas Oratorio," The Sea and the Mirror a "Commentary on Shakespeare's The Tempest," and The Age of Anxiety a "Baroque Eclogue." Each therefore calls for a different basic diction and for different principles of arrangement.[2]

I Oratorio

For the Time Being is a lively pageant of choruses, recitatives, arias, and prose speeches; it is divided into tableaux like the old mystery cycles and possesses, as Edward Callan has shown,[3] an elaborate philosophical structure. The characters, in medieval fashion, present themselves directly to the audience and explain or dramatize their attitudes and situations. The verse often has a Romanesque innocence: "Let us run to learn/How to love and run;/Let us run to Love" (CP, 292).

Since this semi-drama may be performed as well as read, the arias and choruses are usually set in rather plain English. Auden thus has the problem—the same that he had faced in the mid-

147

1930s when he had tried to give flat speech extra resonance (see Chapter 6)—of making the truly simple reverberate with meaning and yet not sound insipid. One course open to him is to change pace frequently in order to keep the familiar story of Christ's nativity brisk and animated; he therefore writes the parts in a variety of verse forms. Since he wishes to show the Nativity from all angles, he is free to throw in some lively satiric pieces on the secular world at the time of Christ; these are, of course, updated so that their objects have recognizable contemporary counterparts. The Incarnation, after all, has both inner and social contexts. Deliberate anachronisms suggest the presentness of these events, for the significance of the Incarnation is less that it happened once than that it is always happening.

The central subject of the piece is the meeting of the ordinary and the miraculous. Mary, Joseph, the Shepherds, even the Wise Men, are all ordinary human beings; Herod himself is an ordinary liberal reformer; and the appearance of the extraordinary among them is the fact to which they must adjust their ordinary perceptions, fears, and desires. For Auden, the Incarnation is at the very center of his metaphysical speculation; for its reconciliation of divinity and humanity is analogous to the reconciliation of the abstract and the concrete, Logos and Eros, event and meaning. It might be thought, then, that of all subjects the Incarnation should be the most perfectly suited to his talents and intellectual concerns.

Alas, not so. Apart from his plays, *For the Time Being* seems to me the least successful of his longer works. For one thing, its echoes of Eliot and Yeats are much too bland, obvious, and lacking in irony. Auden's assimilation of the method of *The Waste Land* in his early verse and of that of *Four Quartets* in his later is much more subtle and original than his adaptation in *For the Time Being* of Yeats's later poems and Eliot's early plays.

Yet even after the echoes die away, as they mainly do after the first two or three tableaux, the problem of simplicity remains; the textures are too smooth and continuous; and, although the characters must be stylized, they still seem too thin, too little human. In this story of the Incarnation, the meeting in Christ of God and Man, the godly element is well represented by a multitude of abstractions; the human is hardly there at all. A heavy philosophical structure rests on a scanty foundation of the convincingly actual. The language of the simple people too often lacks bite and force. Here, for example, is the end of the dialogue between Joseph and Gabriel. Joseph asks:

> How then am I to know,
> Father, that you are just?
> Give me one reason.

> *Gabriel*
> No.

> *Joseph*
> All I ask is one
> Important and elegant proof
> That what my Love had done
> Was really at your will
> And that your will is Love.

> *Gabriel*
> No, you must believe;
> Be silent, and sit still.   (*CP*, 281–82)

Too much of the verse is equally inactive, without notable verbal interest; it is not memorable speech. What is true of the words is true of the people; they are generalized and dull: Mary, sweet and gentle; Joseph, confused and obedient; Herod, whose decision to massacre the innocents is represented as the logical conclusion to a career of liberal reform; the Wise Men, Gilbert-and-Sullivanesque versions of the scientist, metaphysician, and political economist; and the Shepherds, who stand for the proletariat. Nothing individual marks off one character from another; they all represent some abstract position.

Spears, who finds the oratorio in general "a unique and remarkable success both formally and as a whole" and is pleased with "the enormous scope and variety of the piece" (217), thinks the section on the shepherds "would be enough to confute those who say Auden lacks understanding of or sympathy with the common man; it is shrewd, amusing, and without condescension" (212). But the moment the shepherds appear, it is evident from what they say that they are a special class, poorer than the rest of us, with duller (though crucially necessary) jobs, and with certain shrewd insights; Auden's observation is not shrewd really, but is an observation of the shepherds' shrewdness. The significant thing about them, says one of the shepherds, "is that each of us is waiting." And another goes on: "That is why we are able to bear/Ready-made clothes, second-hand art and opinions/ And being washed and ordered about..." (*CP*, 290). Not condescending?

Later, another shepherd says: "The solitude familiar to the poor/Is feeling that the family next door,/The way it talks, eats, dresses, loves, and hates,/Is indistinguishable from one's own" (*CP*, 294). Far from being shrewd or uncondescending, this view of the poor is the one an outsider has—not a view that the poor have of themselves. It is only from outside that the poor—or the rich, or Chinese, or poets—look all alike; for familiarity breeds distinction as well as contempt. Besides, the feeling that the family next door is like one's own does not foster solitude but community, except in the person who, resenting his family's ordinariness, is convinced of his own individual uniqueness. But this conviction is not felt generally by the poor; it is most common among individuals who are not poor.[4]

The fault here is one that Auden never overcame. His characters must all be stylized, all but one. For he can present feelingly, from inside, only the hesitant, sophisticated, anxious modern man taking stock of his situation and wondering where to go next. The best approach he can make to simplicity is to present a complex mind in a simple state, or to show the simple personage from the outside in a characteristic revealing gesture or pose. Hence the generic categories in which his poetry abounds: the lovers, the soldiers, the women, the shepherds, all of whom he categorizes with a sweeping assurance that their background position often justifies. But when the simple types move into the foreground, as they often do in the plays and in *For the Time Being*, they do not convince, because Auden, in drawing them nearer to us, has not seen more deeply into them. His only successful alternative is to satirize them by exaggerating still more the gestures and poses we can see from a distance, and in *For the Time Being* all the best pieces are satiric. But the truly simple seems beyond Auden's ability to dramatize. Aware as we are, even from indications within this oratorio, of the remarkable sophistication of Auden's mind, his attempt to portray the simplicity of these "common ungifted/Natures" (*CP*, 284), though it recalls the graceful naïveté of the medieval Nativity play, must seem, in comparison, at best disingenuous.

Aside from the unconvincing primitivism of *For the Time Being*, its force depends too much on the doctrines that are basic to its drama and that intrude again and again in devout phrases, often drawn from the liturgy—phrases that, we suspect, Auden was rediscovering at this time and whose newfound freshness to his own ears he hoped to convey to ours. We should remember, too, that much of the language is kept simple because it was intended to be set to music, and that Auden was learning a craft which would serve him well when he came to write opera librettos. But, despite the success of a few pieces and the child-like charm of much of the work, *For the Time Being* has little of that human force that distinguishes the best religious poetry: the people are not really people, the sin not really sin; and the exchange between heaven and earth is, therefore, a kind of stylish puppet show. To take the work as simply that is probably enough; to claim for it as much as Spears does is to invite dissent from all those for whom neither the holy phrases nor the Christian fable is sacred in any sense.

II *Triptych*

If *For the Time Being* offers little to those who reject its doctrines, *The Sea and the Mirror* offers much. In it Auden again allows his characters to face us directly and explain their attitudes. One by one the principals of Shakespeare's *The Tempest* step forward to speak, each in a different form, of their common experience and their private hopes, of their wishes and their disappointments, and of the meanings that they now see in what is behind and before them. If there is one thing they all share, it is a kind of radiance; they have all been touched by magic; in their words there is a shining; in their tones, moderated differently in each and missing only in Antonio, there is a joy. They step to the edge of the stage as if in a trance of exaltation, of heightened awareness of their lives and their lives' meanings.

Their speeches—each governed by its formal mode (terza rima, sonnet, ballade, syllabic verse, sestina, villanelle, and others)—are frequently abstract and elliptical, but appropriately so, for these self-declarations seem visionary glimpses into the meaning of what the characters are and have become. And if they are not entirely Shakespeare's people any more, especially in their developed religious consciousness, the polish of the verse and the richness of their reconciliations make them not unworthy transformations of the Shakespearean into the Audenesque.

The main theme of the work is the relation of Art to Life, and its structure (again it is Edward Callan who has pointed out the analogies) owes something to both painting and Kierkegaard. Callan writes:

The structure of this poem is comparable to a triptych: the first panel represents the artist; the second, the work of art; and the third, the audience. In Part I, Prospero, the "personified type of the creative," becomes aware of death as a reality he cannot conjure with. His farewell to Ariel is developed in three stages analogous to Kierkegaard's triad. Part II is an elaborate pageant corresponding to Prospero's masque in *The Tempest*. The group of characters from Ferdinand to Miranda who are "linked as children in a circle dancing" represent the ideal order possible in art; and the arrangement also suggests a "Utopian" social order as Alonso holds the center and the courtly and rustic characters are proportioned on either side of him between the lovers. The attitude of Antonio who stands withdrawn from the group represents the tension between his Ethical world of "will" and their Aesthetic world of "wish"—a tension present in all Christian art. Part III, "Caliban to the Audience," is an artful symposium in which Caliban echoes the Ethical and Aesthetic attitudes of the audience to the relationship of art and reality.[5]

Caliban's speech does even more. Prospero's, in chatty elegiacs, has raised some of the issues: the life to which he is now returning is different from the art he gives up; ethical existence poses problems different from those of the aesthetic order. But Caliban's harangue probes the distinction still more profoundly. In an astonishing reversal of our expectations, the gross Caliban assumes several masks in turn but presents the arguments of each in, of all styles, that of the later Henry James. The parody is superb, but it is more than parody: the Jamesian style is just the right one for explaining, with all the necessary qualifications and illustrative digressions, the subtleties and complexities of the points Auden wants to make about Life and Art. None of the prolixity is really superfluous: through all the syntactical extravagances, the tone is unfailingly colloquial and animated; and at just the right moments it deepens, in its melodramatic way, to reveal those profundities which it normally seems too capricious to reach quite down to. If the characters do not out-Shakespeare Shakespeare, this style out-Jameses James.

Caliban takes up, in his very special fashion, the problems Auden had earlier considered in other works—especially in his reviews and in "New Year Letter." The Sea of life is one thing; the Mirror of art, another. Life is full of disorder, extra paraphernalia, irrelevant perspectives, mess; Art (at least according to the public view, which Caliban begins by voicing) presents only "the perfectly tidiable case of disorder" (*CP*, 328). Its world is one in which everything is patterned; the demands of pattern, in fact, may justify almost any improbability. But in life, pattern is rare and accidental. To introduce real life into art, as Shakespeare has done in creating Caliban, is intolerable, partly because it disturbs art's harmless order, partly because it suggests the corresponding, horrible thought that such aesthetically pleasing ideals as fraternity, romance, and justice might be introduced into life.

Caliban's answer (and Auden's) to this protest is, in effect, that although art and life are different, they are not so entirely cut off from each other as the public and even the usual artist wish to believe. To the would-be poet he explains (on behalf of Shakespeare) that at bottom the image-making faculty (Ariel) is, after all, dependent on the senses, the flesh, and, even deeper than the flesh, the id (Caliban). To the public he explains that their various wishes lead only to despair. The desire to escape from abstraction, from mind, to be completely subjective and to experience only sensations, must end in a totally miscellaneous and undifferentiated perceptiveness, a complete absence of values; it is the "romantic lie in the brain/Of the sensual man-in-the-street" (*EA*, 246), the error of Don Giovanni, that we have met before.

The other and opposite lie, that of Authority, Tristan's error, is the desire not to be absorbed in the sea of sensation but to be delivered from it to a desert of abstract value; but this world turns out to be equally unsatisfactory, for nothing in it has the kind of identity that can only be given by a concrete context. Clearly, the wish for total absorption or total deliverance in this life is mistaken; and we can find no surer road to despair and grief than to fail to recognize the difference between This Life and "that Wholly Other Life from which we are separated by an essential emphatic gulf of which our contrived fissures of mirror and proscenium arch . . . are feebly figurative signs . . ." (*CP*, 340).

Art, whose source is our actual flesh and blood (Yeats's "rag-and-bone shop of the heart"), nevertheless gives us some antici-patory sense of divine perfection: its fidelity to the flesh exposes our actual condition; its formal patterns prefigure divine order and justice. Between the two the human creature wavers, and the artist, "in representing to you your condition of estrangement from the truth, is doomed to fail the more he succeeds, for the more truthfully he paints the condition, the less clearly can he indicate the truth from which it is estranged, the brighter his revelation of the truth in its order, its justice, its joy, the fainter shows his picture of your actual condition in all its drabness and sham . . ." (*CP*, 339).

Whereas in *For the Time Being* the intricate ironic structure of contradictory human impulses, which characterizes all of Auden's best work, had no sufficient material in the simple types of the nativity story, in *The Sea and the Mirror* the simplicities of what are here the minor personages function far more satis-factorily because they are subordinated—and properly, in a work *about* art—to the more complex figures of Prospero, Caliban, and even Alonso. Through most of the first two parts we are invited to understand Auden's general statements about life and art as hard truths or radiant insights achieved by the characters; and, even though Caliban himself, among his several masks, may remain untouched, his language, urbane as it is, often expands the tendency toward melodrama that is inherent in the Jamesian style. Comedy and melodrama steer us unawares into the realm of religious feeling, and the grandness of the subject justifies the excesses of the rhetoric. All the mischief is balanced by classical control, and we are moved by the humanity that speaks through all these masks.

III   *Pastoral*

The masks are multiple enough in *The Age of Anxiety*. Stylized characters in varied stances of self-declaration—a basically operatic mode, complicated by occasional duets, quartets, and other elaborate forms—are nowhere more fully in view than in this last of Auden's longer works of the 1940s and, except for some later, looser poem-sequences, the last of his extended productions not designed chiefly for the operatic stage. In *The Age of Anxiety* (1947) we are already close to opera: the characters do not speak and then retire (as in *The Sea and the Mirror*), but share a setting and a situation. And, although their personal relationships are somewhat abstract, distant, far from the usual passionate intimacies and entanglements of traditional opera, their musical statements proceed out of a series of psychic experiences which they undergo in concert.

Nowhere, in fact, is Auden's work more severely stylized than in this "baroque eclogue," which at first reading, if we have no key, may appear quite impenetrable. Four persons—Malin, Quant, Rosetta, and Emble—meet on All Souls' Night in a Manhattan bar during World War II. Feeling a certain affinity, they talk, take a booth together, go to Rosetta's apartment for a nightcap, and part at dawn. Their conversation during the night turns on such subjects as "The Seven Ages" and "The Seven Stages"— apparently aspects of human existence—and, at the end of the evening, the sexual attraction felt by Rosetta and Emble comes to nothing as Emble passes out and Rosetta achieves some spiritual realization.

The English of the poem is fantastically elaborate. Auden chooses that one of his favorite verse forms which always sounds archaic—four-stress alliterative verse (here varied by a wealth of other often remarkable forms). But his diction, instead of being that of Old or Middle English, as his earlier practice might lead us to expect, is much more suggestive of Renaissance splendor; for it takes a munificent delight in odd words ("watchet," "meeken," "daedal," "dunlins," "pursive") and in whimsical names of persons ("Major Mott joins Millicent Rusk" [*CP*, 382]) and of places (St Dill-in-the-Deep, St Dust, St Alb,/St Bee-le-Bone, St Botolph-the-less" [*CP*, 348]). This grand but difficult diction, along with the highly symbolic landscape imagery, makes the action seem quite cryptic; and, although we recognize the poem's great elegance, we need guidance in reading it—a map to lead us through the maze, a plan to explain the riddles.

Fortunately, such a plan exists; and again Edward Callan has supplied it.[6] In his study of the allegorical machinery of the poem, we discover that Auden is relying principally on "Jung's concept of the disintegration of the psyche into four differentiated functions..." (155). In *For the Time Being* Auden had presented these briefly under their own names; now he elaborates them into four actual people: Malin is Thought; Rosetta, Feeling; Quant, Intuition; Emble, Sensation. The first two represent evaluative functions of the psyche, the others perceptive functions: "The dramatic action in *The Age of Anxiety* consists of an unfolding in the direction of 'wholeness.' Such change will be most obvious in the evaluative functions, and, therefore, the significant dramatic action will be the raising of feeling to the sphere of consciousness (Rosetta's awakening to the world of reality), and also the freeing of thought from exclusive preoccupation with the rational (a deepening of Malin's vision)" (157).

Thus, "the six parts . . . are six stages in a regenerative journey" (157), of which the two longest and most significant stages are, first, the conscious examination of the epochs of human life ("The Seven Ages") and, second and most important of all, the deeper exploration of the unconscious, both the personal and the collective unconscious ("The Seven Stages"). Through these explorations Rosetta's Feeling and Malin's Thought achieve independently a more mature religious consciousness, and each character arrives at some kind of reconciliation with functions opposite to the one he represents: Malin feels more, Rosetta wakes to thought, Emble in passing out at least ceases to be dominated by sensation, and Quant's *anima* makes him stumble at his own doorstep and become aware of the sensory world:

"Why, Miss *ME*, what's the matter? *Must* you go woolgather-ing?" (*CP*, 407).

The four characters behave at once realistically and allegori-cally. The actual events—people meeting in a bar, finding one another's company congenial, and feeling better in the morning because of the levels of themselves that the sudden achievement of temporary communion with others has helped them become aware of—are perfectly ordinary. On the other hand, Auden has deliberately narrowed and deepened his characters' actual lives to fit his allegorical design. If alcohol has made them uncom-monly aware of their own feelings and the atmospheres around them, it is Auden, not alcohol, that has given them an uncanny ability to articulate their awarenesses. Hence their explorations of their own pasts and of their own unconsciousnesses (as well as of their collective unconscious) are full of personal touches as the characters remember "Bud' and Whitey/And Clifford Monahan and Clem Lifschutz,/Dicky Lamb, Dominic Moreno,/ Svensson, Seidel . . ." (*CP*, 370); and their visions of the uncon-scious fit their characters. Yet the experience of each is oddly gen-eral and impersonal. Although Auden sketches in backgrounds for all of them, they are delivered from specific practical problems; none of them has a parent, a spouse, a child, or even, as far as we know, a significant friend; the situation of all of them is that, ordinary as they are, almost their entire concern is with life in general. Like true Existentialists, like Kierkegaard's Abraham, they are alone with the cosmos, confronted, however casually, by the largest questions. Indeed, although each is a person and at least some of them develop during the action, from another point of view all four make up one composite psyche, that of modern man, whose anxieties spring both from his position as a creature subject to and conscious of time (The Seven Ages, Emble's youth, Quant's age) and from the elemental and largely unconscious guilts, fears, hopes, and joys that give to experiences their peculiar quality.

What Auden seeks to do in *The Age of Anxiety*, then, is to convey the very textures of human experience apart from the ordinary contexts of specific events, objects, social circumstances, practical motives. On the other hand, "pure" emotions or phases of feeling must be translated into a language of objects, persons, and situations. The result is an "abstract" poetry—not with the intellectual abstraction of Auden's discussing poems, but in the tradition of Gertrude Stein or of certain early poems of Ezra Pound. Thus Emble begins his exploration of the unconscious with an almost childish glee in his release from ordinary social restraints:

> Bending forward
> With stern faces,
> Pilgrims puff
> Up the steep bank
> In huge hats.
>
> Shouting, I run
> In the other direction,
> Cheerful, unchaste,
> With open shirt
> And tinkling guitar.   (*CP*, 373–74)

At a later, more disturbed stage, when they all fear that they are not loved, Emble and Quant, respectively, sing these stanzas:

> My mother weeps for me
> Who disappeared at play
> From home and hope like all who chase
> The blue elusive bird.
>
> Through gloomy woods I go
> Ex-demigod; the damp
> Awakes my wound; I want my tea
> But needed am of none.   (*CP*, 388)

The severe abstraction of this technique is somewhat forbidding, for every new speech, as it were, rearranges the stage set. Every phrase, by its imagery and syntax, locates a feeling, and we must remain extraordinarily alert to tone in order to catch the nuances. On the other hand, Auden provides structural guidelines that make our path much easier than it ever is in Gertrude Stein's abstract work. For one thing, his plan of development, once we understand it, as we now can easily do with Callan's help, is precise and definite. At almost every phase all four char-

acters experience parallel feelings, so that if one speech blurs
for us, the next may make its significance clear. Besides, the
accompanying narration tells us in plain prose just where we are
and keeps us safely above the obscurest levels of mystification.
And, finally, the general agreement among the characters to use
a common imagery, that of landscape, gives the hard passages
unity and makes simpler our task of seeing the connections between one realm and another, between the physical and social
imagery and its psychological and moral meanings.

Thus the characters' quest for the truth about their own human
position takes allegorical form through a Jungian landscape
imagery which borrows as well from other parabolic forms that
Auden admires: fairy tales, detective stories, childish fantasies,
the dream-vision. The quest, in all its forms, is so attractive
and hypnotic that we are ready to join and to follow the characters even through great obscurity. On the other hand, the
allegorical journey through the psyche, the abstract landscape
imagery, and the alliterative and stylized diction make quite
impossible a too extensive identification with the characters. We
may feel some question, even, as to whether the anti-Romantic
machinery—"the pastoral convention in which a natural setting
is contrasted with an artificial style of diction" (as the book
jacket tells us) and the baroque extravagance to which Auden
carries its refinements—does not overwhelm the reader; whether
the insistence on attention to the riddles of the quest does not
kill our sympathy for the questing figures. Many readers of
poetry, after all, do not love word games. There are moments
when the dramatic situation is conveyed in appropriately moving
tones, particularly in some speeches of Malin and Rosetta, but
through most of the poem the high style characteristically filters
out the feeling.

And yet this is not the whole story. Dr. Johnson felt the same
way about "Lycidas," and the truth is that there is surely feeling
in *The Age of Anxiety*, but it is managed differently from what
we expect or usually like. Certainly 138 pages of cryptic alliterative verse is hard reading, and it is easy to be impatient with
what seems in Auden an unscrupulous ingenuity. What we can
admire, in spite of this impatience, is the workmanship; the verse
is splendidly made. If the meter reminds us of Middle English,

if the fantastic dream-journeys recall Dante and Langland, there is much to remind us also of Spenser: not only the pastoral allegory, the atmosphere of the quest, the whole half-childish world of fantasy, but also the unhurried delight in detail, the loving versification, the joy taken in the decorative. From any point of view that wants the reflection of human affairs in poetry to show a more immediate relation to current social and political urgencies, this new kind of verse, like Spenser's, inevitably seems an evasion—a disappearance into a rarefied atmosphere in which nothing matters but consonant values and metrical refinements. But, ornate as it is, the poem's subject is man and the two atlases, public and inner, in which he lives. The elaborate décor provides the setting for a highly stylized performance, but the drama is still that of the anxious human creature, its phases and variations caught and given form as in eighteenth-century fugues and sonatas.

Deft, witty, beautifully wrought, *The Age of Anxiety* certainly suggests that divine order whose "great coherences," according to Caliban in *The Sea and the Mirror*, art can only imperfectly mirror. If there seems too much of the order and too little humanity, still, as we study the poem more fully, we see more clearly how the actual human condition, with its clumsy component feelings, lies hidden in the beautiful crystals. Thus Malin's muted description of the "ruined rebel" in the hermetic gardens is really (among other possible readings) a picture of any man who, in a bright moment of earthly love, catches a glimpse of Paradise—that is, feels a radiance in the world around him:

> Tense on the parterre, he takes the hero's
> Leap into love; then, unlatching the wicket
>   Gate he goes:
> The plains of his triumph appear empty,
>   But now among their motionless
>
> Avenues and urns with extra élan
> Faster revolves the invisible corps
>   Of pirouetting angels
> And a chronic chorus of cascades and birds
>   Cuts loose in a wild cabaletta. (*CP*, 386–87)

Theatrical yet antirhetorical, carefully selecting the melo-dramatic detail yet depriving us of full melodramatic feeling and of the complacent rhyme, this discreet verse arranges for our pleasure a charming miniature; a pattern of inner feeling becomes a tiny ballet. Is it too discreet, too esoteric? It may not do for everyone; but it repays close study. From its rococo extreme, Auden's own later poems pull back in search of a truth more direct and warm in its speaking.

CHAPTER 17

Truth and Textures

A LTHOUGH little space remains to treat Auden's poems of
the last twenty-five years, they lend themselves, luckily, to
briefer discussion, not because they are inferior to the early
poems, but because they are more of a piece. Auden's Christianity gave him a base for a style for his shorter poems. Mainly, I
want to analyze this style as it appears throughout this period,
and shall discuss only briefly, and later, the development from
one of these volumes to the next: the new poems published in
Collected Poetry and *Collected Shorter Poems* (1945 and 1950);
those published in *Nones* (1951); in *The Shield of Achilles*
(1955); in *Homage to Clio* (1960); in *About the House* (1965);
in *City Without Walls* (1969); in *Epistle to a Godson* (1972);
and in the posthumous *Thank You, Fog: Last Poems* (1974).

I The Everyday Hero

Since Auden became a quieter poet in the 1940s, a poet of
acceptance rather than of rebellion, most critics have not been
kind. To the American Alfred Kazin his poetry seems "terribly
impoverished in recent years";[1] to the British Philip Larkin he
became "an engaging, bookish, American talent, too verbose
to be memorable and too intellectual to be moving."[2] If Auden
is still a considerable influence on modern poetry (especially
American), if everyone knows that he continued to produce
work of admirable craftsmanship while most of his cohorts of
the 1930s wrote less or less well, there is nevertheless a general
suspicion of his elegance and of his chattiness—an impression
that he dribbled away his talent by not being serious enough.
"Surely some dreadfully wrong-headed diffidence is here,"
writes Robert Mazzocco, "some waste, some evasion. It has al-

ways haunted me reading Auden's poems, and now, apparently, it haunts the poet himself. . . ."[3]

Such judgments seem to me entirely mistaken. Casual Auden's poetry often is, but it is not trivial nor evasive. He himself excoriated those who think "that anyone who attempts to deal with things that matter must be a bore, that rather than run the risk of talking nonsense one should play it safe and stick to charming trifles."[4] But virtually the whole problem of the modern poem is that of erecting a poetic structure sufficiently ironic or oblique to permit "things that matter" to be treated without sentimentality or pretentiousness. What are these "things that matter"—Romantic passion, one's own emotional history, intense moments of identity with the cosmos? Mazzocco charges that "so much of his extraordinary complexity rests (can it be denied?) on the commonplace." Far from denying it, Auden would heartily agree. For him, as for Yeats, life rests on the ordinary; about it he builds his later poems—the familiar features of landscape ("Bucolics"), the hours of the day ("Horae Canonicae"), the rooms of a house ("Thanksgiving for a Habitat"). In the daily round can be read all the "things that matter"—intimations of death, God, the deepest patterns of human existence.

The truth about these patterns became increasingly important to Auden. Before his reader "is aware of any other qualities [a poem] may have, I want his reaction to be: 'That's true' or, better still, 'That's true: now, why didn't I think of it for myself?' To secure this effect I am prepared to sacrifice a great many poetic pleasures and excitements. . . . The ideal at which I aim is a style which shall combine the drab sober truthfulness of prose with a poetic uniqueness of expression. . . ."[5]

Since the truth about the patterns of ordinary human existence might make for a highly abstract poetry—the danger is always present—Auden usually presents the truth as it is experienced by someone. This method seems the only way in which the basically undramatic experience of an ordinary man can be presented dramatically. Auden quotes a doubtful Kierkegaard on this point: "If I would represent a hero who conquers kingdoms and lands, it can very well be represented in the moment, but a cross-bearer who every day takes up his cross

cannot be represented either in poetry or in art, because the
point is that he does it every day."[6] Always interested in what
cannot be done, Auden does, in fact, represent in his poetry the
man who every day takes up his cross.

That man is, of course, himself. In using his own experience
as central, however, he takes particular care never to stress his
gifts of insight, wit, and feeling, as a Romantic poet would do.
He always implies that all men may have their points of merit,
but that what he is concerned with in his poems are the respects
in which most of them are equal: their possession of bodies
and souls; their relationship to ordinary and fundamental needs,
desires, satisfactions, disappointments.

The somberness of this description somewhat falsifies Auden's
poems. They have their somber moments, but most of the memorable and ambitious poems are witty and casual in tone. The
poet seems sometimes even garrulous as one subject recalls another and he chatters away like an imperturbable, benevolent,
unstoppable raconteur. But this characteristic dramatic frame
moves constantly between the surfaces and the depths of life,
between the clear and the dark, the personal experience and
the universal, the apparently trivial and its real meaning. Such
oscillation is necessary because total seriousness in poetry is
suspect; the ordinary poet's critical intelligence requires him to
question all his most sacred truths and feelings. So the later
poetry is full of statements that are serious but protected from
both sentimentality and coldness by wit:

> The blessed will not care what angle they are regarded from,
>   Having nothing to hide. (CP, 415)

> After all, it's rather a privilege
> amid the affluent traffic
> to serve this unpopular art which cannot be turned into
> background noise for study
> or hung as a status trophy by rising executives . . . (CP, 522)

Such protective devices, multiplied on every side, form the
basic structure of Auden's later poetry. His work has always
used them, but now more than ever, and more consistently than

ever. Now that his poetry is using himself as a feeling subject, it is essential to protect the work both from banality and egoism; this he achieves not only by mixing levels of seriousness and by presenting the elegant and witty speaker as flawed and ordinary in body and soul, but also by developing farther than ever before those stylistic devices that, even from Auden's earliest poetry, had been suggestive of ambiguities and misgivings beneath a surface certainty.

The later poems are characterized, therefore, by the most extraordinary textures, which Auden creates mainly by his manipulation of syntax, tone color, and rhythms. His aim in doing so is always to surprise us, to attack our certainties with unexpectednesses, to resist the expected patterns of sentence structure, tone, and metrical regularity. But this resistance is not to pattern in general; depriving us of the old, he gives us new ones, new forms, to keep us alert, to stress the newness of the world and the inventiveness of poets, "that joy in beginning/ for which our species was created" (*CP*, 536).

II *Syntax, Tone, Rhythm*

Throughout Auden's career his command of English syntax is always astonishing. No other modern poet has such sovereignty over the syntactical possibilities of the language. Savoring his intricacies has on the admiring reader the same effect as reading late Henry James: after either experience, most other writing of the same genre seems pale and undistinguished. For Auden uses, it seems, every formula, every variation, the language has to offer, from the labyrinthine riddle—"What they were once was what they would not be;/Not liking what they are not is what now they are" (*CP*, 467)—to the direct and choppy—"It hangs, it flogs, it fines, it goes. There is drink./There are wives to beat" (*CP*, 433)—and the wayward, yet precisely articulated—

So few of the Big
Ever listen: that is why you have a great host
Of superfluous screams to care for and

> Why, up and down like the Duke of Cumberland,
>> Or round and round like the Laxey Wheel,
> The Short, The Bald, The Pious, The Stammerer went,
>> As the children of Artemis go,

> Not yours.   (*CP*, 465)

What is constant, even in the most meandering passages, is a crispness, a sharpness of outline, often achieved through parallel phrasing (as in all three examples above), that allows the syntax to get just as casual as it likes. For no matter how rambling the discourse, the sentence structure is almost always perfectly clear. Nevertheless, especially in the late poetry, it resists our expectations. We often expect a sentence to unfold in one way, only to have it turn in an unlooked-for direction. What appears to be the last noun in a series is actually the subject of the next verb:

> We know all about graphs
> and Darwin, enormous rooms no longer
> superhumanize, but earnest

> city planners are mistaken . . . (*CP*, 519–20)

On first reading, too, I mistakenly expect the "but" to lead to a statement of what enormous rooms *do* do. Everywhere in these late poems we have to watch the syntax carefully, through all its snakelike twists.

If syntax has this ability to deceive us, to require alertness from us, so does the shifting tone. Central as never before, the tone keeps us jumping from one feeling to another, one frame of reference to another:

> The sin of Gluttony
> is ranked among the Deadly
> Seven, but in murder mysteries
> one can be sure the gourmet
> didn't do it. . . . (*CP*, 531)

> When I disband from the world,
> and entrust my future to the Gospel Makers,
> I need not fear (not in neutral Austria) being called for

> in the waist of the night by deaf agents, never
> to be heard of on earth again. . . . (*CP*, 536)

Here the poet's seriousness is protected from unbecoming egoism by the wit of "disband" and the ironic reference to literary critics; and it is both protected and deepened by the deliberately melodramatic allusion to the "deaf agents" who escort the protagonist of Kafka's *The Trial* to his death. Every phrase touches the subject with a different light, turns on it a different speech, yet all the speech seems one and whole. Auden seems really to be aiming at a verse equivalent of the rich changes in color and timbre that distinguish operatic voices. But the basis of this poetic fullness of tone is ordinary spoken English. Although the situations of these chatty poems are seldom precisely fixed enough to make them full dramatic monologues, the characteristic tones are basically those of casual conversation, not lyrical reflection. However highly ordered, however rhetorically complex, the sounds are those not of speeches but of speech.

Auden's rhythms, too, in these later poems, do several things at once—resist traditional metric pattern, establish new patterns, and reflect the range and movement of actual good talk. Experimental as always, he tries out many meters and verse forms: a canzone, sestinas, sonnets, haiku, clerihews, limericks, various intricate song forms, rime royal, heroic couplets; there is internal rhyme and apocopated rhyme; one of the most peculiar poems is "Dame Kind" (*CP*, 503), in a meter that mocks Browning's "A Grammarian's Funeral."

In general, despite their variety, these poems divide rhythmically into two groups—the metrical and the syllabic. Throughout his career, however, Auden's metrical poems have been of two kinds—those measured by the foot and those measured by the stress. The poems with strictly counted feet (those which tend to have a regular number of short syllables with each long one) are usually his more abstract or more obviously humorous pieces: sonnets, sestinas, jocular verses. Yet this category also includes a quietly personal poem like "New Year Letter" and some splendid heroic couplets. But from his earliest work his more sublime effects—the hawk's-eye imagery at its grandest, the large, prophetic tone—have been cast in a looser, accentual line, in which we count the stresses because the feet, though guided by a generally iambic or anapestic feeling, vary in the number of minor syllables.

We can find this pattern in very early poems—in *1928*, XVI (*EA*, 26), for example, where these lines are pentameter: "It is seen how excellent hands have turned to commonness./One, staring too long, went blind in a tower;/One sold all his manors to fight, broke through, and faltered." But Auden began very soon to carve a stanza out of such rough lines—in imitation of similar stanzas used in Greek and Latin poetry. Though he varies this stanza repeatedly and uses most of his variations only once, he develops one form that is almost standard for him—the quatrain whose first two lines are longer than the last two, and whose stress pattern, though varied much even within each poem, is most often 5-5-3-4 or 5-5-4-3. Examples in *The English Auden* are "Casino" (164–65), "Certainly Our City" (165–66), and "Journey to Iceland" (203–204). The poems on Spain, Dover, Oxford, schoolchildren, and "A Bride in the 30's" are all variations of the same metrical scheme. The flexible rhythm of all these pieces—I think of them as Alcaic because they recall that ancient four-line meter—helps them to achieve distance, elevation, ironic largeness:

> Without, the rivers flow among the wholly living,
> Quite near their trysts; and the mountains part them; and
> > the bird,
> > Deep in the greens and moistures of summer,
> > Sings towards their work. (*EA*, 164)

This flexibility, the careless air with which each line meets its formal requirements (learned, no doubt, from Yeats), must have appealed to Auden as parabolic even of the human situation: man must be free to choose his Necessity. The language's normal rhythms struggle to evade the Necessity of the line-pattern, just as man struggles to avoid the knowledge and choices that alone can set him free. We need not push this kind of reasoning too far; it is enough to recognize Auden's interest in designs that combine regularity and looseness, surface disorder and underlying pattern. No wonder, then, that after he became acquainted in the 1930s with the quiet-toned syllabic poetry of Marianne Moore, he should investigate the possibilities of this new kind of patterning.

He began to write syllabics in two poems composed in 1939: "Where do They come from?" (*EA*, 243–44) and the elegy on Freud (*CP*, 215–18). On the page these poems look like the earlier Alcaics, but the measure is now one of syllable, not stress; both poems have a syllable count of 11-11-9-10. This is the pattern also of the two poems Auden once called "Spring 1940" (*EA*, 457–58) and "Autumn 1940" (*CP*, 222–23), which he included as "Prologue" and "Epilogue" to *The Double Man*. As he worked over the form in the next few years, trying out different stanzaic shapes or stichic lengths (examples can be found in *CP*, 245–46, 254–55, 255, 293, and 307), especially as he was seeking to rid his poetry of a too pretentious prophetic note and to center it in the ordinary life, he discovered the perfect suitability of syllabics to the poem expressive of quiet personal concern. The early syllabic poems are a bit stiff; still Alcaic in feeling, they have not arrived at a feeling of their own. But by the time of *The Sea and the Mirror*, Alonso's form (*CP*, 320–22) has both dignity and personal warmth; and Prospero's long speech (*CP*, 312–16) catches the tone of most of Auden's later syllabic poems—witty, self-critical, a bit garrulous, very human.

Many of the most memorable poems in the last four volumes are written in this important form—notably "In Praise of Limestone" and half the poems in the three sequences that dominate the later volumes—"Bucolics" and "Horae Canonicae" in *Shield*, and "Thanksgiving for a Habitat" in *House*. As Auden uses it, the syllabic verse has something of the same effect as the surprising syntax and changing tone color: one line may suggest one meter, but the next matching line will contradict it. Thus, "Homage to Clio" begins:

> Our hill has made its submission and the green
>   Swept on into the north: around me,
> From morning to night, flowers duel incessantly,
>   Color against color, in combats . . .

If these lines do not conclusively reject our stress-counting impulses (the syllable-pattern is *11-9-11-9*, adjacent vowels as in

flowers and *duel* being counted as one), the next lines will.
Again the point is to forestall the too complacent participation
of the reader; it is also to suggest the extent of the speaker's
casualness: no rigid meter for *his* talk, but a liquid flow of the
language. Just as the syntax and the tone must never fall into
obvious patterns, the syllables must never accidentally, for more
than about a line, fall into some accentual pattern. The skill is
in endlessly varying the design, the triple design of meter, sentence, and feeling.

But though the thought seems, from moment to moment, un-
kempt and formless, though the lines are hard for the ear to
measure, we still do feel most of the lines as lines, feel an order
in the palaver. This evident combination—*in the same words*—
of elegance and disorder, of control and laxity, has great power.
Life, it seems to say, is at once form and process; the order
develops out of the formlessness; the reflective meandering of
chat, which, like life itself, rambling through all the dimensions
of the trivial, does arrive somewhere at last—what else does it
turn out to be but form?

III   *Horace*

In a sense, the basic theme of all Auden's later books is this
assertion. Despite the blur of ordinary life, everything makes
sense; pattern is everywhere. We never see all of it, but nonetheless it is there. Ubiquitous parables show us, for all our
troubles, how finely life is arranged. Auden's poetry does not
slight its difficulties; social distress and personal anxiety are
always central in his work. But where the early poetry arraigns
and ridicules the guilty and the weak, and rebels against authority and tradition, the later work affirms even authority. The war
between an irreconcilable We and They in which nothing would
do for Them but total abolition has given way to a common human order of which We and They are alike indispensable members. The authorities, administrators, managers, Utopians—all
temperamentally antipathetic to Auden—he recognizes as having
their part to play (unsavory it may be, but his own is not blame-
less) in the working out of the world's form.

This reconciliation with the world (it is no accident that one of his finest works is based on *The Tempest*) is inevitably less exciting than the youthful stance of rebellion and challenge. Firmly classical, Auden's later poetry rejects most of the values attractive to energetic young readers—passion, revolt, defiance. On the other hand, its wisdom, its awareness of the sides of ordinary life, its balancing of multiplicities and unities, confusions and clarities, recommend it to seasoned readers. As the syllabic poems issue out of Latin meters, so Auden's poetry of his last twenty-five years benefited from his long visits to Italy. Although the syllabic style may still owe something to Rilke and much to Marianne Moore, the intricate textures of these poems, their unpredictable formal progress, their sly development of balances and contrasts, are strongly reminiscent of Horace. Both poets are highly civilized and highly ironic; both know the country and the town but give us few details of their personal lives; both have a strong sense of the limitations of life and the satisfactions of small pleasures; both want us to recognize what they tell us as true, as wise.

Nietzsche's description of Horace's poetry as "a mosaic of words" certainly fits Auden's, except that Auden does with phrases what Horace's language permits him to do with words—move them around into the most expressive order. And single words can balance whole phrases, as in Auden's remark to the shade of Louis MacNeice (my italics): "Though neither of our dads, like Horace's/*wiped his nose on his forearm,*/neither was *porphyry-born* . . ." (CP, 521). One modern critic notes in Horace what is always in Auden, "the curious parallel existence of bold and tame, old and new." And, when we recall Auden's later distaste for translatable imagery (see above, p. 123), it is startling to hear the same critic observe of Horace that "the sensitivity of expression which some poets achieved through an intuitive perception of unsuspected likeness [that is, striking imagery] is matched in Horace's lyric by experiments in the contrastive and combinatory potentialities of words."[7]

Horace, too, uses the casual excursus, the chatty parenthesis, the fanciful exaggeration, especially the witty suggestion that quite ordinary behavior owes something to the intervention of supernatural beings (in Auden: imps, demons, Dame Kind, Greek gods and goddesses). The structure of Horace's poems, as of Auden's, is often elusive and subtle; and the apparently irrelevant detail or digression comes only gradually to be seen as functional. He, too, seems to many readers a poet of the intellect rather than of feeling; but, although the outlook of both Horace and late Auden is generally sunny, each is capable of flaring out into quick bursts of feeling; and there is more feeling, anyway, in both poets, than one first thinks. Horace's poems often end without much flourish, with an almost antirhetorical flatness; Auden, in Horatian fashion, finishes many poems (like the one to MacNeice) quietly: ". . . dear Shade, for your elegy/ I should have been able to manage/something more like you than this egocentric monologue,/but accept it for friendship's sake" (*CP*, 523). Finally, both poets are acute observers of people and of social and human patterns; and both discern the fundamental patterns and conflicts of life from within a framework of acceptance.

This poetry, then, requires time, leisure, maturity for its enjoyment. Retirement to the Sabine farm does not appeal to twenty or twenty-five, and even older readers sometimes think the quiet contemplation of life's follies and ironies to be politically irresponsible. Still, now that Western culture, like the Roman, has stirred the world with Romantic expectations of the impossible, there is much to be said for the poet who, beyond all the immediate and miscellaneous distress, can make out, quietly and elegantly, meanings that endure and fortify.[8]

IV   *The Later Volumes*

Since the later volumes of Auden show less development than the earlier, the foregoing description can serve as a general guide to his shorter poems and sequences from 1941 to 1973. Nevertheless, the successive volumes do vary in quality and character, and a word should be said about each. In the early and middle 1940s Auden was busy with his impressive long poems; therefore, the new pieces in *Collected Poetry* (1945) are comparatively unambitious. I have already referred to the three poems in syllabics (CP, 245–46, 254–55, 255), and to the highly polished stanzaic poems such as "Kairos and Logos" and "Canzone" (see p. 114). There are several metrical poems in a relaxed style that

derives from the earlier Alcaic poems and leads to the later
syllabic and accentual poems: "Mundus et Infans" and "At the
Grave of Henry James."

Equally important is the poem in strict meter which is polished enough to be pleasing but also relaxed and somewhat
(sometimes) personal in feeling—a genre that continues Auden's
indebtedness to such poets as Frost, Robinson, Housman, Jonson.
Such slight, graceful, but concentrated pieces rely largely on
word-play, epigram, the neatness with which the thought is
turned:

> Few as they are, these facts are all
> The richest moment can recall,
> However it may choose to group them,
> And, simple as they look, enough
> To make the most ingenious love
> Think twice of trying to escape them.   (*CP*, 253)

All the subsequent volumes contain many such poems of low
intensity but of elegant design and, often, of subtle idea. With
the more deliberately casual poems that are usually syllabic,
they form the bulk of Auden's later work.

Nones (1951) carries farther the development of these two
main styles, the syllabic poems being especially numerous, various, and attractive. A highly experimental volume, *Nones* feels
out new possibilities of arrangement, from blank-verse syllabics
("Not in Baedeker") to the highly operatic "The Duet." Several
of the poems have an Italian setting, and Classical allusions
begin to abound. If there is one series of ideas that can be read
in most of the poems, it is something like this: The Just City,
which all of us would like to see exist, depends mainly on the
conduct of our inner lives, on loving God and our neighbor
instead of ourselves. To bring about such a condition requires us
to make the best use of the gifts we have and of our immediate
situations, not to expect too much of life or of ourselves. We can
also distinguish here and there between what is truly valuable
and what is only apparently so; we can try to see the meanings
that underlie the surfaces of life; and we can *"Bless what there
is for being"* (*CP*, 450).

The Shield of Achilles (1955) is much less miscellaneous than

Nones. It begins with the seven-poem sequence "Bucolics" and, after fourteen other pieces, ends with the seven-poem sequence "Horae Canonicae." These very impressive sequences are beautifully constructed out of poems in various forms; finely wrought, rich in texture, they move continually from one mood or tone to another. Both try to see what realities lie below ordinary surfaces we do not usually subject to such penetrating scrutiny. To the water in streams, for example, Auden says, you

> still talk to yourself: nowhere are you disliked;
> arching your torso, you dive from a basalt sill,
>   canter across white chalk, slog forward
>   through red marls, the aboriginal pilgrim,
>
> at home in all sections, but for whom we should be
> idolators of a single rock, kept apart
>   by our landscapes, excluding as alien
>   the tales and diets of all other strata.   (*CP*, 434)

Nor is this talk merely idle and ingenious: streams, like everything else, are parables and show man things about himself. This volume, too, contains, outside the sequences, a few poems that are surely masterpieces: "The Shield of Achilles," " 'The Truest Poetry Is the Most Feigning,' " and "The Willow-Wren and the Stare." Auden's poetry achieves in this book a classical order and beauty marred only by an occasional blandness or archness—in the flat "Epitaph for the Unknown Soldier," for example; or in sly references to some loved one: "while, near enough, a real darling/Is cooking a delicious lunch" (*CP*, 430).

A major theme in all these volumes (and in all Auden's poetry) but one that receives special emphasis in *Homage to Clio* (1960) is the opposition between History and Nature. Nature, represented by Dame Kind and by "the appetitive goddesses" Aphrodite and Artemis, governs animals, plants, kings, warriors, and fleshly lovers; though important in human life, it lacks final point, for it offers imperatives, not choices. An organism is driven to act as it does; it does not decide. Clio, on the other hand, the Muse of History, is, more precisely, "Muse of the unique/Historical fact." In short, what makes a man fully human is his involvement in the actual details of ordinary living. The great conquerors matter less than "those who bred them better horses,/ Found answers to their questions, made their things,/Even those fulsome/Bards they boarded . . ." (*CP*, 457).

Not the natural drives, then, but an interest in them, a thirst to understand and manipulate nature, begins to make human beings historical, sets them in a world of moral choices. "The significant difference" between men and animals "is not that man has speech, but that he talks to himself, not that he has reason, but that he reasons about reasoning."[9] On the other hand, still loyal to Kierkegaard's leap and even Homer Lane's love, Auden continues to insist that reason, planning, purpose may be less effective guides to a man's best life than instinct or luck. The road to that life is "Unlookable for, by logic, by guess:/ Yet some strike it, and are struck fearless" (*CP*, 462). Mistakes have their uses. History and Nature together make man what he is.

If *Homage to Clio* is less rich stylistically than *The Shield of Achilles*, it has its brilliant moments. It also has more fun: the poet writes limericks and clerihews, and celebrates bathtubs and kitchens. But, as to whether or not serious poems can be written on such subjects, Auden himself, in 1955, is skeptical: "There are some products of technology—kitchen refrigerators, for example—which seem to me an unqualified good; but however grateful I may feel towards mine at cocktail time, I cannot see myself writing a panegyric ode to it as I could have written centuries ago to a king who at his marriage ordered wine to flow from the public fountains."[10]

Auden goes on to say that the modern poet "can only produce genuine work about events to which he has a personal relation"; yet if he risked more, "he would find that the possible area of the personal is larger than he supposes." When the impressive prose piece, "Dichtung und Wahrheit," in *Homage to Clio*, doubts the feasibility of writing a good personal love poem, it is really raising the broader question of whether any intensely personal poem can be written. It decides not. But many later poems by Auden seek, through the mannered and witty treatment of physical surroundings, to move ever closer to the poet himself in order to show him, an example of man, as fully and meaningfully involved in Nature and History.

His next volume, *About the House* (1965), is, in fact, richly personal. He writes not only of kitchens but of all the rooms in his Austrian house, even the water closet (a hilarious poem). And, as he writes with disarming casualness of his intimate connections with rooms, his more personal affections slip in; his feelings for his friends are more openly stated than ever before, not directly but in poems ostensibly about something else. Postscripts, haiku, transliterations, slight occasional poems—all give us the sense of a man engaged in verbal experiments: poetry is the milieu of this particular creature, the thing he does that makes him historical, as other men create coins or weapons or music.

Careful always to avoid Romantic egoism, Auden again makes no claims for this speaker's moral valor: he is weak, flawed, not a great villain (to claim that would be equally Romantic); he is merely an ordinary sinner. But he *is* an artist, he has written fine poems, possibly just *because* of the yielding to temptation that in the moral sphere is deplorable. So he can think of no worse nor more fitting punishment for an artist than that God should set him, on Judgment Day, to "reciting by heart/the poems you would/have written, had/your life been good."[11] We find, altogether, in these poems, an impressive picture of an ordinary man, one fully committed to living, working, loving, and, finally, praising in an age of anxiety, and even in ignorance: "about/catastrophe or how to behave in one/what do I know, except what everyone knows—/if there when Grace dances, I should dance" (*CP*, 560).

Auden's last three volumes continue this pattern. The poems are most attractive when in a variety of tones (modest, wry, irritated, poignant, whimsical) they acknowledge Auden's faults and guard against his natural tendency to pontificate, to categorize, "to hold forth" (*CP*, 581). But without these subdued failings we would have no poems at all, for they all spring out of intellectual perceptions of similarities, differences, connections, and out of an irrepressible impulse to exhibit them formulated, embodied in comic instances, and embedded in a comic style. But whatever the comic treatment, the subject is still very serious: how to live in an age of disastrous change as a human creature whose cities, habits, and values are becoming out of date or turning grotesque.

The title poem of *City Without Walls* (1969), for example, uses the regularly thumping beats of four-stress alliterative verse to pound out its vision of the modern city where " 'hermits, perforce, are all today,/with numbered caves in enormous jails' ":

> "A key to the street each convict has,
> but the Asphalt Lands are lawless marches
> where gangs clash and cops turn
> robber-barons: reckless he
> who walks after dark in that wilderness." (*CP*, 563)

This is the most impressive poem in the volume, and the most grim. But even the end of "City Without Walls" questions, in a mock interior dialogue, the poet's enjoyment of his own apocalyptic vision. The defensive reply, " 'So what, if my words are true,' " though it fails to win the argument, nevertheless sums up much of the spirit of Auden's last poems: If what I am saying is true and important, the word-games I play as I tell you the truth should only please both of us.

The poems in *City Without Walls* tell us the truth about human weakness, love, poem-making, aging. Among the volume's thirty-seven poems, ten are songs (eight of them translations from Brecht's *Mother Courage*), four are commissioned texts, five are occasional poems (tributes to various persons esteemed by Auden), and two are series of haiku and haikulike five-line stanzas ("Profile" and "Marginalia"). In this last group, in some of the more personal longer poems ("Prologue at Sixty," "Since"), and, indeed, in the whole volume, the wisdom of the aging poet words its awareness of time passed, values tested, perceptions refined. The meters used are as various and inventive as ever, and Auden's delight in odd words ("frore," "nauntle," "disembogueing," "wastemantle," to give examples from only one poem, "River Profile") and in such rhetorical figures as anthimeria (using one part of speech for another—"When has Autolycus ever solemned himself?" ["Forty Years On"]) is everywhere evident and persists through the next two volumes.

Epistle to a Godson (1972) is a thinner collection. It contains

no such striking assessments of modern life as "City Without
Walls," and its poems mainly divide into three kinds: (1)
"Shorts": brief, fragmentlike observations on poetry, the human
condition, horse-flies, TV; (2) more substantial poems on topics
suggested by Auden's reading or by recent public or personal
events ("Moon Landing," "A Bad Night," "Loneliness," and
poems to friends recently dead or retired); and (3) longer, reflective poems on, once again, the difference between human and
other life ("Natural Linguistics," "The Aliens," "Talking to Dogs,"
"Talking to Mice"). Here again the title poem is probably the
largest in scope, exploring as it does the difference in perspective
between the aging Auden and his godson, young Philip Spender.
In a sense, the volume shows us nothing new in Auden's view of
the world, but it is full of vigorous, inventive, humorous phrases,
lines, and stanzas, in a variety of meters and forms. Some lines
that pass for verse are certainly prosy: "I suspect that without
some undertone of the comic/ genuine serious verse cannot be
written to-day" (*CP*, 643). But one can also enjoy amusing and
acute remarks about animals:

> Since in their circles it's not good form to say anything novel,
>   none ever stutter on *er*, guddling in vain for a word,
> none are at loss for an answer: none, it seems, are bilingual . . .
> If they have never laughed, at least they have never talked
>   drivel . . .   (*CP*,636)

Though some readers will think of this sort of verse as mere
rattling on, and though Auden had become by this time an almost
compulsive versifier, ready to turn almost any occasion, any perception, into ingenious verse, there is still in almost all this last
work a precise touch, a feeling for words, phrases, and sentences
that is impressive and that can give pleasure to anyone willing to
follow his curious ideas through all their devious shiftings. The
Master is at the end of his life, but he is still a Master.

Certainly there are signs in *Epistle to a Godson* that Auden
was preparing to die. One of his "Shorts" reads: "What is Death?
A Life/ disintegrating into/ smaller simpler ones" (*CP*, 642).
And the last poem, "Talking to Myself," addressed to Auden's
body, ends:

> Remember: when *Le Bon Dieu* says to You *Leave him!*,
> please, please, for His sake and mine, pay no attention
> to my piteous *Dont's*, but bugger off quickly.   (*CP*, 654)

Auden did die quickly, on September 29, 1973, and the poems
he had written after *Epistle to a Godson* were collected in *Thank
You, Fog* (1974). One of his last poems, "Lullaby," seems clearly
in part a farewell to the world; Edward Mendelson appropriately
places it at the end of *Collected Poems*, with its unmistakably
Audenesque last line: *"Sleep, Big Baby, sleep your fill."* And in
his Note to *Thank You, Fog* Mendelson tells us that the last poem
Auden wrote was this:

> He still loves life
> but O O O O how he wishes
> the good Lord would take him.[12]

In all these late poems an aging "I," not personally happy but
content with his lot, aware of his luck, and ready to cope with
loneliness, "to live with obesity/ and a little fame" (*CP*, 585),
talks as if to one person in a consistently conversational, sometimes joking but essentially serious tone about the life we all
share and some of us try to understand. This "I" talks in verse,
and what it says can be paraphrased; it makes points that are
meant to be followed and understood, however elusive the
vocabulary or syntax that robes them; it plays with words and
their associations, their double or multiple meanings; it discusses
our human plight, our debts to Nature and History, our differences from other lives, and the symbolism implicit not only in
our behavior but in our condition. But it avoids the reverberating language which poets in our century have characteristically
used to evoke and reenact the mysterious processes of symbolism.
Anti-Romantic to the last, Auden continues to condemn "all/
self-proclaimed poets who, to wow an/ audience, utter some resonant lie" (*CP*, 609).

One striking recurrent situation in these last poems is the address by Auden to some other part of himself, usually by his soul,
or whatever is "I," to the body, or "You." If Auden has always
been the poet of divided consciousness, recommending integration, as some critics say, he appears to recognize in these poems

how separate our selves may feel. "Bound to ourselves for life,/ we must learn how to/ put up with each other" (*CP*, 666). Whatever harmony or self-content one achieves, these parts never merge entirely; rather, they look forward, with relief or foreboding, to complete separation at death. The stylistic separation of content and form, of truth and that capricious style in which Auden presents it, reflects the division between body and soul. In an age concerned with the organic unity of poems and the integration of the personality, this may seem an odd development, but Auden is, as usual, being true to what we sense in our own lives, rather than to the rhetoric we use to talk about it. It is in the service of the same truthful Muse that, instead of envisioning Utopian futures, Auden can only sadly, and still gratefully, acknowledge that what we have got is probably the best we are going to get—essentially, the decency of most individuals, the evil of collective man (*CP*, 667); and not Perfection, the Great Good Place, but "the Mansion of Gentle Joy/ it is our lot to look for" (*CP*, 670).

CHAPTER 18

Atlantic Goethe

POETRY was only one of Auden's careers. Teacher, critic, playwright, translator, librettist, he was a remarkably versatile man of letters, as active and energetic as the Goethe whose *Italian Journey* he helped to translate and whose career he saw in a late poem as parallel with his own: "I should like to become, if possible,/a minor atlantic Goethe . . ." (*CP*, 522). Although Auden did not dominate his age's culture as Goethe did, the breadth of his interests and activities gave some substance to the claim. In his last three decades his libretti and his criticism especially were marked with distinction. These genres, however, raise large questions that this study must discuss only briefly.

As for the criticism, I have already indicated that Auden's early essays and reviews, though often provocative, are commonly insistent and strident in tone. In accord with the more relaxed manner of all his later work, the essays of his last thirty years are almost always charming, genial, richly suggestive, and modest. The great strength of his critical intelligence was in making distinctions and in pursuing them farther than anyone else would believe possible or useful. This exercise is often a fascinating one and can result in such extraordinary assertions as that (each the last step in quite convincing arguments) Falstaff is emblematic of Christian charity, or Iago of modern science. Auden's first volume of criticism *The Enchafèd Flood, or The Romantic Iconography of the Sea* (1950) systematically pursues Romantic literature through its recurrent and various imagery of sea, desert, and city. The result is an extraordinary anatomy of Romantic image-making, illuminating at once much poetry and fiction of the nineteenth century and some of Auden's own work (e.g., *The Sea and the Mirror*) that makes extensive use of the central contrasts he points to here.

The essays in *The Enchaféd Flood* were delivered as Page-Barbour Lectures at the University of Virginia in 1949; a later collection of essays, *Secondary Worlds*, presented as the T. S. Eliot Memorial Lectures at the University of Kent in 1967, treats several kinds of word-systems, notably opera and Icelandic saga, to the same acute systematic analysis. A larger and wider-ranging volume, *The Dyer's Hand*, collects many of Auden's engaging later essays into one of the most readable, witty, perceptive, and profound critical books of the century.

In all these books, Auden's distinctive style of criticism is evident. In particular, his skill in ferreting out the parable hidden in every literary or actual situation; his insight into perspectives of all kinds—fantasy, science, or subjective experience—and his awareness of them as sometimes opposed, sometimes complementary, sometimes interdependent; his power of thinking himself into any point of view and developing all its moral and intellectual tendencies to their logical conclusions—these gifts are not merely instructive, they are almost terrifying. In a century dominated very largely by psychoanalytical inquiry, political fairy tales, the middle-class search for roles and stances, Auden both as a poet and as a critic is the man who, more than any other, is determined to show us—obliquely or directly—what we are *really* doing, what our wishes, our actions, our values *really* mean. Even where we feel he may not be right, his procedure has a frightening clarity which warns us that if total truth is not precisely here, it is not far off; that this is, indeed, the way in which the human contraption works, through emblems and allegories, myths and habits; that every social and personal structure conceals and expresses some truth about its anxious makers.

Auden's activity in translating and writing opera libretti occupied him considerably in his last twenty-five years—so much so that since 1947, except for his poem sequences, all his longer works were libretti. He and Chester Kallman translated Mozart's *The Magic Flute* and *Don Giovanni*, Karl Ditters von Dittersdorf's *Arcifanfano, King of Fools*, and Brecht's *The Rise and Fall of the City of Mahagonny*. Auden worked alone on the libretto for Benjamin Britten's opera *Paul Bunyan* (1941), a work they thought so little of that after its first performance it was neither published nor produced again for more than thirty years. But when Igor Stravinsky suggested to Auden that they collaborate on an opera based on Hogarth's series of paintings, *The Rake's Progress*, Auden and Kallman began seriously to produce opera libretti. *The Rake's Progress* (1951) was followed by the one-act *Delia or a Masque of Night* (1953), which still awaits its music, by libretti for two operas by Hans Werner Henze: *Elegy for Young Lovers* (1961) and *The Bassarids* (1966), and by a still unpublished libretto for *Love's Labour's Lost* (1973), an opera by Nicolas Nabokov. Since these works are only partly Auden's, partly his collaborator's, partly the composer's, and (in the case of translated libretti) partly the original librettist's, they cannot altogether be regarded as representative of Auden's art, but they cannot, either, be altogether ignored in an account of Auden's poetic productions. Indeed, they throw considerable light on his attitudes toward his art and on his technical concerns during his last quarter-century of literary work.

As we might expect, these operas are all allegorical fables, and their themes are familiar ones. *Paul Bunyan* shows us the necessity of stages in a people's history: in effect (in Brecht's phrase), "Grub first, then ethics," a time for the rough pioneer, followed by a civilized stage in which the pioneer is discarded. *The Rake's Progress* adapts Hogarth's eighteenth-century series of paintings to accommodate at once a fairy-tale story of the rake's three wishes (which turn out to be versions of Christ's three temptations) and a Faustian fable of contract and corruption; the rake is redeemed, but only in part, when he sees that he must make choices guided by Love. *Elegy for Young Lovers* shows us "the artist-genius of the nineteenth and early twentieth century,"[1] who is willing to use other people, and even to send them to their deaths, if, as a consequence, his art may prosper; for such a man (as not for Auden), Art is to be set above Life, a valuation made explicit at the moment when the great poet in the opera, irritated by all the helpful people around him, explodes: "Why don't they all DIE?"[2]

The most ambitious of all the operas is *The Bassarids*, which returns, in what seems at times a high-camp adaptation of Euripides' *The Bacchae*, to the theme of the Truly Strong Man. Pentheus, the rational, Apollonian king of Thebes, is no match for the maddened women who worship Dionysus. When Dionysus exposes his weakness, the women tear him to pieces. It is the old destructive struggle between Eros and Logos, but the power of Agape is nowhere present to resolve the contest—except implicitly, perhaps, in a Christ who does not appear but who is traditionally associated with Dionysus. As Spears reminds us, Dionysus is "the only Greek god born of a mortal mother and thought to die and rise again, celebrated in mystery cults which involved the ritual eating of the flesh and drinking of the blood of a sacrificial victim who incarnates the god."[3] But his very similarity to Christ insures that his taste for lust and vengeance will remind us of Christ's more gracious Love.

The essays Auden has written about opera show, as usual, his remarkable acuteness in isolating the distinguishing elements of an art or of an art's subspecies. Several such essays are included in *The Dyer's Hand*, and one of the T. S. Eliot Memorial Lectures later published as *Secondary Worlds* is entitled "The World of Opera." Here Auden discourses brilliantly on the relations of opera to "everyday experience," the difficulties facing the librettist, and his own and Kallman's problems in writing libretti for the three operas on which they collaborated. He concludes with a passage that explains much of his own interest in opera:

Judging by the poetry they have written, all the modern poets whom I admire seem to share my conviction that, in this age, poetry intended to be spoken or read can no longer be written in a High, even in a golden style, only in a Drab one to use these terms as Professor C. S. Lewis has used them. By a Drab style, I mean a quiet tone of voice which deliberately avoids drawing attention to itself as Poetry with a capital P, and a modesty of gesture. Whenever a modern poet raises his voice, he makes me feel embarrassed like a man wearing a wig or elevator shoes.[4]

Auden goes on to say that, while lyric poetry can survive in the *sotto-voce* style, dramatic poetry is poorer without its traditional elevation, and

as an art-form involving words, Opera is the last refuge of the High style, the only art to which a poet with a nostalgia for those times past when poets could write in the grand manner all by themselves can still contribute, provided he will take the pains to learn the metier, and is lucky enough to find a composer he can believe in.   (116)

Opera must deal with passionate or willful, not passive, characters, and its setting must be fairly distant from our ordinary world, but it must still have "something significant to say . . . about our present life" (95). The best central figures in opera "are mythical figures" who "embody some element in human nature, some aspect of the human condition which is of permanent concern to human beings irrespective of their time and place" (95). Hence, Auden's (and Kallman's) choice of mythic figures as the chief protagonists in their own libretti: Paul Bunyan, the personification of the pioneer spirit; Tom Rakewell, whom they made into a kind of Everyman (99); Mittelhofer, the artist-hero; and Pentheus, the would-be rational ruler. The verse has to be simple if it is to be heard at all and understood, but the composer can provide music that will do justice to the complex passions of the characters.

In writing for a composer, then, the librettists inevitably sacrifice some of the richness of verbal texture that Auden's poetry usually has; but if the verse is sometimes bland, the moral problems are nicely posed, the apparently simple verse is sometimes weighted with considerable meaning, occasional scenes are richer in suggestion, verbally denser and more subtle than we usually think possible in opera, and something of Auden's complex virtuosity is conveyed by the formal pageantry.[5]

Even if, as Auden claims, only the writing of a libretto offers to a modern poet the chance to participate in a High-style enterprise, the collaborative nature of that enterprise suggests to what an extent Auden has rejected Romantic egoism. Writing libretti (not to speak of translating them) requires a poet to subordinate his own personality to that of the composer's, his own art to music. Indeed, Auden's whole career exhibits a talent for collaboration unprecedented in any important English writer since the Jacobean dramatists. He collaborated not only on translations and libretti but on travel books, poems, plays, textbooks, anthologies, films, and a pamphlet on education. There was nothing aloof about this poet; Auden was a man who took part, who participated actively in the common literary life.

Even his conversion to Christianity and his repudiation of secular humanism did not in any sense represent a withdrawal from responsibility, as critics have often unfairly charged. On the contrary, no fine writer of the twentieth century was so sensitive to its intellectual currents, so ready to try on hats, to grant a hearing to every claimant, and to do so with sympathy and yet with discrimination. Perhaps because he was so fully of his time, so deeply involved in it, so quietly yet unmistakably an influence on it, we have tended to take for granted his wit, his elegance, his art, and his insight.

Yet Auden's involvement seems especially valuable because it is balanced by his detachment—his insistence on seeing the immediate moment (which includes his own feeling and action) from a distance, from estranging and therefore illuminating perspectives. Critics who complain of his lack of commitment are usually unsympathetic to what he was committed to. The deepest things to which important writers are committed are not often political causes or religious doctrines; their loyalties are rather to certain ways of thinking and feeling—to *patterns* of commitment, of hesitation, of active or passive acceptance or denial. If our own commitment to an author is to anything less deep in him than this, if it is merely to his Anglicanism or his Marxism, it may not survive the next doctrinal debate.

Thus Auden—despite his devotion to Freud and Marx, the Christian poems which occasionally seem too positive and knowing, the arrogant tone of his early essays and the assured categorical distinctions of the later ones—is fundamentally a poet of doubt, of uncertainty, of insecurity, of hesitations, second thoughts, qualifications—in short, of anxiety. In an age when nothing is clear, all the certitudes gone, perhaps the best we can do is to lunge after one idea or another, to embrace some orthodoxy, to make the leap of faith. The extravagance, the frequency, of Auden's leaps confirm the undercurrent of worry beneath even the tones of joy. So, from time to time, he finds a sage (Freud, Marx, Kierkegaard) or a career (teaching, film work, free-lance writing) or a new literary form, or a new country, a new church, a new home for spring and summer. What makes all this turning and turning most impressive poetically is that it is all done in the open: there is no hiding the doubts and hesitations, the other thoughts.

This anxiety, which is only intensified by the early poetry's tones of total certainty, even reaches at times to a fear that there will be no meaning, no intercourse between realms of being. Such intercourse—between parts of our lives, between people, between God and man, abstract and concrete, meaning and object—is what chiefly validates experience, the Incarnation that wakes the Sleeping Beauty, Life. In Auden's poetry the one intolerable possibility that is not often looked at as such, but which provides the unspoken source of all its anxieties, is that such intercourse will stop, or that it is only an illusion. The nightmare basic to his work is not that the world is evil but that it is meaningless. If Tennyson is, as Auden says, "the great English poet of the Nursery," who must constantly assure himself of his own identity,[6] Auden's work seems rooted in a similar primal fear—that of losing touch, of being really alone. Freud, Marx, Christ in turn give hope of recharging a dead world—imaged successively in glaciers and abandoned mines, in the blank physical surfaces of a decadent society, in the trivial joys, despairs, and insights of a prosperous one.

The problem of an Auden poem, from this point of view, is to certify reality, and the technique for doing this is fundamentally Jamesian: truth (that benevolent classical light to which we can be led only by Romantic processes of derangement) illuminates the world and, by showing us its patterns filled with moral significance, redeems it from unmeaning. Poetry affirms this process and, through this process, life itself.

In Auden's later years (especially after 1950), the need to be sure that the world is really substantial seems much less desperate. By the time his religious faith has become habitual, he seems more assured that everything really *is*: faith in God for Auden is largely faith that things exist, for things exist only when they exist meaningfully. I have suggested that Auden's later poetry has a wise complexity, quite grand in its way, but what many readers feel as comparatively unexciting in it is, I think, that it has passed through, has survived, and no longer therefore fully expresses this terrifying anxiety as to whether the world, or

anything, is really there. What this poetry does remain expressive
of is the high perspective and the broad sympathies of a man
who has come through decades of feeling such anxiety and of
seeing it all around him, and who knows and can tell us the
value of everything in a world now assuredly real but still filled
with real anxieties.

One irony of this development is worth noting. The early
poems often show an arrogance of manner, a certainty of tone,
so exaggerated as to contribute to Auden's general portrait of
our anxiety and desperation, just as Kafka's narrative style, with
its meticulous emphasis on physical fact, contributes to his picture of a world where one can be sure of nothing. In later years,
though his work is as precise as ever, Auden's tone and manner
are more modest, his confession of weakness more honest and
simple. The irony is that critics have interpreted this loss of
bluster as a loss of personal confidence—as a sign that Auden
came to see that he had wasted his talent. Precisely the opposite
is probably true; it is only the man who has become strong (even
Truly Strong) who can afford to speak with such candor.

Some of Auden's early techniques he discarded along the
way; some he kept and refined. The banal phrase, the casual
style, the hawk's-eye vision survived in one form or another, but
he stripped his work of the unintentional overtone, the vague
reverberation, on which Romantic poetry too often rests its appeal. In general, we can say that in resisting the art of the
rhapsode he developed two principal methods. The less remarkable is the direct, objective explanation of truth, using traditional
figures such as personification, hyperbole, amplification; but the
abstraction of this technique limits its largeness.

The second method is to present the truth more dramatically,
as something desired, pursued, and perhaps achieved by someone whose unfolding feeling is the basic design of the poem.
All his early work in parody, in establishing his myth of rebellion and exile, in constructing the situations out of which the
speakers of his songs and ballads emerge, taught him much
about the subtleties of having a flawed dramatic character tell
the truth. His best poems can be seen as experiments in balancing the perception with the perceiver, in achieving between
them a classical poise that mediates between the human reader

and the impersonal truth. His poetry learns to be instructive without being didactic, personal but not Romantic; what it means it often says indirectly, through ironic frames, but it says, on the whole, no more than it means. It gives us allegorical designs to figure out, and memorable words to repeat, but Auden scrupulously refuses to lure our vaguest emotions into the service of his own sacred beings or events.

Central and crucial in his work is the opposition between enchantment and disenchantment. In a sense, he hardly writes of anything else. The distinctions between Art and Life, the frequent combination of hope and skepticism, the techniques of ironic perspective—all dramatize an attitude that recognizes both the charm of magic and illusion ("the delicious lie") and the superiority of goodness and truth. Auden's poetry explores finely and without sentimentality the pathos (even at times the evil) of those who, living in one world, try to escape into another. Still, all such wish is not bad: it foreshadows the divine, it rescues us from the untruth of mere fact, it suggests varieties of action and feeling that we need to live in the light of. The problem is to reconcile enchantment with disenchantment, Art with Life, to know which is which, and when each (or a union of both) is appropriate.

Through all his work runs a basic fable and a basic character: man as a lucky and gifted third son whose quest for meaningful life can succeed only if he discovers its paradoxical key. Being lucky is necessary, but it is not enough. It is not enough, either, to work out the answer by careful study and logic; for life, however logical in its structures here and there, in its deepest currents defies logic, is all trapdoors, sudden darknesses, exceptions. Seeing this, the third son recognizes his limitations, submits to the conditions of his existence, and in the very act of submission (which must, however, be repeated for the rest of his life) achieves the object of his quest: continous existence. For the basic condition to which he has submitted, though it looks like defeat and death, turns out to be love.

How good is Auden's poetry? How long will people read it? No one, of course, is in a position to say. Comparison with Yeats and Eliot is inevitably misleading, for in our judgments of greatness in poetry we still use Romantic standards. When we speak of Yeats as greater than Eliot, and of both as greater than Auden, we still have some notion, even as we ridicule Arnold, that greatness involves grandeur. The poets we think of as great are all grand—Homer, Dante, Shakespeare, Milton; and although we have finally managed to include Chaucer sometimes in such lists, it is mainly because he has been dead so long. What we still want from contemporary poets is uplift, moments of exaltation and wonder, a feeling that life is lofty and rich. The canny poet, like Horace, Chaucer, Dryden, or Auden, seems to be operating on a different level. His usual subject is not the heroic and the transcendental but the normally human, and he achieves depth by other means than reverberating symbols and resonant tones.

As critics study Auden more fully in years to come, I suspect we shall see more clearly not only his psychological penetration but the force of his delicate poetic strategies, his superb balances, his unprecedented uses of the comic, his careful arrangements of surprises that disturb our expectations and yet fulfill them, the harmonies that are at once resolved and disconcerting. He disconcerts us so oddly that we think he must be at fault. We have hardly any previous experience with literary irony pushed so far, made to do so many things, in single poems and throughout a long career. But we ought by now to guess that the reason a poet like Auden puzzles is that we have not yet understood him and to think it likely, as in similar past cases, that as the world we live in grows clearer to us, these intricate ironies will seem more and more appropriate to it.

CHAPTER 19

But Leaders Must Migrate

S INCE 1969, when the first edition of this book was published, many books and articles have appeared, and they tend, on the whole, to support the prediction in the final paragraph of the previous chapter. Scholars are clearer now about the meanings and contexts of the early work of Auden, and the later poetry is beginning to be better understood and appreciated, as a result of studies by Replogle, Johnson, and others (see Bibliography). Anthologists still suffer from the lazy habit of using only early poems to give students an idea of Auden's work. Occasionally, they include "In Praise of Limestone" (1948) or "The Shield of Achilles" (1952) but almost never a syllabic poem written by Auden during his last quarter-century as an active poet. Until they begin to do so, new readers of Auden will continue to get a distorted notion of what his work is like.

We now know much more, too, about Auden's personal life, and his death in 1973 permits us to begin to see his life and poetic career as a whole. One question bound to be debated is whether Auden was happy. In his last years he certainly became very lonely in his New York apartment during the half-years that Chester Kallman spent in Greece. Still, he could write in 1965 that the three months he had traveled in Iceland in 1936 were "among the happiest in a life which has, so far, been unusually happy."[1] He appears to have thought of himself as having been blessed in his life and in his talent, and he appreciated, as most of us do not, what a privilege it is to lead a comfortable life unmarked by personal catastrophe.

Yet many of his friends report his closing years to have been increasingly lonely. At one point in the early 1970s, Auden proposed to his younger friend Orlan Fox, with whom he had been dining on Friday nights for years, that they should share an

191

apartment. Fox declined but realized later that "it was a cry for help, for companionship."[2] Finding his isolation unbearable, and physically threatening (he told reporters: "If I should have a coronary, friends may not find me for days"[3]), he decided, after more than thirty years, to give up his residence in New York and to spend his winters instead at his old college at Oxford, Christ Church. He had taught for five seasons at Oxford (1956–61) as Professor of Poetry and hoped to find there a more companionable setting for his winter months. In December 1972 he accordingly left New York, spent the next few months at Oxford, where, it appears, he was too old and formidable a lion to get close to,[4] and in the spring moved on to the little house in Kirchstetten, Austria, which he and Kallman had shared during springs and summers since 1957.

Although Auden's health in these years is often described as failing—his corns had long required him to wear house slippers everywhere and to walk with a shuffling gait, his "breathing was labored and he was blue around the lips," his heart was "playing up a little," and he had had "an attack of severe vertigo"[5]—at least one visitor to Kirchstetten in the summer of 1973 found him lively, "rejuvenated," talkative, and charming.[6] In late September, having closed up the house for the season, he was preparing to return to England after spending the weekend in Vienna. There he gave a poetry reading on September 29, retired to his hotel room, and was found dead the next morning. He had evidently suffered a heart attack. "I shall probably die in a hotel to the great annoyance of the management," he had written to Ursula Niebuhr in 1947.[7] He was buried in Kirchstetten, but a plaque in the Poet's Corner of Westminster Abbey also commemorates his life. Whether Kallman had any intention of writing at length about his famous life-companion is not known; but he, too, died of a heart attack in Athens less than two years later.

I *Auden's Influence*

The influence of Auden on contemporary American poetry has still to be studied in detail. Hardly any poet in English history has been so intensely admired as Auden in the early part of his career, and even in 1956 Allen Ginsberg and Gregory

Corso on meeting him tried to kiss "the turn-ups of his trousers."[8]
But as early as 1941 Randall Jarrell was shocked by Auden's
changes in style, which he anatomized in two brilliant essays
(see Bibliography), and in later years Auden's reputation
among poets was mixed. He continued to be admired for his
prodigious craftsmanship, but as more young writers learned
to write free verse or to explore what came to be known as
deep-image poetry, they found more congenial models in Pound,
Williams, and others. For some time Auden's easy conversational style—the classic example is "Musée des Beaux Arts"—was
much praised and imitated by poets eager to avoid the hyper-
Romantic bardic chanting of Dylan Thomas, but only a few
American poets have found it possible or desirable to mix that
easy style with formal verse. Similarly, although Auden, following Eliot's lead, showed later poets with what strong ironic
effect ordinary phrases and slang could be used in modern
poems, it was the Beat poets, not Auden, who extended the
principle so far as to make available to contemporary poets
any English words or locutions, no matter how obscene they
might have been thought by earlier writers.

Even relatively traditional poets, such as Adrienne Rich,
James Wright, W. S. Merwin, and John Ashbery—all chosen by
Auden as winners in the Yale Series of Younger Poets—in time
moved away from stricter to freer styles. On the other hand,
Richard Wilbur, Anthony Hecht, John Hollander, James Merrill, and other poets influenced by Auden have continued to
explore the possibilities of metrical verse and regular stanzaic
forms. Merrill's allegiance has been carried even further: mainly
in iambic pentameter lines, often in rhymed couplets, he has
made Auden one of the chief characters in an elaborate three-
volume account of his experiences with the Ouija board.[9]

It is still too early to tell whether free verse will become the
characteristic mode of American poetry in the future, or
whether formal verse—iambic, accentual, or syllabic—will continue to be composed by our chief poets. In England the question is, if anything, even more open. In any event, the formality
of Auden's verse is less and less likely to be considered a ground
for reproach as his life recedes further into the past, for to
write a formal poem in an age of free verse is to make a polemi-

cal statement; twenty years later all that matters is whether
the poem is, of its kind, as good as it might be. If poets do
continue at all to write in formal verse, they are bound to pay
homage to Auden, who is one of the art's great practitioners.

In addition to assisting contemporary poets to develop more
conversational styles in their verse, Auden also helped them
to feel more at home with symbolism. He is, from first to last,
a symbolist poet who in his own way carries on the tradition
of the great modernist writers Yeats, Joyce, and Eliot. But,
unlike them, he repudiated the idea that symbolist poetry must
be portentous in manner, grandiose in scale and design. Whereas they saw in symbols a means of transcending or aggrandizing
commonplace reality, Auden succeeded, as it were, in domes-
ticating symbolism. His way of seeing everything in our lives,
no matter how trivial, as symbolic—streams, waking up, the
bathroom, killing mice—implies, and is meant to imply, that
our symbolic habits are themselves commonplace, that symbolism, far from justifying flights of romantic emotion, is merely
part of the ordinary furniture of our lives. It has been exciting,
even fun, to become aware of it; we need to understand how
it works; we need, especially, to see how largely it figures in
our lives, and how necessary to us are the "secondary worlds"
(like poetry or opera) that we construct with our symbolic
imaginations. But our aim is to understand, not to be trans-
ported out of time, not to seek those eternal moments so valued
by Yeats and Eliot, but to develop an accurate understanding
of the conditions, both inner and outer, under which we live
and the behavior we characteristically use to cope with those
conditions.

Although Auden's almost nonchalant use of symbolism has
undoubtedly helped make it easier for some contemporary poets
to incorporate it without fuss into their own work, it is still
uncertain what influence Auden's later, less resonant poetry may
have. For if Auden was at all a revolutionary poet, this well-
made comic verse of his mature period was his most revolutionary work. It goes against a two-hundred-year-old tradition
of Romantic verse, in which we expect a poet to lift us out of
ourselves, to offer archetypal sufferers and symbolic experiences
with which we can deeply identify, to present human life es-

sentially through images of successful or failed transcendence. Auden's highly original later poetry goes counter to this whole tradition, and most other poets have not yet become aware of its force, its meaning, and its possibilities. In time we can reasonably expect that other poets of merit will find in his work a classic model of a poetry strong in feeling, large in scope, but centered in the perception of truth rather than in the emotional transport.

II *Anti-Romantic Hyperbole*

In declining to overstate the importance of our passionate moments, and in turning an essentially comic glance on our most intense feelings, Auden in his later years incurred the doubt and even the hostility of many writers and readers of poetry. Often committed to fuzzy ideas about myth, religion, or mystical sources of self, or at least convinced of the primacy of personal or political feeling in any account of human values, they sometimes found Auden's subjects trivial, his manner frivolous, his concern with forms mere playing. And it is difficult still for many readers to go all the way with Auden in his views of life and art. Refusing to exaggerate the role of poetry in the world, recognizing that it can have almost no political impact and is enjoyable simply for its own sake, content to have been fortunate enough to excel at it and to have spent his life as a maker of poems, Auden has seemed to some to be concerned with a poetry whose passional center is missing. The *angst* is gone, and what remains is a brilliant but fussy verse-maker: Hans Sachs has turned into Beckmesser.

Poets who felt this way became increasingly aware that Auden's way of producing poetry was radically different from theirs. The visionary poetry of his early phase gave way to a verse of intellectual insight in which ideas—often comically presented, and always with panache—are central. Although it is hard to imagine a poet without an idea, there are many contemporary poets who hold a much more organic theory of poetry. For them the poem is likely to begin with an image or a rhythm which serves as a kind of mystical vortex around which the poem in all its phrases gathers like a thunderstorm.

Or, in more moderate versions, the poem should at least con-
fess its origins in some more passionate center than the brain.
If Auden would regard all such views as fatally Romantic ("The
romantic lie in the brain/Of the sensual man-in-the-street"—
EA, 246), his own later poetry has seemed to many readers too
directly concerned with ideas, and its whimsical or even at
times its precious tone has been heard as a ghastly thinning
of the prophetic voice that rang out so impressively in his
youth.

The figure Auden cut in his last years in literary circles contributed something to this picture. A great, aging presence in
American poetry, Auden had brought many younger poets into
prominence when, as editor of the Yale Series of Younger Poets
from 1947 to 1958, he had chosen to publish their first volumes.
By 1972, however, he had stopped reading the new poets. "One
hasn't the time!" he said in an interview,[10] and it is clear that
as he grew older his ideas became codified, his receptiveness
to new ones diminished. Again and again in interviews, lectures,
readings, conversations, and letters the same formulated convictions, the same canonical examples, are trotted out, almost
verbatim. When interviewers continually ask Auden the expected questions, he provides the expected answers. More and
more, too, those formulations—often phrased with beautiful
clarity and conciseness, and proceeding out of extremely intelligent observation of people and life—are disturbingly systematic: there are only two ways of doing this, or three ways
of doing that. All life is analyzed schematically, and sometimes
one senses that the beauty of the scheme has been more important to Auden than the accuracy of the observation.

In *Secondary Worlds,* for example, Auden makes the point
that statements in poems, as opposed to statements in life, are
neither true nor false:

> Similarly, if a boy says to a girl 'I love you,' she may with good
> reason wonder if he really means what he says, or is only pretending
> in order to seduce her, but if I read the lines
>> My dear and only love, I pray
>> That little world of thee . . .
> I cannot raise the question of sincerity: the words mean neither
> more nor less than they say.[11]

But, like many statements in the later criticism of Auden, the conclusion is too downright. Such lines as Auden quotes may be ironic or insincere, and we regularly raise questions about the sincerity of speakers in poems. Or again, he writes:

In a secondary world [art, as opposed to life], we are omniscient, aware of everything which exists and happens in it, and understanding exactly why.[12]

But this is obviously not true: we value some works for their ambiguity, for their being open to different readings, and after several hundred years we are still not sure why Hamlet acts as he does. When he makes such statements, Auden seems to have mainly in mind the lucid, unambiguous poetry that he himself came to write in his later years.

But if such statements suffer from an exaggerated lucidity, an overstatement of what is generally the case, it is exactly this quality that readers have often found most exciting in Auden's early poetry. His art strangely mixes crisp, logical statement with hyperbole; its discourse constantly proceeds as if something were literally true that can only be understood as metaphor. Throughout his career, from the spy-imagery of the early poems to the quest of *The Age of Anxiety,* from the notion that Yeats, as his body breaks up, *becomes* his admirers to the transformation of Caliban into our most sophisticated fleshly selves, from the exegetical reading of desolate early landscapes to that of "Streams" and "Islands," Auden's technique has been to overstate his insights. That his prose, that his talk, often did the same—" 'Only the "Hitlers of the world" work at night; no honest artist does' "[13]—serves to remind us how deeply the habit was ingrained and how inseparable it was from his quest for truth. Truth hides in our lies; lies peep out at us from behind our truths. In an odd way, Auden's finished work stands as an express, and also as an implicit, warning against the excessive claims of any abstract system.[14] The most uncanny strength of his hyperbolic art is that it warns us against hyperbole.

III   *Yes, Love, You Have Been Lucky*

For many British critics, Auden's apostasy has seemed of

several kinds—the abandoner of his country in time of crisis, and of his commitment to politics in a troubled age. As expatriate, Anglican, and homosexual, he appears to have made all the wrong choices; at the very least, everyone can accuse him on *some* score. Radical enough to begin with, and always at odds in some ways with traditional measures of respectability, he nevertheless traveled his own odd path toward a modified *rapprochement* with conventional good behavior. As François Duchene puts it:

Yet, for all his cosmopolitan activity and catholic interests he has, in his attitudes, seemed more and more a caricature of an Edwardian upper-middle-class Englishman of his year of birth. His clerihews, his whimsy, his faintly stiff-upper-lip emphasis on the decencies . . . his nonsense rhymes, his daydreams of lawns and rain-gauges, his dislike of ash in teacups or his assumption that a *nurse* will first point out the moon to the infant poet-to-be, have vanishing English privilege written all over them. To emerge as a posthumous Victorian is a curious consummation for the marxist *enfant terrible* of the Thirties and naturalised postwar American. It is a distinguished and well-earned retirement, but a kind of retirement all the same.[15]

Most writers, as they grow older, lose some of their creative energy, and their imaginative work falls increasingly into a familiar mold. Some go on writing, but their novels and poems repeat each other; they have trouble finding anything new to say. Shakespeare retired before he was fifty; Wordsworth was not quite forty when his verse began to cool; when Eliot gave up poetry (for verse plays), he was fifty-five. The contrary example of Yeats in our century has perhaps led us to expect too much of our poets' stamina. But those who are disappointed by Auden's later career are probably troubled not merely because a fine poet abandoned a successful early style or the right views, but because his whole later life was a deliberate repudiation of his earlier position as a poetic *leader,* not merely one of many admired young writers but the poet who established the tone, the idioms, the imagery, of a whole generation of poets and fiction writers, or at least of many among them. (No one has cared very much when Robert Lowell took up, or put down, his religion.) Probably no poet since Wordsworth, not even Eliot to the same degree, has been regarded in this way, as the poet who could show the way to new modes of writing. What becomes increasingly clear in retrospect, and increasingly remarkable, is that Auden deliberately resigned this position at the age of thirty-two, and that he did so out of profound conviction. Always interested in leadership, both personally and as a subject to explore in poems and plays, he was never really comfortable with it, and he writes most often about the inadequacy of leaders. He came to feel, with the help of Kierkegaard, that the single ordinary man is a better subject, and that is what, in his gifted way, he tried to become. In the private world, where everyone is alone, there are no leaders. Every poet must write his own poems, not those that belong to another's style or thought, so that to be a poetic leader is really to falsify the whole enterprise. Honesty, in poetry as in life, is the best policy.

To be gifted and ordinary at once may seem a paradox, but it is a paradox at the very heart of Auden's view of life. Every human being is special, but no one is heroic in all respects, and Auden from the beginning is fascinated by the coexistence in the same person of remarkable and commonplace qualities—to cite one example, the great writer of "Who's Who," full of "honours" but "Love made him weep his pints like you and me" (*EA*, 150). For Auden, being human means being divided, and among the divisions that count in his work is that between having great talent and being an ordinary muddled mortal. "The Arts? Well, FLAUBERT didn't say/Of artists: '*Ils sont dans le vrai*'" (*CP*, 171). The maker of poems is also a liver of life, and no better than most at that. Auden seems to have known that in his own life he never quite got over being a precocious boy, slovenly in his habits, inordinately fond of jokes, and caustically critical of obtuse people: "I was . . . insufferably superior with anybody who, when speaking about matters in which I was interested, said something I thought stupid."[16] Contempt for stupidity goes along with cleverness, the character fault with the intellectual virtue. And one of Auden's recurrent themes (notably in *Elegy for Young Lovers*) is the knowledge that to be brighter than everyone else is not at all to be better.

Auden's work is divided in other ways, too. It is a strange

mixture, for example, of the caustic and the bland, of satire and praise. It seems to go in for praise on principle, not by nature, and this is partly what irritates critics—that his gift for the absurd detail, the comic instance, should have been used, finally, in the service of relatively bland statements about the nature of man, or even of more trivial notions, instead of in the service of some overwhelming tragic or Swiftian vision of twentieth-century life. We keep asking Auden to have been some other kind of poet, instead of noticing exactly the kind of poet he was. For Auden's own nature appears to have been divided along lines that his poems reflect, between personal disorder and an exaggerated intellectual clarity, between a neurotic untidiness in the spaces where he lived and a compulsive punctuality, between his sense of himself as quicker and cleverer than almost anyone else in the world and his sense of himself as unloved, unattractive, lonely, fat, faulty. There are other oppositions—between the one-night sexual stand and his enduring life with Chester Kallman, in the division of his life into a European spring and summer and an American autumn and winter, between his English youth and his American maturity, between a professional fame that enabled him to meet and influence great numbers of the world's, and especially New York's, artists and intellectuals and a personal life of sordid encounters with barmen, drifters, and call-boys. His firm intellectual control of abstract ideas and formal structures seems clearly to have been Auden's way of coping magisterially with elements in his nature that remained perpetually adolescent; his insight into secondary worlds at once brilliantly clarifies the role they play in everyone's life and confesses the miseries of his own primary world.

Yet even those miseries were the limited ones of loneliness and isolation, and critics who discuss his personal foibles as if they could constitute a convincing moral case against Auden have been beautifully answered by Elizabeth Hardwick:

Auden's eccentricities were harmless and had the good fortune to be predictable, sparing his conduct thereby from rushes of paranoia, violence, and pettiness. If he knocked off at nine, his example was not of sufficient tyranny to drag anyone else along with him. His mind, his loneliness, his ability to love, his uncompetitive sweetness of character survived his ragged bedroom slippers and egg-spotted tie. And his genius, the high seriousness of his life, survived his death.[17]

If Auden failed to develop the promise of his numinous early poetry into a later work of great power and presence, he did so out of conviction that to write such a poetry in our age was, at least for him and probably for everyone, a dishonest act. The best poetry he wrote after 1940 is certainly stunning and impressive; it glows with insight and intelligence, and its forms and rhythms are richly inventive. He managed to survive his own divided life and to make its disorder into art, to turn Caliban (Wystan) into Ariel (W. H. Auden). From his own art, as well as from the reminiscences of others, the picture we get of Auden's own life is of a brilliant, only fitfully happy boy turning gradually into a world-weary roué, his growing irritation with the world relieved only by bouts of elegant mischief and cleverly phrased *aperçus*. For many readers this vision seems insufficiently large: too little of the inner man, the sufferer, appears, too much of the comic diminisher. The imposing art which his early poetry promised, a poetry which would provide a ringing appraisal of an age, of our public as well as our private problems, never materialized, or not in the looked-for guise. In the early 1940s Auden's verse ceased to refer to current public events, and a generation of readers that had hoped to find in him a continuing commentator on political events was disappointed.

Their expectations, of course, were unrealistic, even Romantic. Auden knew that he could not continue as a cultural spokesman, that his insight into day-by-day or year-by-year political affairs was that of an amateur, and that his continuing to claim to have more than a distant general perception of the cultural anxieties of his time would be dishonest. Looking at Europe in the 1930s, Auden could see an Inferno of damned leaders, driving their peoples blindly to war or stumbling stupidly in ignorance of what to do:

> And still all over Europe stood the horrible nurses
> Itching to boil their children.   (*EA*, 240)

Unlike Voltaire, the subject of this poem, Auden was wise

enough not to think that "Only his verses/Perhaps could stop them." But if a poet could not change the world, if he could not even, in conscience, lead a poetic revolution, he could still tell the truth in his poems.

We can now begin to see Auden's whole career in perspective, and it is his whole career that will have to be understood if we are to judge his achievement. This is still not easy to do, and most critical studies have concentrated either on the poetry before 1940 or on the poetry after, on the English Auden or the American, or have seen these phases as deeply opposed and inconsistent. What we may come to see in his whole career is a powerful but erratic imaginative talent scattering its striking images of inner and European life but gradually corrected and controlled by an art that regularly exchanges mythic power for intelligence, elegance, comedy, and truth. If Auden was not happy in his life, he was happy in his art: he achieved what he wanted to achieve.[18] Over nearly half a century he composed an impressive array of masterful poems and other writings, and these should assure him a prominent place among the great poets who have written in English.

Notes and References

A Note on Auden's Texts

1. Edward Mendelson, "A Note on Auden's Text," *W. H. Auden: A Tribute*, ed. Stephen Spender (New York, 1975), p. 251.

Chapter One

1. Randall Jarrell, "Changes of Attitude and Rhetoric in Auden's Poetry," *Southern Review* 7 (Autumn 1941): 326–49.
2. Christopher Isherwood, *Lions and Shadows* (New York, 1947).
3. "Henry James and the Artist in America," *Harper's*, July 1948, p. 40.

Chapter Two

1. Monroe Spears, *The Poetry of W. H. Auden: The Disenchanted Island* (New York, 1963), p. 3.
2. "As It Seemed to Us," *Forewords and Afterwords* (New York, 1973), p. 502. Originally published in *New Yorker*, April 3, 1965, pp. 159–92.
3. Spears, p. 13.
4. Stephen Spender, *World Within World* (New York, 1951), p. 46.
5. *F & A*, p. 508.
6. C. Day Lewis, *The Buried Day* (London: Chatto & Windus, 1960), p. 176.
7. Spears, pp. 82–83.
8. Carlo Izzo, "The Poetry of W. H. Auden," in Spears, ed., *Auden* (Englewood Cliffs, N.J., 1964), p. 127.
9. Auden married Erika Mann, Thomas Mann's daughter, in 1935 to give her a British passport at a time when her German citizenship was in jeopardy. She proposed the idea first to Isherwood, who demurred; Auden, who had never met her, agreed. The couple never lived together but remained on friendly terms, and the marriage continued in force until Mrs. Auden's death thirty-five years later.

See Charles Osborne's biography, *W. H. Auden: The Life of a Poet* (New York, 1979), pp. 222–23, for a brief account of Auden's only heterosexual love affair.

10. See, for example, the caricatures of such guardians in *The Dog Beneath the Skin* and *The Ascent of F6*.

11. *F & A*, p. 511.

12. See Justin Replogle's "The Gang Myth in Auden's Early Poetry," *Journal of English and German Philology* 61 (1962): 481–95, or pp. 7–30 in Replogle's *Auden's Poetry* (Seattle, 1969).

Chapter Three

1. Barbara Everett, *Auden* (Edinburgh, 1964), pp. 25–27. Everett's whole discussion of the ambivalences of the early verse is illuminating.

2. See Groddeck's *Das Buch vom Es* (1923), translated as *The Book of the It* (New York: Funk & Wagnalls, 1950).

3. Homer Lane, *Talks to Parents and Teachers* (London: Schocken, 1928), p. 177.

Chapter Four

1. This is why I have not adopted Monroe Spears's picturesque term, "the Nordic mask" (*The Poetry of W. H. Auden*, p. 22), to describe these poems. To me, what distinguishes them from others is their imagery, not the Norse landscape and not even the Old English style. In Spears's classification (see note 7, below) the poems of war that lack the landscape or the alliterative devices have to be moved into some other category even when their texture, along with the oracular, elliptical manner, links them to the Norse poems in feeling. Anyway, since every poem combines the several elements of the style in a different way, its limits should not be set too strictly.

2. Everett, p. 22.

3. A fair example is F. W. Cook's "Primordial Auden," *Essays in Criticism* 12 (October 1962): 402–12. Cook analyzes the 1928 *Paid on Both Sides* as a Marxist piece.

4. See Replogle's "Social Philosophy in Auden's Early Poetry," *Criticism* 2 (Fall 1960): 351–61; and his "Auden's Marxism," *PMLA* 80 (December 1965): 584–95. Recast in *Auden's Poetry* (Seattle, 1969), pp. 3–16, 30–50.

5. Everett, pp. 20–21.

6. See Auden's review of *The Complete Works of John Skelton*, ed. Philip Henderson, in *Criterion* 11 (January 1932): 316–19.

7. It is useful to know Spears's names for six styles he distinguishes in the early poems (22–27; 34–35): the Nordic mask (see note 1, above); "the clipped lyric"—that is, the elliptical poem in Skeltonic style; the middle or colloquial style, in casual and easy English; a high style ("florid, extravagant, elevated, profuse; usually it is written in long lines, and it often exhibits baroque incongruities of diction" [25] and aims at mock-heroic effects); "the Rilkean sonnet"; and the popular style in which "the trite and flat language of popular songs and speech is used for satirical effect, and the poem is spoken by a *persona*" (34–35).

8. See the preface to *Collected Poetry* (1945); and the foreword to the revised edition of *The Orators* (1966).

9. Spears reads it differently (47–48).

10. Stephen Spender, *The Destructive Element: A Study of Modern Writers and Beliefs* (London: Jonathan Cape, 1935), p. 268.

11. Peter E. Firchow, "Private Faces in Public Places: Auden's *The Orators*," *PMLA* 92 (March 1977): 253–72, esp. 266–69.

12. See Clive James, "Auden's Achievement," *Commentary* 56 (December 1973): 53–58. As far as I know, this is the first essay to suggest in public that Auden's early poems have a hidden but unmistakable homosexual content.

13. "Honour," in *The Old School: Essays by Divers Hands*, ed. Graham Greene (London: Jonathan Cape, 1934), p. 17.

14. John Fuller's account of *The Orators* in *A Reader's Guide to W. H. Auden* is helpful and accurate, but students of this work should also consult Firchow's important article cited above; W. H. Sellers, "New Light on Auden's *The Orators*," *PMLA* 82 (October 1967): 455–64; and Edward Mendelson, "The Coherence of Auden's *The Orators*," *ELH* 35 (March 1968): 114–33. Samuel Hynes's *The Auden Generation* (New York, 1977), by far the best commentary on Auden's political attitudes and political writing in the later 1930s (and on everyone else's), offers some important insights also into the political background of *The Orators*.

Chapter Five

1. See, for example, "Mimesis and Allegory," *English Institute Annual, 1940*, ed. Rudolf Kirk (New York, 1941), pp. 1–19. A relevant quotation from this essay appears below on p. 108.

2. "A Literary Transference," *Southern Review* 6 (Summer 1940): 83–84.

3. Review in *Criterion* 12 (January 1933): 289.

4. Replogle, "Auden's Marxism" (See note 4 to Chapter 4).

5. Introduction to *The Poet's Tongue* (London, 1935), p. x. See this introduction, passim, and the essay listed in note 8, below.

6. See Spears, p. 86.

7. Ibid.

8. "Psychology and Art," *The Arts To-day*, ed. Geoffrey Grigson (London, 1935), p. 19   (*EA*, 341).

Chapter Six

1. See Lucy S. McDiarmid, "W. H. Auden's 'In the Year of My Youth,'" *Review of English Studies*, n.s. 29 (1978): 267–312, which provides text, notes, and an intelligent commentary. The lines quoted are 1–4 and 866–71.

2. The influence of Eliot is still much felt in the poem: the narrator, like Eliot's speaker in *The Waste Land*, is hurried from scene to scene of contemporary life, and even the first line, "In the year of my youth when yoyos came in," ironically echoes and undercuts the opening line of Langland's poem ("In a somer seson whan soft was the sonne") in exactly the same way that Eliot's somber opening ("April is the cruelest month") echoes the sunnier lines of Chaucer that begin *The Canterbury Tales* ("Whan that April with his shoures soote . . .").

3. But see Replogle's "Auden's Marxism," esp. pp. 585–86, for the best study of this play, which he sees as mainly non-Marxist. Note that "New Year Letter" shows Auden at a later stage between two views of life, just in the process of changing.

4. *The Dance of Death* (London, 1933), p. 16.

Chapter Seven

1. *New Country*, ed. Michael Roberts (London: Hogarth, 1933), p. 207.

2. Auden uses this term to describe "Letter to Lord Byron"   (*EA*, 172).

Chapter Eight

1. See John G. Blair, *The Poetic Art of W. H. Auden* (Princeton, 1965), pp. 130–34; Spears, pp. 110–12; Cleanth Brooks and Robert Penn Warren, *Understanding Poetry*, 3d. ed. (New York: Holt, Rinehart & Winston, 1960), pp. 332–35; Edward C. McAleer, "As Auden Walked Out," *College English* 18 (February 1957): 271–72.

2. See, for example, *Poets of the English Language*, ed. Auden and Norman Holmes Pearson (London, 1952), esp. Auden's Introduction to Vol. III (xv) and to Vols. IV and V (passim).

3. *New Republic*, November 25, 1940, p. 716.

4. In *Best Broadcasts of 1939–40*, ed. Max Wylie (New York: McGraw-Hill, 1940), p. 37.

Chapter Nine

1. The Roman numerals given here are taken from *Journey to a War* (New York, 1939) and are retained in *EA*. Auden's later revision of the sequence resulted in the sonnets being shifted around and given the new numbers they have in *CP*.

Chapter Ten

1. "Living Philosophies. VII. Morality in An Age of Change," *Nation*, December 24, 1938, p. 691.

2. "Rilke in English," New Republic, September 6, 1939, p. 135.

3. "A Great Democrat," *Nation*, March 25, 1939, p. 352 (*EA*, 387).

4. "Tradition and Value," *New Republic*, January 15, 1940, p. 90.

5. See "Jacob and the Angel," *New Republic*, December 27, 1939, pp. 292–93.

6. "Eros and Agape," *Nation*, June 28, 1941, p. 757.

7. "A Note on Order," *Nation*, February 1, 1941, p. 132.

8. "Eros and Agape," p. 756. The next four quotations are also taken from this essay.

9. "Tradition and Value," p. 90.

10. Spears, "The Dominant Symbols of Auden's Poetry," *Sewanee Review* 59 (Summer 1951): 413.

11. Ed. James A. Pike (London, 1956), pp. 31–43. Two quotations that follow cite page numbers from this book.

12. Introduction to *The Living Thoughts of Kierkegaard* (New York, 1952), p. 13.

13. *Ibid.*, p. 14.

14. *Ibid.*, p. 16.

15. The term Agape he draws mainly from the influential book of the 1930s, Anders Nygren's *Agape and Eros: A Study of the Christian Idea of Love* (New York: Macmillan, 1932), and from the later, popular *Love and the Western World*, by Denis de Rougemont, which Auden reviews in the above-cited essay, "Eros and Agape."

16. "Mimesis and Allegory," *English Institute Annual, 1940*, ed. Rudolf Kirk (New York, 1941), pp. 18–19.

Chapter Eleven

1. It ought to be noted that a few of the discursive poems in *On This Island* have this remote bleakness of outlook—"Casino" and "Epilogue." These chronological layers overlap; the powerful harmonies coexist with the toneless despair. But then the harmonies subside for a while or are pressed into the service of severely ironic ballads, while the deadly despair continues. On Dante, see "New Year Letter," *CP*, 164.

2. Cf. "A Great Democrat," cited above in note 3 to Chapter 10. This review of a book on Voltaire is relevant to both the Voltaire and the Pascal poems.

Chapter Twelve

1. Rainer Maria Rilke, *Duino Elegies*, tr. J. B. Leishman and Stephen Spender (New York: Norton, 1939), pp. 37, 39. Auden's review of this volume is listed in the next note.

2. "Rilke in English," *New Republic*, September 6, 1939, p. 135.

3. Isherwood, "Some Notes on Auden's Poetry," *New Verse*, No. 26–27 (November 1937): 4.

4. *The Collected Poems of W. B. Yeats* (New York: Macmillan, 1956), p. 206.

5. *The Contemporary Poet as Artist and Critic*, ed. Anthony Ostroff (Boston, 1964), p. 186.

6. Blair, esp. Chapters 2 and 3.

7. Blair's book is excellent in its description of Auden's devices for achieving generality. At the same time, it seems to me to err somewhat in depicting Auden as too much the calculating strategist. Blair himself acknowledges this (193). But not only does the unconscious contribute a good deal to the working out of an Auden poem; the poetry very largely speaks of, and dramatizes, the impingement of unconscious and irrational forces on ordinary conscious life. The id, the It, the specter of Caliban, the "gibbering fist-clenched creature" (*CP*, 333), "the dark thing you could never abide to be with" (*CP*, 334), is always present or virtually present, and so is Grace, God, the Unconditional: meaning always lurks in the shadows, is seen through "chinks of the forest," stands ready to invest ordinary things with life. Auden's severe hostility to Romanticism, after all, confesses some Romantic impulses.

Chapter Thirteen

1. Orlan Fox, "Friday Nights," in *W. H. Auden: A Tribute*, ed. Stephen Spender (New York, 1975), p. 173.
2. *Christopher and His Kind* (New York, 1976), p. 304.
3. Osborne, p. 213.
4. Hannah Arendt, "Remembering Wystan H. Auden," in *W. H. Auden: A Tribute*, p. 182.
5. Robert Craft, *Stravinsky: Chronicle of a Friendship, 1948–1971* (New York, 1972), p. 40.
6. The phrase appears frequently in writing about Auden—e.g., in Michael Yates, "Iceland 1936," in *W. H. Auden: A Tribute*, p. 65.
7. Craft, p. 25.
8. Louis Kronenberger, "A Friendship Revisited," in *W. H. Auden: A Tribute*, p. 157.
9. Robert Craft, "The Poet and the Rake," in *W. H. Auden: A Tribute*, p. 150.
10. Arendt, pp. 184–85.
11. "The Municipal Gallery Revisited," *The Collected Poems of W. B. Yeats*, p. 318.

Chapter Fourteen

1. *The Double Man* (New York, 1941), p. 20.
2. See Callan's articles referred to below in note 1 to Chapter 15, and in notes 3, 5, and 6 to Chapter 16.
3. Lane, *Talks to Parents and Teachers*, p. 177.

Chapter Fifteen

1. Edward Callan, "Auden's *New Year Letter*: A New Style of Architecture," *Renascence* 16 (1963): 13–19, reprinted in Spears's *Auden*, pp. 152–59.
2. Charles Williams, *The Descent of the Dove* (London: Collins, 1963), p. 176. The Montaigne passage appears on p. 175.

Chapter Sixteen

1. Blair, p. 106.
2. This chapter tries mainly to suggest the general nature and value of these complex works. Anyone studying them closely can find valuable analyses of their philosophical structure and image-patterns in the essays cited below.

3. Edward Callan, "Auden and Kierkegaard: The Artistic Framework of *For the Time Being*," *Christian Scholar* 48 (Fall 1965): 211–23.

4. G. S. Fraser has criticized this passage as snobbish along somewhat different lines. See Spears, ed., *Auden*, pp. 90–91.

5. Callan, "Auden's *New Year Letter*. . . ." I quote from Spears's *Auden*, p. 159. See also Callan's longer study of *The Sea and the Mirror* in "Auden's Ironic Masquerade: Criticism as Morality Play," *University of Toronto Quarterly* 35 (January 1966): 133–43; Blair's discussion, pp. 106–17; Justin Replogle, "Auden's Religious Leap," *Wisconsin Studies in Contemporary Literature* 7 (Winter-Spring 1966): 47–76; Lee M. Whitehead, "Art as Communion: Auden's 'The Sea and the Mirror,'" *Perspective* 14 (Spring 1966): 171–78; and Thomas R. Thornburg's monograph cited in the Bibliography.

6. Callan, "Allegory in Auden's *The Age of Anxiety*," *Twentieth Century Literature* 10 (January 1965): 155–65.

Chapter Seventeen

1. Alfred Kazin, "The Function of Criticism Today," *Commentary* 30 (November 1960): 104.

2. Philip Larkin, "What's Become of Wystan?" *Spectator*, No. 6890 (July 15, 1960): 104.

3. Robert Mazzocco, "The Poet at Home," *New York Review* 5 (August 5, 1965): 7.

4. "One of the Family," *New Yorker*, October 23, 1965, p. 242.

5. *The Contemporary Poet as Artist and Critic*, pp. 185–86 (see note 5 to Chapter 12).

6. "A Preface to Kierkegaard," *New Republic*, May 15, 1944, p. 686.

7. N. E. Collinge, *The Structure of Horace's Odes* (London: Oxford, 1961), pp. 13, 19. See also Steele Commager, *The Odes of Horace* (New Haven: Yale, 1962).

8. Much still remains to be said about the influence on Auden throughout his career not only of Horace but of Roman or Classical poetry in general. Cf. his interest in epigrams, epitaphs, tributes, and the genre of the occasional poem.

9. "The Dyer's Hand," Part I, *Listener*, June 16, 1955, p. 1066.

10. "The Dyer's Hand," Part III, *Listener*, June 30, 1955, p. 1152.

11. *About the House* (New York, 1965), p. 13. Mazzocco (see pp. 162–163 and note 3 above) misreads this poem, thinking that Auden is saying his poems would have been *better* if his life had been

better. Cf. *Elegy for Young Lovers*, where precisely the same point is the opera's main theme.

12. *Thank You, Fog* (New York, 1974), p. viii.

Chapter Eighteen

1. "Genesis of a Libretto," in *Elegy for Young Lovers* (Mainz, 1961), p. 62.

2. *Elegy for Young Lovers*, p. 46.

3. Monroe K. Spears, "Auden and Dionysus," *Shenandoah* 18 (Winter 1967): 92.

4. *Secondary Worlds* (New York, 1968), pp. 115–16.

5. Blair has an excellent essay on *The Rake's Progress* (154–84); Spears discusses the earlier operas at length (262–89), and *The Bassaids* in the *Shenandoah* article cited above in note 3 (85–95). *Delia or a Masque of Night* appeared in *Botteghe Oscure* 12 (1953): 164–210. See also Ulrich Weisstein, "Reflections on a Golden Style: W. H. Auden's Theory of Opera," *Comparative Literature* 22 (Spring 1970): 108–24; and Robert Craft's discussion of *The Rake's Progress* and its 1968 production in Phoenix, Arizona, in *Stravinsky: Chronicle of a Friendship, 1948–1971* (New York, 1972), pp. 348–55.

6. *Tennyson: An Introduction and a Selection by W. H. Auden* (London, 1946), p. xv. Cf. Isherwood's report on Auden's smoking, p. 34 above.

Chapter Nineteen

1. "Foreword," *Letters from Iceland*, by W. H. Auden and Louis MacNeice (New York, 1969), p. 9.

2. Fox, p. 174.

3. *Minneapolis Tribune*, February 19, 1972, pp. 1A, 8A.

4. David Luke, "Homing to Oxford," in *W. H. Auden: A Tribute*, pp. 202–17.

5. Dr. Oliver Sacks, "Dear Mr. A . . . ," in *W. H. Auden: A Tribute*, pp. 192–93.

6. Anon., "Auden at Kirchstetten," *South Atlantic Quarterly* 75 (Winter 1976): 12.

7. Ursula Niebuhr, "Memories of the 1940s," in *W. H. Auden: A Tribute*, p. 118.

8. Osborne, p. 246.

9. See "The Book of Ephraim" in *Divine Comedies* (New York, 1977), pp. 47–136; *Mirabell: Books of Number* (New York, 1978); and *Scripts for the Pageant* (New York, 1980).

10. Daniel Halpern, "Interview with W. H. Auden," *Antaeus* 5 (1972): 139.

11. *Secondary Worlds*, p. 50.

12. Ibid., p. 52.

13. Fox, p. 173.

14. As Hannah Arendt summed up his thoughts, in words quoted earlier: "The main thing was to have no illusions and to accept no thoughts, no theoretical systems that would blind you against reality." ("Remembering Wystan H. Auden," in *W. H. Auden: A Tribute*, pp. 184–85.)

15. François Duchene, *The Case of the Helmeted Airman: A Study of W. H. Auden's Poetry* (London, 1972), pp. 179–80.

16. "As It Seemed to Us," *F & A*, p. 508.

17. Elizabeth Hardwick, "Love It or Leave It!" (review of Peter Conrad, *Imagining America*), *New York Review of Books* 27 (April 3, 1980): 27.

18. I owe this assessment to Stephen Spender, who ventured it during a visit to the University of Minnesota some years ago.

Selected Bibliography

PRIMARY SOURCES
(in chronological order)

1. Books (with abbreviations used in the text)

Poems. Oxford, 1928. Printed privately by Stephen Spender.

Poems. London: Faber and Faber, 1930.

The Orators. London: Faber and Faber, 1932. (Revised edition, 1966.)

The Dance of Death. London: Faber and Faber, 1933.

Poems. Second edition. London: Faber and Faber, 1933.

Poems. New York: Random House, 1934. Includes *The Orators* and *The Dance of Death.*

The Dog Beneath the Skin (with Christopher Isherwood). New York: Random House, 1935. For convenience I quote from the London Faber and Faber edition of 1935.   Dog

The Ascent of F6 (with Isherwood). New York: Random House, 1937. For convenience I quote from the London Faber and Faber edition of 1936.   F6

On This Island. New York: Random House, 1937. (British edition: *Look, Stranger!* London: Faber and Faber, 1936).   OTI

Letters from Iceland (with Louis MacNeice). New York: Random House, 1937. Second edition, 1969.

Spain. London: Faber and Faber, 1937.

On the Frontier (with Isherwood). New York: Random House, 1938. For convenience I quote from the 1938 Faber and Faber edition.

Journey to a War (with Isherwood). New York: Random House, 1939.

Another Time. New York: Random House, 1940.

The Double Man. New York: Random House, 1941. (Issued in London by Faber and Faber, 1941, as *New Year Letter*).   DM

For the Time Being (including *The Sea and the Mirror*). London: Faber and Faber, 1944.

The Collected Poetry of W. H. Auden. New York: Random House, 1945.

The Age of Anxiety. New York: Random House, 1947.

Collected Shorter Poems, 1930–1944. London: Faber and Faber, 1950.

The Enchafèd Flood. New York: Random House, 1950.

213

Nones. New York: Random House, 1951.

The Shield of Achilles. New York: Random House, 1955.

Selected Poetry. New York: Random House, 1959.

Homage to Clio. New York: Random House, 1960.

The Dyer's Hand. New York: Random House, 1962.   *DH*

About the House. New York: Random House, 1965.

Collected Shorter Poems, 1927–1957. London: Faber and Faber, 1966.

Secondary Worlds. New York: Random House, 1969.

Collected Longer Poems. New York: Random House, 1969.

City Without Walls. London: Faber and Faber, 1969.

Academic Graffiti. London: Faber and Faber, 1971.

Epistle to a Godson and Other Poems. New York: Random House, 1972.

Forewords and Afterwords, selected by Edward Mendelson. New York: Random House, 1973.   *F & A*

Thank You, Fog: Last Poems. New York: Random House, 1974.   *Fog*

Collected Poems, ed. Edward Mendelson. New York: Random House, 1976.   *CP*

The English Auden: Poems, Essays and Dramatic Writings, 1927–1939, ed. Edward Mendelson. New York: Random House, 1977.   *EA*

Selected Poems, ed. Edward Mendelson. New York: Random House, 1979.

2. Libretti

The Rake's Progress (with Chester Kallman). London: Boosey and Hawkes, 1951.

Delia: or a Masque of Night (with Kallman). Botteghe Oscure 12 (Autumn 1953): 164–210.

Elegy for Young Lovers (with Kallman). Mainz: B. Schott's Söhne, 1961.

The Bassarids (with Kallman). Mainz: B. Schott's Söhne, 1966.

Paul Bunyan. London: Faber Music Limited, 1976. (Written in 1941.)

Love's Labour's Lost (with Kallman). Not yet published separately from the music by Nicholas Nabokov.

3. Translations

Bertolt Brecht and Kurt Weill, *The Seven Deadly Sins* (with Kallman.) *Tulane Drama Review* 6 (Autumn 1961): 123–29.

Mozart's *The Magic Flute* (with Kallman). New York: Random House, 1956.

Mozart's *Don Giovanni* (with Kallman). New York: G. Schirmer, 1961.

Goethe's *Italian Journey* (with Elizabeth Mayer). New York: Pantheon, 1962.

Dag Hammarskjöld, *Markings* (with Leif Sjöberg). New York: Knopf, 1964.

Andrei Voznesensky, *Antiworlds*, ed. Patricia Blake and Max Hayward. New York: Basic Books, Inc., 1966. Includes Auden's Foreword and seven poems he translated, along with translations of Voznesensky poems by other poets. Reprinted in 1967 in the Doubleday Anchor series.

The Elder Edda (with Paul B. Taylor). London: Faber and Faber, 1969.

Bertolt Brecht, *The Rise and Fall of the City of Mahagonny* (with Kallman). Boston: David R. Godine, 1976.

4. Books Edited

The Poet's Tongue: An Anthology (with John Garrett). 2 vols. London: G. Bell & Sons, 1935. An original selection of poetry for schoolboys, with a sensible introduction (included in *EA*).

The Oxford Book of Light Verse. Oxford: Clarendon Press, 1938. Shows a wide acquaintance with light verse, and the introduction (included in *EA*) is an important discussion of the nature, value, and history of English light verse.

A Selection of the Poems of Alfred Lord Tennyson. New York: Doubleday, 1944. Auden sees Tennyson as "the great English poet of the Nursery" and explores surprising parallels between his work and Baudelaire's. Introduction included in *F & A*.

Yale Series of Younger Poets, 1947–58. Perceptive introductions to the verse of new young poets.

The Portable Greek Reader. New York: Viking, 1948. Contains a valuable analysis of Greek ideals and attitudes (included in *F & A*).

Poets of the English Language (with Norman Holmes Pearson). 5 vols. New York: Viking, 1950. The introductions, all by Auden, show us his mature view of English poetry and of the philosophical, social, and formal currents that have helped to shape it.

The Living Thoughts of Kierkegaard. New York: David McKay, 1952. The introduction (included in *F & A*) summarizes what Auden takes to be central in Kierkegaard's work.

The Criterion Book of Modern American Verse. New York: Criterion Books, 1956. (British edition: *The Faber Book* . . . etc. London: Faber and Faber, 1956.) A key to Auden's taste. The introduction is included in *DH*.

The Viking Book of Aphorisms (with Louis Kronenberger). New

York: Viking, 1962. (British edition: *The Faber Book of Apho-risms*. London: Faber and Faber, 1964.) Splendid and original collection, with a brief introduction.

19th Century British Minor Poets. New York: Delacorte Press, 1966. Brief selections from eighty poets, with a brisk and perceptive introduction.

A Certain World: A Commonplace Book. London: Faber and Faber, 1971. A charming collection of quotations, arranged by subject and culled from an astonishing variety of sources.

5. Contributions to Books

"Psychology and Art." *The Arts To-day*, ed. Geoffrey Grigson. Lon-don: John Lane, 1935. An apparently hasty but useful summary of the significance for art of psychology, i.e., of the "attitude to life and living relationships" best represented by Freud. In-cluded in *EA*.

"Mimesis and Allegory." *English Institute Annual, 1940*, ed. Rudolf Kirk. New York: Columbia University Press, 1941. An important, wide-ranging essay in which, with special reference to Wagner, Auden discusses the connections between art and life, art and beliefs.

"Criticism in a Mass Society," *The Intent of the Critic*, ed. Donald A. Stauffer. Princeton: Princeton University Press, 1941. An ex-tended discussion, pontifical but illuminating, of the problem of belief in art and of the responsibilities of critic and artist in a social democracy.

"K's Quest." *The Kafka Problem*, ed. Angel Flores. New York: New Directions, 1946. Analysis of the elements of different types of quest narratives, from the fairy tale to Kafka's kind. Only a bit of it appears in *DH*.

Untitled essay in *Modern Canterbury Pilgrims*, ed. James A. Pike. London: A. R. Mowbray, 1956. A revealing examination of Au-den's personal religious history.

6. Articles and Reviews in Periodicals (see also those cited in the notes to Chapter 10)

"A Literary Transference," *Southern Review* 6 (Summer 1940): 78–86. "I cannot write objectively about Thomas Hardy because I was once in love with him." Describes Auden's youthful in-fatuation with Hardy's poetry and the permanent marks it left on his own work.

"A Preface to Kierkegaard," *New Republic*, May 15, 1944, pp. 683–86. Important summary of Kierkegaardian existentialism: "what he would teach is an approach to oneself, not a conclusion, a style of questioning to apply to all one's experience . . ."

"Augustus to Augustine," *New Republic*, September 25, 1944, pp. 373–76. Discusses ideas important to Auden's later poetry. Included in *F & A.*

"The Dyer's Hand," *Listener*, June 16, 23, 30, 1955, pp. 1063–66, 1109–13, 1151–54. Significant observations on the poet, the poetic process, and the special problems that face today's poet.

"On W. H. Auden's 'Change of Air,'" by George P. Elliott, Karl Shapiro, Stephen Spender, and Auden, in *The Contemporary Poet As Artist and Critic*, ed. Anthony Ostroff. Boston: Little, Brown, 1964. [First appeared in *Kenyon Review* 26 (Winter 1964): 190–208.] An amusing exchange in which, replying to exasperatingly weak criticism, Auden brilliantly explains what he is currently trying to do in his poems.

"As It Seemed to Us," *New Yorker*, April 3, 1965, pp. 159–92. A generously autobiographical review of two other writers' autobiographies. Included in *F & A.*

SECONDARY SOURCES

1. Bibliographies

BLOOMFIELD, B. C., and EDWARD MENDELSON. *W. H. Auden: A Bibliography, 1924–1969.* Second edition. Charlottesville: University Press of Virginia, 1972. A beautifully produced and presented volume, as nearly complete and as perfectly arranged as any extensive bibliography is likely to be. It lists not only Auden's books, pamphlets, introductions and forewords, articles and reviews, but a dozen other varieties of authorial work, along with bibliographical and critical work about him. An indispensable aid to Auden scholars.

CALLAN, EDWARD. *An Annotated Check List of the Works of W. H. Auden.* Denver: Alan Swallow, 1958. List and notes are very helpful.

————. "W. H. Auden: Annotated Checklist II" (1958–1969), *Twentieth Century Literature* 16 (January 1970): 27–56. Continues Callan's earlier list.

GINGRICH, MARTIN E. *W. H. Auden: A Reference Guide.* Boston: G. K. Hall & Co., 1977. An annotated list of the main books, dissertations, articles, and other important published work on Auden, arranged chronologically from 1931 to 1976. An index lists titles and authors alphabetically and also shows which Auden works have been discussed by which Auden scholars.

218 W. H. AUDEN

2. Biography

OSBORNE, CHARLES. *W. H. Auden: The Life of a Poet*. New York: Harcourt Brace Jovanovich, 1979. A workmanlike compilation, largely from published sources, of the main events and periods of Auden's life. Osborne was a friend of Auden's, and his account is thorough, friendly, tactful, and honest.

3. Critical Books

BAHLKE, GEORGE W. *The Later Auden: From "New Year Letter" to About the House*. New Brunswick, N. J.: Rutgers University Press, 1970. Defends the unity and sincerity of Auden's later Christian work. Examines especially the four long poems of the 1940s and, more briefly, the shorter poems in volumes from *Nones* to *About the House*, "in an effort to reveal the consistency and cogency of the thought lying behind them."

BEACH, JOSEPH WARREN. *The Making of the Auden Canon*. Minneapolis: University of Minnesota Press. Puzzles over the quirks of Auden's collections.

BLAIR, JOHN C. *The Poetic Art of W. H. Auden*. Princeton: Princeton University Press, 1965. A perceptive general study of Auden's poetic techniques, which are seen as consistently anti-Romantic and allegorical.

BROPHY, JAMES D. *W. H. Auden*. New York: Columbia University Press, 1970. (Columbia Essays on Modern Writers.) Briefly surveys some verbal techniques and comic poems that make Auden balanced and Horatian, "a moderate poet."

BUELL, FREDERICK. *W. H. Auden as a Social Poet*. Ithaca: Cornell University Press, 1973. Studies the relationship of Auden and his poems "to a public world," in particular the development of a political consciousness and "political voices" in the early work.

DAVISON, DENNIS. *W. H. Auden*. London: Evans Brothers, 1970. (Literature in Perspective.) A cursory survey of Auden's work.

DUCHENE, FRANÇOIS. *The Case of the Helmeted Airman: A Study of W. H. Auden's Poetry*. London: Chatto & Windus, 1972. A discerning and eloquent presentation of the case for Auden's early poetry. Praises the numinous early poems and their intimation of deep personal experience; is more dubious about, but ultimately respectful of, the intelligent later poems that have resolved the struggle but, he feels, omit the sense of it. Full of valuable insights, but extremely judgmental, sometimes patronizing, and even careless ("James Warren Beech" is a noted Auden critic).

EVERETT, BARBARA. *Auden*. Edinburgh: Oliver and Boyd, 1964. (Writers and Critics Series.) A brief survey of Auden's poetry, especially sensitive on the early work.

FULLER, JOHN. *A Reader's Guide to W. H. Auden.* New York: Noonday Press, 1970. Informative poem-by-poem survey of Auden's work through 1966. Direct and clear readings, not always right but especially good on the early poems, notably *Paid on Both Sides* and *The Orators,* and on Auden's debt to Old English poetry.

GREENBERG, HERBERT. *Quest for the Necessary: W. H. Auden and the Dilemma of Divided Consciousness.* Cambridge: Harvard University Press, 1968. A lucid, subtle, and convincing account of Auden's poems as variations on the central theme of the divided self.

HOGGART, RICHARD. *Auden: An Introductory Essay.* London: Chatto and Windus, 1950. An early sympathetic study, strangely organized, sometimes mistaken or misleading, but often perceptive.

————. *W. H. Auden.* London. Longmans, Green, 1957. (British Council Pamphlets, No. 93.) Collected, with similar pamphlets on Eliot and Dylan Thomas, in *British Writers and Their Work* No. 5. Lincoln: University of Nebraska Press, 1964. A brief survey and appraisal of Auden's work.

HYNES, SAMUEL. *The Auden Generation: Literature and Politics in England in the 1930s.* New York: Viking, 1977. Shows, year by year, through the extremely perceptive analysis of a few key works, how the political and literary consciousness of the Auden generation developed through the decade. Hynes has a thorough knowledge of the era (especially, a grasp of its political and social issues), an eye for the revealing detail, a lively style, and a superb ability to cut through cant and get to the basic issues. His book makes most other writing on Auden seem tedious and academic.

JOHNSON, RICHARD A. *Man's Place: An Essay on Auden.* Ithaca: Cornell University Press, 1973. Studies the variety of ways in which Auden's ideas about man's place in the world are realized through formal designs and techniques. Some good close readings of poems, including the later sequences ("Bucolics," "Horae Canonicae," and "Thanksgiving for a Habitat"), which he shows to be much more profound and systematic than their often chatty surface leads most readers to expect. The last few pages provide an intelligent discussion of the sense in which Auden continued throughout his career to be "a profoundly political poet." An essential book for understanding Auden's later poetry.

NELSON, GERALD. *Changes of Heart: A Study of the Poetry of W. H.*

Auden. Berkeley: University of California Press, 1969. (Perspectives in Criticism Series, No. 21.) Focuses on the long poems of the 1940s, the shorter poems of the next two decades, and on the development of Auden's later persona.

REPLOGLE, JUSTIN. *Auden's Poetry.* Seattle: University of Washington Press, 1969. Incorporates material from Replogle's valuable articles on Auden's early poems and ideas, and adds, most notably, (1) a long and suggestive, if perhaps too schematic, analysis of Auden's "Poetic" and "Antipoetic" personae, (2) some original observations on Auden's conceptual style (pp. 186–97) and his genius for mixing levels of usage (pp. 208–13), and (3) a brilliant anatomy of the comic perspective and style that give scope to Auden's later poems and make them his best work.

SCARFE, FRANCIS. *Auden and After: The Liberation of Poetry, 1930–1941.* London: George Routledge & Sons, 1942. Generally hasty and superficial in treating Auden.

————. *W. H. Auden.* Monaco: Lyrebird Press, 1949. Better than Scarfe's earlier book, most apt on Auden's existentialism, but fails to see his work in its own terms.

SPEARS, MONROE K. *The Poetry of W. H. Auden: The Disenchanted Island.* New York: Oxford University Press, 1963. The first really important work of scholarship on Auden's poetic career, full of useful information and perceptive in tracing the basic patterns in Auden's work.

STOLL, JOHN E. *W. H. Auden: A Reading.* Muncie, Indiana: Ball State University Press, 1970. (Ball State Monograph Number Eighteen.) Mainly traces Auden's development of a mature philosophical view of psychological duality, under the influence of Lawrence, Jung, and Blake.

THORNBURG, THOMAS R. *Prospero, the Magician-Artist: Auden's The Sea and the Mirror.* Muncie, Indiana: Ball State University Press, 1969. (Ball State Monograph Number Fifteen.) A brief study (35 pp.) of *The Sea and the Mirror.*

4. Collections of Writing on Auden (arranged chronologically)

NEW VERSE, No. 26–27 (Nov., 1937). ("Auden Double Number.") An early collection of essays and comments on Auden by such notable writers as Spender, Day Lewis, Isherwood, MacNeice, Pound, Masefield, Dylan Thomas, and Graham Greene.

SPEARS, MONROE K., ed. *Auden: A Collection of Critical Essays.* Englewood Cliffs, N. J.: Prentice-Hall, 1964. (Twentieth Century Views Series.) Thirteen essays on Auden's work. (Abbreviated in my text as *Auden.*)

SHENANDOAH, XVIII (Winter, 1967). Special issue on Auden.

HARVARD ADVOCATE, CVIII (1975). Special issue commemorating Auden's life and work.

SPENDER, STEPHEN, ed. *W. H. Auden: A Tribute.* New York: Macmillan, 1975. Handsomely produced memorial volume, with essays by many personal friends and colleagues.

5. Interviews and Reported Conversations (arranged chronologically)

"Auden on Poetry: A Conversation with Stanley Kunitz," *Atlantic*, August 1966, pp. 94–102.

PLATT, POLLY. "W. H. Auden," *American Scholar* 36 (Spring 1967): 266–70.

PRYCE-JONES, DAVID. "Conversation with W. H. Auden," *Holiday*, June 1969, pp. 56, 66–67.

LEVY, ALAN. "On Audenstrasse—In the Autumn of the Age of Anxiety," *New York Times Magazine*, August 8, 1971, pp. 10ff.

HALPERN, DANIEL. "Interview with W. H. Auden," *Antaeus* 5 (1972): 134–49.

NEWMAN, MICHAEL. "W. H. Auden" (1972), in *Writers at Work: The Paris Review Interviews: Fourth Series.* Hammondsworth, England: Penguin, 1977, pp. 243–69.

CROSSMAN, RICHARD. "Remembering and Forgetting—W. H. Auden Talks to Richard Crossman about Poetry," *Listener*, February 22, 1973, pp. 238–40.

ANON. "Auden at Kirchstetten," *South Atlantic Quarterly* 75 (Winter 1976): 8–19.

All of these are full of lively remarks by Auden—on poetry, on his own writing, and on his own life.

See also H. Griffin's seven reports of conversations with Auden (1949–53), published in *Accent* (X, XII, XIII), in *Hudson Review* (III), in *Partisan Review* (XX), in *Poetry* (LXXXIII), and in *Avon Book of Modern Writing*, I.

See also the books by Craft, Isherwood, Spender, and Stravinsky listed below in the final section.

6. Critical Essays

BAYLEY, JOHN. *The Romantic Survival: A Study in Poetic Evolution.* London: Constable & Co., 1957. Esp. pp. 129–85. A stylish, much praised study, which, along with some good analyses and sensible judgments, seems to me full of misinformation and mistaken insights.

BLOOM, ROBERT. "W. H. Auden's Bestiary of the Human," *Virginia*

Quarterly Review 42 (Spring 1966): 207–33. An illuminating study of Auden's animal imagery.

————. "The Humanization of Auden's Early Style," *PMLA* 83 (May 1968): 443–54. Convincingly refutes Jarrell's 1941 claim that Auden's progress in the 1930s was in the direction of impersonality and inhumanity.

CALLAN, EDWARD. "Allegory in Auden's *The Age of Anxiety*," *Twentieth Century Literature* 10 (January 1965): 155–65. An indispensable guide to this poem.

————. "Auden and Kierkegaard: The Artistic Framework of *For the Time Being*," *Christian Scholar* 48 (Fall 1965): 211–23. Analyzes the poem's structure, its thought- and image-patterns.

————. "Auden's Ironic Masquerade: Criticism as Morality Play," *University of Toronto Quarterly* 35 (January 1966): 133–43. Shows how *The Sea and the Mirror* presents Auden's literary theory.

————. "Auden's *New Year Letter*: A New Style of Architecture," *Renascence* 16 (Fall 1963): 13–19. Reprinted in Spears, *Auden*, pp. 152–59. Admirable analysis of the poem's Kierkegaardian structure.

————. "The Development of W. H. Auden's Poetic Theory Since 1940," *Twentieth Century Literature* 4 (October 1958): 79–91. Accurate and helpful.

————. "Exorcising Mittenhofer," *London Magazine* 14 (April-May 1974): 73–85. A brief study of the attitudes in Auden's later verse, especially of his debts to Horace, Hammarskjöld, and Isaiah.

————. "W. H. Auden: The Farming of a Verse," *Southern Review*, n.s. 2 (Spring 1967): 341–56. Discusses Auden's view of formal composition and the way it works in such key poems as the elegy on Yeats and some later, anti-Romantic works.

ENRIGHT, D. J. "Reluctant Admiration: A Note on Auden and Rilke," *The Apothecary Shop: Essays on Literature*. London: Secker & Warburg, 1957. Perceptive, if harsh, study of Auden's use and misuse of Rilke.

FIRCHOW, PETER E. "Private Faces in Public Places: Auden's *The Orators*," *PMLA* 92 (March 1977): 253–72. Especially useful in arguing that there *was* an Auden group and in showing connections between *The Orators* and John Layard's 1930 articles on the Malekula Bwili, or "flying tricksters" (266–70).

FOWLER, HELEN. "The Faces and Places of Auden," *Approach* 57 (Fall 1965): 6–14. Good discussion of Auden's intimate style: "The tone is that of two people talking together, describing what it feels like to be inside a small private circle, having the freedom to joke and banter about their difficulties, to display their small perceptions and their shy evanescent feelings without being overheard and reproached for their odd and dismaying sensibilities."

HARDY, BARBARA. "The Reticence of W. H. Auden," *Review*, No. 11–12 (1964): 54–64. Enlightening on Auden's combination of reticence and strong feeling.

JAMES, CLIVE. "Auden's Achievement," *Commentary* 56 (December 1973): 53–58. Interesting on the homosexual content of Auden's early imagery.

JARRELL, RANDALL. "Changes of Attitude and Rhetoric in Auden's Poetry," *Southern Review* 7 (Autumn 1941): 326–49. Witty and exhaustive analysis of the rhetorical devices used in Auden's poetry as he moved from early myth to later abstraction. A brilliant article, technically accurate and highly unsympathetic. Reprinted in his *The Third Book of Criticism*. New York: Farrar, Straus and Giroux, 1969.

――――. "Freud to Paul: The Stages of Auden's Ideology," *Partisan Review* 12 (Fall 1945): 437–57. A later, more cranky, less convincing attack. Reprinted in his *The Third Book of Criticism*. New York: Farrar, Straus and Giroux, 1969.

LARKIN, PHILIP. "What's Become of Wystan?" *Spectator*, July 15, 1960, pp. 104–105. From the eminence of his own assured greatness, Larkin looks down disdainfully on the ruins of one who "no longer touches our imaginations."

McDIARMID, LUCY S. "W. H. Auden's 'In the Year of my Youth . . . ,' " *Review of English Studies*, n.s. 29 (1978): 267–312. Studies, annotates, and gives the text of a long (1,235 lines), unfinished, early poem by Auden.

ORWELL, GEORGE. "Inside the Whale," *Inside the Whale and Other Essays*. London: Victor Gollancz, 1940. Some hard but just words on the politics of Auden and his group.

THURLEY, GEOFFREY. "W. H. Auden: The Image as Instance," *The Ironic Harvest*. New York: St. Martin's Press, 1974, pp. 54–78. Like Duchene's book on Auden, Thurley condemns the later work from a superior and very Romantic perspective. But he is good in noting, in the early poetry, Auden's "uncanny aptness in the selection of image to demonstrate thesis . . . [his] instantaeous conversion of thinking into relevant image."

WEISSTEIN, ULRICH. "Reflections on a Golden Style: W. H. Auden's Theory of Opera," *Comparative Literature* 22 (Spring 1970):

108–24. Careful study of Auden's views on opera, as he expressed them in various writings.

7. Especially Interesting Collateral Books

CRAFT, ROBERT. *Stravinsky: Chronicle of a Friendship*. New York: Alfred A. Knopf, 1972. Includes some marvelous portraits of Auden, extensive quotations from his conversation ("easily . . . defending his title as the world's most delightful wit"), and acute criticism of the libretto for *The Rake's Progress*. This volume includes much of the material contained in the earlier *Themes and Episodes* (1966) and *Retrospectives and Conclusions* (1969).

ISHERWOOD, CHRISTOPHER. *Lions and Shadows*. New York: New Directions, 1947. Delightful account of Isherwood's early days, including much about Auden ("Hugh Weston").

———. *Christopher and His Kind*. New York: Farrar, Straus and Giroux, 1976. A franker account of Isherwood's homosexual life (and of Auden's), 1929–39.

MERRILL, JAMES. *Divine Comedies*. New York: Atheneum, 1977.

———. *Mirabell: Books of Number*. New York: Atheneum, 1978.

———. *Scripts for the Pageant*. New York: Atheneum, 1980.

These three books detail Merrill's adventures with the Ouija board and with Auden as a principal communicant from The Other Side. One passage offers this trenchant summary self-judgment by the character "Auden":

MY DEARS IT IS ME   MY MINERALS MINED OUT EARLY,
I SPENT SLOW DECADES COVERING THE SCARS.
HAD I SUNK SHAFTS INTO MY NATURE OR
UPWARDS TO THE DEAD I WD HAVE FOUND RICH VEINS
INSTEAD I LOOKD FOR INSPIRATION TO
RITUAL & DIFFY MORAL STRICTURES
SO WRONG   (*Mirabell*, 70)

SPENDER, STEPHEN. *World Within World*. New York: Harcourt, Brace, 1951. A sensitive autobiography that throws much direct and indirect light on the young Auden.

STRAVINSKY, IGOR, and ROBERT CRAFT. *Memories and Commentaries*. London: Faber and Faber, 1960. Stravinsky devotes a long section of this memoir to his collaboration with Auden on *The Rake's Progress*.

SYMONS, JULIAN. *The Thirties: A Dream Revolved*. London: The Cresset Press, 1960. Useful account, by one of the minor writers of the thirties, of the decade's main directions, movements, feelings, events.

UPWARD, EDWARD. *Journey to the Border*. London: The Hogarth Press, 1938. An odd novel, full of Audenesque ideas and imagery, by the "Chalmers" of Isherwood's *Lions and Shadows*.

WARNER, REX. *The Wild Goose Chase*. New York: Knopf, 1938. A novel, by one of Auden's friends, that develops much of the group's imagery.

Index

86, 112; "New Year Letter," 28, 87, 111, 114, 135, *140–43*, 144–47, 153, 167; *On the Frontier*, 67, 77–78, 90; *The Orators*, 41, 48, *56–62*, 70, 72, 87, 93, 205n14; *Paid on Both Sides*, 39, 41, *51–52*, 87; "The Quest," 87, 92, 124, *144–46*; *The Sea and the Mirror*, 28, 62, 87, 135, 147, *151–55*, 160, 169, 181